Democratic Rights

◆

Democratic Rights

The Substance of Self-Government

◆

Corey Brettschneider

PRINCETON UNIVERSITY PRESS

PRINCETON AND OXFORD

Published by Princeton University Press, 41 William Street, Princeton, New Jersey 08540
In the United Kingdom: Princeton University Press, 3 Market Place,
Woodstock, Oxfordshire OX20 1SY

Library of Congress Cataloging-in-Publication Data
Brettschneider, Corey Lang.
Democratic rights : the substance of self-government / Corey Brettschneider.
p.   cm.
Includes bibliographical references and index.
ISBN-13: 978-0-691-11970-0 (hardcover : alk. paper)
ISBN-10: 0-691-11970-8 (hardcover : alk. paper)
1. Democracy. 2. Civil rights. 3. Citizenship. I. Title.
JC423.B784 2007
321.8—dc22
2006038310

British Library Cataloging-in-Publication Data is available

This book has been composed in Adobe Caslon with Bauer Bodoni for display.

Printed on acid-free paper. ∞

pup.princeton.edu

Printed in the United States of America

10 9 8 7 6 5 4 3 2 1

FOR ALLI

◆ Contents ◆

◆ Acknowledgments ◆

This book reflects the belief, at the heart of both my teaching and research, that incorporating political theory into the study of public policy and constitutional law enhances all of these fields of inquiry. In this pursuit I follow mentors and colleagues at a variety of institutions who have paved the way for such work. At Princeton I had the privilege of being supervised by Amy Gutmann, George Kateb, and Stephen Macedo. I thank them for managing to be both encouraging and demanding at the same time. Although this book moves well beyond my dissertation in both its scope and its main argument, many of the ideas in it began to take shape during conversations and emails with these supervisors. I will always remain deeply in their debt. At my dissertation defense Charles Beitz, who served as a fourth reader, also suggested ways to make some of the ideas in the dissertation the basis for a new book. I am particularly grateful to Amy Gutmann and George Kateb for their continued support throughout the process of writing the book.

I began this project during my first year at Brown University, after a lunch meeting with John Tomasi and David Estlund. Both have been ideal colleagues; through multiple sessions at our political philosophy workshop, they have served as guides and critics. David Estlund was writing his own book on democratic theory as I developed this project, and our many conversations about both topics contributed significantly to my final product. Together we organized an APSA panel on democratic theory. Our discussant, Chris Eisgruber, led me to rethink key portions of the book project and to write the concluding chapter.

The Cornell University Center for Ethics and Public Life presented me with its "Young Scholar Award" for article versions of chapters 1 and 5. I am grateful to Michelle Moody Adams, Henry Shue, and Burke Hendrix for organizing a weekend conference on this work at Cornell during the spring of 2004 and for the comments of the participants. In particular I thank Don Moon for his remarks, which led me to rethink the arguments of chapter 5.

Susan Okin, Steven Kelts, and Robert Reich also provided much helpful feedback during my presentation at the Stanford University Political Theory Tea. I would especially like to acknowledge Susan Okin for her encouragement of this project and of a separate book, currently in progress, that deals in depth with her own work. Her death was a great loss for political theory.

Paul Hurley introduced me to political theory at Pomona College when I was seventeen. His influence is still present in this work. I am grateful also for his invitation to lecture at my alma mater and for the many helpful comments I received there from Lee McDonald and John Seery, among others.

I completed most of the final stages of this manuscript during a leave from Brown as a visiting scholar at Stanford University's Political Science Department. I am grateful both to the department for providing me with space and for a grant financed by the American Council for Learned Societies and Brown University. At Stanford, Nannerl Keohane was particularly generous in her attention to this manuscript and in her suggested improvements in regard to chapter 2. I would also like to thank Tom Grey of Stanford Law School for his support of this project and his colleague, Lawrence Lessig, for input on related work. Finally, the Brown University Humanities Center and its director, Michael Steinberg, deserve thanks for providing a grant that allowed me to reduce my teaching load as I put the final touches on this book during the spring semester of 2006.

Simone Chambers, Eamonn Callan, and Leif Wenar all served as reviewers for this book, and I am extremely grateful for their careful work on the manuscript and for their many helpful suggestions. I would also like to thank my editor, Ian Malcolm, who was supportive of this project from the proposal stage to completion.

Thanks are due to the following people for comments on this project at various stages: Wendy Brown, Joshua Cohen, Alon Harel, Loren King, John McCormick, James Morone, Robert Post, Nancy Rosenblum, Austin Sarat, Dennis Thompson, and Mariah Zeisberg. Sharon Krause and Frank Michelman gave especially helpful feedback on the final draft.

For excellent research assistance I am indebted to Isaac Belfer, Nate Goralnik, David Grant, David McNamee, and Paul Neufeld.

Article versions of three of these chapters have been published previously. A version of chapter 1 was published as "The Value Theory of Democracy" in *Politics, Philosophy, and Economics* (October 2007). A version of chapter 5 was published as "The Rights of the Guilty" in *Political Theory* (April 2007). A version of chapter 7 appeared in *Political Studies* (July 2005) as "The Balance Between Outcomes and Procedures Within Democratic Theory: Core Values and Judicial Review."

This book is dedicated to my wife, Allison, who read the manuscript and suggested many editorial and substantive improvements. It is much better than it would have been without her precision and attention to the details of the argument. She is everything anyone could want in a life partner.

Democratic Rights

◆

◆ Introduction ◆

In 2003 the Supreme Court of the United States overturned its decision in *Bowers v. Hardwick* and struck down a Texas law that prohibited homosexual sodomy.[1] Writing for the Court in *Lawrence v. Texas,* Justice Kennedy argued that the Court's guarantee of a right to privacy, which it had earlier extended to areas such as contraception, marriage, and abortion, also included a protection of sexual relationships for gay and straight couples.[2] The privacy doctrine invoked in *Lawrence* was based, he argued, in the Fourteenth Amendment's guarantee of "substantive due process."

One prominent critique of this privacy doctrine and of the decision in *Lawrence* is that an appeal by the Supreme Court to a set of substantive rights is antidemocratic: it was never endorsed by a legislature or a constitutional convention. The word "substantive" does not appear in the Fourteenth Amendment or anywhere else in the Constitution. At its base, "substantive" is defined as "not procedural," or "procedure-independent." Substantive matters pertain to issues of justice, such as protecting individual rights against abuses of power. In contrast to procedural rights, such as the right to vote, substantive rights are often thought to be at the heart of a just society but not integrally connected to citizens' ability to partake in the democratic process. In addition to the right to privacy, they include rights to property and against excessive punishment. Because of this clear distinction between substantive and procedural rights, many think that the phrase "substantive due process" is not only bad doctrine, but an oxymoron: the terms "substantive" and "process" are at loggerheads.

Although the *Lawrence* decision was hailed by many as a gain for the rights of gay citizens, as this critique makes clear, it poses a dilemma for democratic theory. The Texas law had been passed according to the procedures established by the Texas legislature. The representatives of that legislature had been elected by a majority of Texans, and thus their decision not to repeal the Texas law was arguably majoritarian.[3] Although critics of the law might find it repugnant, it would seem to have been democratically authorized. Therefore, while critics of the Court's decision might agree that the legislation at issue in *Lawrence* was "uncommonly silly," some argue that the Court acted without democratic

---

[1] 478 U.S. 186 (1986).

[2] 539 U.S. 558 (2003).

[3] Although *Lawrence* struck down a Texas law, the precedent it sets is binding for legislation in every state as well as on federal congressional decisions that would affect the entire polity of the United States. Justice Scalia's dissent expresses his concern with the countermajoritarian nature of

1

authority in striking down the law.[4] Defenders of the Court's decision in *Lawrence*, as well as of the general concept of "substantive due process," face what Alexander Bickel calls the "counter-majoritarian difficulty."[5] Such defenders must explain why, in a society guided by democratic principles, a majority of the Supreme Court can override a majority of voters in an entire polity.[6]

Although the question of whether the Court should ever act contrary to democratic will is a live issue in political and legal theory, the case of *Lawrence v. Texas* raises another distinct issue: What is required for a society to be an ideal democracy in the first place? Are substantive rights an essential aspect of ideal democracies? Those who point to the countermajoritarian difficulty often assume that democracy is to be defined exclusively by adherence to majoritarian procedures. They adhere to what I call a "pure procedural" definition of democracy.[7] This means that a decision is democratically legitimate only if it is produced by citizens participating in a set of sanctioned processes. As such, there is nothing intrinsically democratic about outcomes of such decisions aside from the fact that they were produced by democratic procedures. On a pure procedural view, then, even when democratic processes produce results that are unjust or violate individual rights, such as the antisodomy law in Texas, they are democratic. According to pure proceduralists, concerns about the justice or injustice of policy outcomes, apart from procedural issues, are not matters of democratic concern. In other words, these thinkers suggest that procedure-independent evaluations of outcomes, what I call "substantive evaluations," are not rightly characterized as democratic.

In this project, however, I offer an alternative to the traditional divide between procedural theories of democracy and substantive theories of justice. I

---

the decision: "But persuading one's fellow citizens is one thing, and imposing one's views in absence of democratic majority will is something else. I would no more require a State to criminalize homosexual acts—or, for that matter, display any moral disapprobation of them—than I would forbid it to do so. What Texas has chosen to do is well within the range of traditional democratic action . . ." (*Lawrence v. Texas,* 539 U.S. 558 [2003]).

[4] In *Lawrence,* Justice Thomas called the Texas law "uncommonly silly."

[5] See Bickel, *The Least Dangerous Branch: The Supreme Court at the Bar of Politics* (New Haven: Yale University Press, 1986), 16.

[6] In *Romer v. Evans,* 517 U.S. 620 (1996), for example, the Supreme Court upheld an inferior court decision striking down a Colorado plebiscite that prohibited local antidiscrimination ordinances protecting gays. In reaction to this decision, critics of the Court charged it with acting contrary to a clear democratic will expressed through a plebiscite. Moreover, the suggestion that the law was based on animus seemed to critics an illegitimate attack on the motives of a democratic majority.

[7] See David Estlund, "Democratic Theory," in The Oxford Handbook of Contemporary Philosophy, ed. Frank Jackson and Michael Smith (Oxford: Oxford University Press, 2005), 208–30.

argue that democracy is an ideal of self-government constituted by three core values—political autonomy, equality of interests, and reciprocity—with both procedural and substantive implications. I contend that what are often thought of as distinctly liberal substantive rights to privacy, property, and welfare can be newly understood within a theory of democracy. I do not aim merely to provide new democratic justifications for traditional rights; in many instances, I argue that democracy requires rights less often invoked in the liberal tradition. I argue, for example, that rights to welfare are central to democratic legitimacy, as are free speech rights for convicted criminals and the right not to be executed by the state. Moreover, once democracy has been reformulated in this manner, I suggest that we can reexamine *Lawrence's* legitimacy with a new lens. Rather than being counterdemocratic, the Court's substantive due process doctrine and its decision in *Lawrence* help to guarantee a set of basic, democratic rights.

I begin by challenging the idea that the only proper criterion by which a decision can be judged democratic is whether it resulted from a majoritarian procedure. In contrast to pure procedural theories of democracy, I propose the *value theory of democracy* as a way of articulating the fundamental idea that self-government should respect each individual's status as a ruler. The three core values serve as the independent standards by which to judge whether citizens' democratic status is respected through procedural rights to participate in governance and substantive rights that protect against undemocratic outcomes of democratic procedures. Thus, democratic procedures and substantive rights are both distinct yet necessary aspects of ideal democracies.

In a broad sense, the value theory of democracy draws on the idea of "co-originality" present in the work of Jürgen Habermas and arguably implicit in the work of Jean-Jacques Rousseau and John Rawls. Co-originality suggests that participatory rights and the right to be free from government intervention are not conflicting ideals, but rather are complementary aspects of a good theory of political legitimacy. These theories thus aim to reject the conflict between what Berlin termed "positive" and "negative" liberty and what Constant called the "liberty of the ancients" and the "liberty of the moderns."[8] On my understand-

---

See also his *Democratic Authority* (forthcoming, Princeton University Press), in which Estlund defines "intrinsic democratic proceduralism" as the view that "only democratic political arrangements are legitimate, and the value of their being democratic does not depend on any qualities of democratic decisions other than whether they are democratic in two senses: (a) decisions must be made by democratic procedures, and (b) they must also not unduly undermine or threaten the possibility of democratic procedure in the future" (Estlund, "Democratic Theory," 213). Estlund rejects such a view in favor of one that views democracy as instrumental to good outcomes, a view that I take up in chapter 6.

[8] See Isaiah Berlin, "Two Concepts of Liberty," in *Liberty*, ed. Henry Hardy (Oxford: Oxford

ing, rights and procedures are co-original in that each is founded on the three core values that best define the democratic ideal of rule by the people.[9]

My argument for the value theory of democracy begins in chapter 1, where I consider and reject procedural accounts of democracy. I instead defend the value theory and elaborate why its three core values should be the standard for judging democratic legitimacy.

In chapter 2, I argue that the core values give rise to rights of citizens. These rights, I suggest, not only protect citizens in their capacity as makers, or "authors," of the law, but also provide substantive entitlements to citizens as they are coerced, or "addressed," by law. The rights of addressees, I argue, are best justified with reference to reciprocity's requirement of reasonable treatment for all democratic citizens.[10] In defending the idea that democratic rights should not merely protect citizens as political participants but should also guarantee substantive limits on state coercion, I avoid a top-down theory that merely proposes a standard and then applies it. Instead, I ground the idea of the rights of citizens as addressees in our intuitions about the requirements of paradigmatic democratic institutions such as the rule of law and free speech.

University Press, 1997), 166–217, and Benjamin Constant, "The Liberty of the Ancients Compared with That of the Moderns: Speech Given at the Athénée Royal in Paris," in idem, *Political Writings,* trans. and ed. Biancamaria Fontana (Cambridge: Cambridge University Press, 1988), 307–28. Isaiah Berlin helped popularize the notion that democracy and individual rights are drawn from two distinct traditions. He argued: "There is no necessary connection between individual liberty and democratic rule" (Berlin, "Two Concepts of Liberty, 177). For Berlin the linguistic and conceptual contrast between positive liberty, or self-rule, and negative liberty, or freedom from coercion, served to highlight what he regarded as a valid historical and philosophical distinction between democracy and individual rights. He believed that the tradition of positive liberty, from which the concept of democracy stems, draws on the fundamental question, "Who governs me?" Democratic conceptions argue that citizens are most free when they rule themselves. In contrast, the tradition of negative liberty attempts to respond to the separate question: "How far does government interfere with me?" (ibid.). Drawing on Benjamin Constant's distinction between the democratic liberties of the ancients and the rights of the moderns, Berlin sought to show that a good political theory would demonstrate how individual rights could constrain democracy while at the same time avoiding a conflation between these two basic concepts.

[9] In the first chapter I distinguish my view from what I deem sophisticated proceduralists' accounts of co-originality, such as that of Habermas. See Jürgen Habermas, *Between Facts and Norms: Contributions to a Discourse Theory of Law and Democracy,* trans. William Rehg (Cambridge, Mass.: MIT Press, 1996), 104. For a reading of Habermas's procedural notion of co-originality that contrasts it with Ronald Dworkin's constitutional conception of democracy, see Frank I. Michelman, "Democracy and Positive Liberty," *Boston Review* 21, no. 5 (November 1996). See also the introduction to Dworkin, *Freedom's Law: The Moral Reading of the American Constitution* (Cambridge, Mass.: Harvard University Press, 1996), to which I respond in chapter 6.

[10] Although I draw in this chapter from Habermas, I argue against him that this concept suggests a capacity of citizens that is normatively independent of any appeal to democratic procedure.

In chapter 3, I draw on the insights gleaned from my analysis of paradigmatic democratic rights of addressees of law to develop a framework for democratic justification that can be extended to some of the most contentious contemporary debates about rights. I call this framework for interpreting the core values of democracy "democratic contractualism" to emphasize its debt to Rousseau and Rawls. The framework contains two standards for judging the democratic limits of coercion and those rights to which citizens are entitled. The first standard, "democracy's public reason," serves as an initial way of identifying coercion that is inconsistent with the core values of democracy by examining whether its justification respects citizens as autonomous and equal. A second standard, the "inclusion principle," focuses on the impact of coercion on individuals in their particular contexts and with their distinct interests.

Chapter 4 begins the project of extending the ideas developed in chapter 3 to more controversial areas. I appeal to democratic contractualism to illustrate that the right to privacy is a necessary condition for an ideal democracy. Democratic contractualism articulates an understanding of the substantive right to be free from state intervention in matters of consensual sexual relations, such as that at issue in *Lawrence v. Texas*. Moreover, the democratic account of privacy can take into account feminist arguments about the need to develop and maintain theories of privacy that respect the core value of equality.

In chapter 5, I explore the implications of democratic contractualism for the rights of convicted criminals against certain forms of state punishment. I argue that the ideal of democratic citizenship should be extended to even the most violent offenders in our society. The democratic ideal requires certain restrictions on the forms of punishment that a legitimate democracy can rightly invoke.

In chapter 6, I discuss democratic contractualism's account of the right of private property and the right of welfare. While the right to private property plays a fundamental role in ideal democracies, I argue that a necessary condition for justifying its enforcement is that all citizens should be entitled to a basic right of welfare. I suggest three forms that this right could reasonably take: a right to a job, in-kind resources for basic needs, and basic income. Unlike the right to privacy and the rights of the incarcerated, the right of welfare is a positive right that provides for citizens to be given certain goods by the state. This right distinguishes democratic contractualism from libertarian theories.

Central to this project is an articulation of the democratic meaning of privacy, criminal justice rights, and property in an ideal democracy. Once this meaning has been established, however, it is necessary to explore a potential conflict between aspects of the democratic ideal. Although both democratic procedures and democratic rights are necessary conditions for ideal democracies, these two aspects at times will conflict in real democracies. What is the most democratic response when democratic procedures produce outcomes that violate democratic rights? Such an instance characterizes the *Lawrence* case discussed above. In chapter 7, I argue that in certain instances, such as cases related to privacy, judicial review in defense of democratic rights is justified. Although this form of judicial review results in a loss to the procedural integrity of democracy, it can be defended on the grounds that it represents an overall gain for the democratic ideal. One can, however, also embrace the value theory of democracy as articulated in chapters 1 through 6 without accepting the implication I suggest it has for judicial review; I examine such a position in this final chapter.

Now that I have explained the outline and ambition of my argument, I want to clarify its limits. My argument is limited in that I hope to articulate what a commitment to democracy means for an account of rights, not to provide a comprehensive account of all rights. Similarly, as I suggest in chapter 2, the core values are not intended to serve as an exhaustive list of *all* values relevant to democracy but rather as a collection of those that are most fundamental. These values may be consistent with a wide range of other values present in a democracy, such as fiscal responsibility and aesthetics. Finally, while I argue for rights as an implication of democracy, I do not seek to provide a justification of democracy itself; such a justification is outside the scope of this project. Indeed, another project might pursue the question of whether the rights I examine are ever trumped by nondemocratic reasons and values. I leave open this possibility in my discussion of supreme emergencies in chapter 2.

The ideals of the value theory of democracy and democratic contractualism suggest a new understanding of the meaning of democracy. Given how widely "democracy" is invoked in political discourse, the debate over the term's meaning is essential for understanding what is required of the state and citizenry for moving society toward an ideal democracy. Defenders of the democratic ideal rightly seek the power of all to participate, but they should also demand the rights that are the substance of self-government.

CHAPTER 1

THE VALUE THEORY OF DEMOCRACY

If, therefore, the populace promises simply to obey, it dissolves
itself by this act, it loses its standing as a people. The very
moment there is a master, there no longer is a sovereign,
and thenceforward the body politic is destroyed.
—*Rousseau, "On the Social Contract"*

I. INTRODUCTION

The notion that individual rights are distinct from, and often in tension with, democracy is widespread in the literature of liberal political theory.[1] This view needs to be rethought, however. Most contemporary liberal theorists understand democracy as a set of procedures intended to manifest the ideal of rule by the people.[2] In contrast, substantive individual rights, such as those that protect privacy and property and limit state punishment, are thought to be "procedure-independent." Rights are distinct from democracy, according to these theorists, because they are linked to substantive values of justice. Furthermore, liberal theorists believe that because there are good reasons to respect these rights when they conflict with outcomes dictated by democratic procedures, the rights should be taken as more fundamental than democracy itself. Liberal theory,

---

[1] "Liberal" refers here not to the left wing of the Democratic Party in the United States, but rather to the tradition of political theory that emphasizes a public/private distinction and the protection of individual rights. John Locke is a paradigmatic example. For contemporary discussions, see Ronald Dworkin, "Liberalism," in idem, *A Matter of Principle* (Cambridge, Mass.: Harvard University Press, 1985), 181–204, and Samuel Freeman, "Illiberal Libertarians: Why Libertarianism Is Not a Liberal View," *Philosophy and Public Affairs* 30, no. 2 (April 2001): 105–51.

[2] For a procedural defense of democracy with reference to an account of equal political resources, see Thomas Christiano, *The Rule of the Many: Fundamental Issues in Democratic Theory* (Boulder, Colo.: Westview, 1996). Jeremy Waldron defends a specifically majoritarian procedure as inherently valuable on the basis that it is the best manifestation of persons' capacity to make their own decisions in his *Law and Disagreement* (New York: Oxford University Press, 1999), 109, 250, where he elaborates upon this argument as rights-based. Both Christiano and Waldron explicitly reject any attempt to synthesize substantive and procedural concerns in an account of self-government.

therefore, defends substantive rights on the grounds that they are not only distinct from, but also more fundamental than, democracy.

The view that a theory of basic rights both has a root distinct from democracy and also constrains democracy is present in major historical and contemporary accounts of liberalism. It is implicit in Locke's argument that natural property rights should constrain any theory of consent, as well as in liberal theories that tie rights to a concept of "intrinsic dignity."[3] Finally, a popular understanding of the substantive guarantees implicit in the Bill of Rights, such as the Eighth Amendment, and of the doctrine of substantive due process elaborated in the twentieth century is that a general theory of justice must constrain a democratic polity if the latter is to be legitimate.

The theoretical distinction between democracy and rights is also reflected in ordinary language. The term "democracy" is often used to refer to majority decision making. Rights violations, by contrast, are often associated with distinct moral principles of justice, principles that serve to limit majority tyranny. The definitional implication would seem to be that democratic decisions could violate substantive individual rights. For instance, a polity could decide democratically to violate an individual's privacy rights.

The common distinction between democracy and substantive individual rights introduces a major normative problem—that of constraint—suggesting that this distinction is flawed. An appeal to the will of the people is often thought the best justification of political coercion because the very people who are coerced are also the source of the coercion. In contrast, however, rights that are substantive seem to constrain the will of the people because of their reliance on principles external to democracy. The reasons that support the protection of substantive rights need to be more fundamental than democratic will if they are to trump it when the two conflict.[4] To sum up, the problem of constraint is how to reconcile external constraints on democratic procedures with the belief that democracy is the fundamental basis for legitimate polities.

A theory that could explain why an ideal democracy would protect substantive individual rights would resolve the problem of constraint. In this book I lay out such a theory, conceptualizing democracy as an ideal that accounts for both

---

[3]John Locke, *Two Treatises of Government*, ed. Peter Laslett (Cambridge: Cambridge University Press, 1988), 412, where Locke discusses property. See also Harvey Mansfield, *America's Constitutional Soul* (Baltimore: Johns Hopkins University Press, 1993).

[4]On some accounts, democracy is merely instrumentally valuable because it tends to protect rights. When it fails to do so, however, it should be overridden. In contrast, as will become evident, I offer an account whereby democracy and rights are not in tension but part of a coherent, unified theory of self-government. As I noted in the introduction, to some extent, I share this ambition with Rawls and Habermas.

procedural guarantees and basic rights. As an alternative to the notion that rights are conceptually distinct from democracy, I attempt to recast the idea of substantive rights as an aspect of the democratic ideal.

This move has a semantic implication. Whereas the adjective "substantive" is widely thought to mean "distinct from democracy," my argument suggests why the term should be taken to mean "distinct from democratic procedures but central to the ideal of democracy." A similar implication holds for the common phrase "liberal democracy."[5] Since the adjective "liberal" is associated with substantive rights, it is often thought to constrain the word "democracy." After demonstrating why individual rights need not be thought of as constraints on democracy, I suggest a new understanding of the phrase: liberal rights do not constrain democracy; they are required by it. With this understanding, I do not object to my view of democracy being considered "liberal."

Broadly, my aim is to demonstrate that a core set of substantive values implicitly underlies pure procedural theories of democracy. I articulate three *core values of democracy:* equality of interests, political autonomy, and reciprocity. These values are central to the idea of democracy because they support the notion of democratic citizens as free, equal, and reasonable rulers. My thesis is that the core values require the guarantee of substantive individual rights as well as rights to participate in democratic procedures. I call this account *the value theory of democracy.*

There are two advantages to conceptualizing both substantive and procedural rights within a theory of democracy. First, such a theory does not rely, as do traditional human rights and natural rights theories, on an assumption of inherent human dignity. Both human rights and natural rights accounts are "metaphysical" in character because they attempt to ground rights in a theory of what it is to be human. Traditionally, such theories defend rights by appealing to often controversial conceptions of personhood that posit an inherent dignity.[6] However, several schools of contemporary theory, including post-

---

[5] I owe this formulation in part to William Galston during a discussion of his manuscript in progress on value pluralism.

[6] This idea is arguably enacted by Germany's constitution. Specifically, Article 1 of the 1949 German Basic Law (*Grundgesetz*) reads, "The dignity of man shall be inviolable. To respect and protect it shall be the duty of all state authority." In contrast, the fact that the Constitution of the United States begins in the preamble with reference to "we the people" could suggest that it and its rights protections should be read as democratic. Prominent contemporary defenders of metaphysical dignity include George Kateb, who writes, "I can't here spell out this notion of equal human dignity. . . . But the core is quite familiar: government is entrusted with the task of doing its necessary work within the limits of recognizing basic individual rights. Unless these rights are recognized, the equal dignity of human beings is not recognized, and people are reduced in their status as human beings to the level of animals or machines or things or wayward children who can never grow up" (Kateb, "What do Citizens Owe Their Constitutional Democracy?" Delivered at the

9

modernism, have challenged what some scholars think is the essentialist assumption at the heart of this doctrine.[7]

It is an advantage of my theory that it need not take a stand about whether dignity is inherent in personhood.[8] I avoid this question not because I think any one school has answered it, but because in politics it is a virtue to take a widely shared concept as one's starting point. I believe this is an advantage of viewing the democratic ideal as the first principle of democratic legitimacy. Because the value theory of democracy focuses on what it means to be a democratic citizen instead of engaging in metaphysical arguments about what it means to be a person, it is compatible with a plurality of metaphysical conceptions and therefore serves as a widely held starting point for thinking about substantive individual rights.

The second advantage of the value theory of democracy over liberal theories of rights is that it resolves rather than replicates the problem of constraint. Liberal theories face the daunting task of demonstrating that substantive rights are more fundamental than democracy in order to justify a constraint on democratic procedures. If rights are formulated with the concept of democracy as a guide, however, a defense of substantive individual rights need not answer such a challenge. Instead, when these rights are formulated in democratic terms, the injury that comes with their violation can be articulated in terms of, rather than in conflict with, the ideal of self-governance. Although the notion of substantive democratic rights is commonly viewed as a contradiction given democratic theory's unresolved problem of constraint, I argue that this notion is essential to self-government rightly understood.[9]

Unlike other attempts to reconcile the ideal of self-government with the tra-

---

Center for Human Values Twentieth-Anniversary Celebration, unpublished ms., 2000). For an elaboration of Kateb's view, see Kateb, *The Inner Ocean: Individualism and Democratic Culture* (Ithaca: Cornell University Press, 1992).

[7] One well-known statement of the postmodern perspective is Richard Rorty, *Contingency, Irony, and Solidarity* (Cambridge: Cambridge University Press, 1989).

[8] Regardless of whether metaphysical theorists are correct to claim that all humans possess inherent dignity, many people find it difficult to identify dignity in those citizens who commit the most brutal crimes. A theory of rights that relied on democratic, as opposed to metaphysical, values, would not face the task of showing that the rights of criminal defendants, among the most basic for individual rights theorists, rest on a dignity they seem to have rejected. A similar point is made by Hugo Adam Bedau, "Abolishing the Death Penalty Even for the Worst Murderers," in *The Killing State: Capital Punishment in Law, Politics, and Culture,* ed. Austin Sarat (New York: Oxford University Press, 1999). For an alternative to the dignity-based criticism of capital punishment, see Austin Sarat, *When the State Kills: Capital Punishment and the American Condition* (Princeton: Princeton University Press, 2001). Also see my "Dignity, Citizenship, and Capital Punishment: The Right of Life Reformulated," *Studies in Law, Politics, and Society* 25 (2002): 119–32.

[9] Some thinkers contrast the concept of "self-government" with "democracy." My understanding of democracy is that it is an account of self-government, and I therefore use the terms inter-

ditionally liberal concern to protect substantive individual rights by appealing to an account of ideal procedure, I appeal to a set of values that underlie the democratic ideal. But why begin with the premise that democracy itself is an ideal? Certainly in life there are other relationships with more value than those rightly considered democratic. Love and friendship, for instance, are better candidates for ideal social relationships. While this might be correct, my ambition is not to assume democracy is the highest ideal of life, but rather that it is the best way to understand the relationship between the state and its citizens and, more specifically, the best way to legitimize the state's use of force. I proceed with the stipulation that the ideal of democracy is the most promising reference point for understanding political legitimacy.

Of course, much inquiry in political theory is devoted to comparison of regimes, and scholars might fruitfully ask why democracy is preferable to other political systems. Though this is a worthy question, I do not take it up here. Rather, I aim to clarify what actions and understandings are required by the democratic ideal, and specifically to argue for them as a way of debating the justifiability of coercion and individual rights. It is possible that the more expansive ideal of democracy that I develop will be attractive to those who might favor other regime types devoted to the protection of individual rights, such as constitutionalism and liberalism. Fundamentally, however, my question is not what justifies democracy, but what democracy means.

The argument in this chapter proceeds in three stages. First, I reveal the limits of purely procedural democratic theories by pointing to the substantive values that underlie them. Second, I argue that these substantive values are in fact democratic values, and I demonstrate how they ground the value theory of democracy. Third I demonstrate that democratic procedures should be constrained when they threaten to undermine the core values of democracy. This chapter sets the stage for the central argument of this book: that such constraints on democratic procedure should be understood as a set of democratic rights retained by all citizens.

II. Procedural Democratic Theories

Before I articulate the value theory of democracy, I will explore the flaws in commonly held accounts of democracy that are purely procedural.[10] Pure pro-

---

changeably. For a different view contrasting self-government with democracy, see Christiano, *Rule Of The Many*, chap. 1.

[10] The use of the term "pure" in this section is elaborated in Brettschneider, "Balancing Proce-

ceduralists are characterized by their belief that a decision is democratically legitimate because it is produced by citizens participating in a fair procedure.[11] According to such a view, there is nothing intrinsically democratic about such decisions aside from the fact that they were produced by democratic procedures. Thus, pure proceduralists see no way to use a procedure-independent standard to evaluate the democratic legitimacy of an outcome. In contrast, my aim is to show that the democratic legitimacy of an outcome is rightly determined by its adherence to a set of democratic ideals. To demonstrate the feasibility of relying on such procedure-independent ideals, I explain why even procedural views implicitly appeal to a set of independent standards. I then demonstrate, in the next section, in what sense these standards are regarded as democratic and why the rights demanded by these standards are also properly considered democratic.

I explore several theories that can be characterized as exclusively procedural but suffer from a critical inconsistency. Despite their ostensibly pure proceduralism, such theories implicitly assume procedure-independent values, values whose presence they deny. I begin by critiquing what I regard as the weakest of these theories, majoritarianism, and then move on to more sophisticated variants.

Perhaps the appeal of procedural accounts of democracy stems from the commonly held definition of democracy as majoritarianism, that is, the notion that the decisions of more than 50 percent of an entire polity are democratically binding for all. Belief in the fairness of majoritarianism is so deeply held that many might not see it as requiring a justification at all. But any good procedure, like any good theory, must have reasons and principles that support it. Majoritarianism must appeal to more than the self-evident validity of the procedure. Relying only on the intuition that majoritarianism is "common sense" would simply be using the procedure to validate itself.[12]

However, the principles that lie outside of the procedure of majority rule might come into conflict with the very procedure to which they give rise. For example, imagine that the justification for majoritarianism is that it gives as many individuals as possible the ability to participate in political decision making. In other words, this procedure both allows all citizens to have a voice in decision making and offers resolution in the face of conflicting views. In this case,

---

dures and Outcomes Within Democratic Theory: Core Values and Judicial Review," *Political Studies* 53, no. 2 (June 2005): 423–41. In this article, I contrast pure proceduralism with impure proceduralism, a view recognizing that substantive rights limit, but do not trump, democratic procedures.

[11] See Estlund, "Democratic Theory," 211.

[12] Ibid.

the justification of majoritarianism could easily conflict with outcomes of majority rule. Consider a case in which a majority disenfranchised one quarter of the population. Here the justification of democracy, that it includes as many citizens as possible in an act of self-rule, conflicts with the results of majoritarian procedure. The result is a tension between the procedure and the reasons that underlie it. Accordingly, if it is not to be self-defeating, majoritarianism should recognize some limits on policy outcomes to ensure that its fundamental justification is not undermined.

In response to such challenges, democratic theorists have developed more sophisticated theories of democracy. Some of these theories remain committed to majoritarian procedures as the core of democracy while avoiding the mistakes of pure majoritarianism. One version of such a theory holds that democracy requires a procedural right of all to participate in democratic decisions as a "precondition" of majority voting. This theory therefore avoids the specific problem of disenfranchisement by recognizing that rule by the people means that no citizen, despite procedural decisions to the contrary, is excluded from the right to participate in democratic procedure. Unlike pure majoritarianism, this view can explain why limiting the franchise based on race or gender is blatantly undemocratic: such a policy would deny some individuals and groups the basic rights of participation essential to democratic governance.

Although it resolves the specific issue of disenfranchisement, however, this version of proceduralism contains a similar flaw to majoritarianism. Despite guaranteeing a right to vote, it does not ensure that participation is meaningful because it might allow for a crippling lack of preparation or education among citizens participating in the procedure. Part of the justification for majoritarianism is that it does not simply allow everyone to partake in decision making, but it recognizes that all have an equal say in voting. Aristocratic voting procedures that gave multiple votes to the educated, for instance, could appropriately be dismissed as undemocratic by majoritarians.[13] But at the same time, merely to give an equal vote to some citizens who lack the capacity to make informed decisions could violate the principle of equality implicit in a democratic procedure. For instance, individuals guaranteed the right to vote might be denied information about the matters before them. For such persons, the concept of universal participation would have no worth.

Because of the realization that participation must be meaningful, some prominent theorists have developed a view that I call "rights as procedural preconditions" to democracy. On this account, the preconditions necessary for citizens to participate as equals must be guaranteed in a legitimate democracy.

---

[13] I elaborate on this point later in the chapter.

Supporters of these theories often claim, therefore, that the rights they defend are procedural, not substantive, because they only serve to enable a good democratic procedure.

Defenders of this view include Alexander Meiklejohn, who suggests that the right of free speech is a precondition for good democratic procedure. Similarly, John Hart Ely at times argues that a variety of rights, including the right to travel, are justified at least partially as necessary preconditions to democratic procedures, and thus are "democracy-reinforcing."[14] Similarly, others have attempted to defend welfare rights as instrumental to democratic procedure. Without adequate means of subsistence, these theorists argue, one cannot go to the polls as an equal participant in democracy.[15] For instance, Carole Pateman has argued on these grounds that an inalienable right to a basic income is essential to democratic citizenship. Another account suggests that even a right of privacy or decisional autonomy is necessary if citizens are to have the conceptual space to decide how best to cast their vote.[16] All of these theorists argue that their frameworks are still procedural because they maintain the ideal of majoritarian procedure at the core of democracy.

The identification of rights as procedural preconditions could be employed as a strategy for defending democratic individual rights. For two reasons, however, I find this view to be too weak a defense. First, it is possible that an empirical study could show that participation was causally unaffected by the preconditional rights these theorists have posited. The result of such a study would undermine purely preconditional defenses of democratic rights.

Second, participants within a procedure who are guaranteed preconditional rights might make a decision to jettison the very rights they have been guaranteed. For instance, imagine that citizens participating in a procedure that guaranteed them a right to free speech as a precondition of voting decided that this right hindered their voting ability and thus decided to revoke it. Such a circumstance is problematic for the preconditional theorist because it forces her to claim both that, on the one hand, the source of legitimacy is the actual participation in the procedure, and, on the other hand, that preconditional rights

---

[14] See Alexander Meiklejohn, *Political Freedom: The Constitutional Powers of the People* (New York: Harper and Brothers, 1960), and John Hart Ely, *Democracy and Distrust: A Theory of Judicial Review* (Cambridge, Mass.: Harvard University Press, 1980), 178.

[15] See Carole Pateman, "Freedom and Democratization: Why Basic Income is to be Preferred to Basic Capital," in *The Ethics of Stakeholding*, ed. Keith Dowding, Jurgen De Wispelaere, and Stuart White (London: Palgrave Macmillan, 2004). Pateman suggests that basic income rights are inalienable because of their essential role as a precondition to political participation.

[16] Michelman suggests that the civic republican tradition can offer a defense of the right of privacy on the grounds that it is a precondition to meaningful political participation; see idem, "Law's Republic," *Yale Law Journal* 97, no. 8 (July 1988): 1493–537.

are necessary for the procedure to be legitimate. The problem here is that the view is supposed to be justified fundamentally on procedural grounds. However, this would mean that those participating in the procedure could decide to revoke the preconditional rights this theory posits.

The tension between procedures and the principles that underlie them leaves the precondition theorist with a choice. Either she can abandon the notion that preconditions are intrinsic to procedural legitimacy, or she must suggest a justification for preconditional rights that does not depend on their affirmation by those participating in a procedure. The latter strategy requires a justification of rights that is tied not to the procedure itself, but rather to principles independent of the procedure. Precondition theorists might be reluctant to follow this strategy on the grounds that it would reintroduce the problem of constraint and therefore take away from the fundamentally democratic nature of rights. I think this concern is unfounded. An appeal to procedure-independent values, I argue, is potentially an appeal to democratic values. The problem of constraint can be avoided if the procedure-independent values are tailored in such a way as to articulate a democratic ideal. Before I elaborate on this approach, however, it is important to examine what is perhaps the most prominent defense of proceduralism in the literature of contemporary democratic theory: Jürgen Habermas's theory of deliberative democracy.

For Habermas, the ideal democratic procedure relies not on the will of the majority but on a conception of unanimity. He writes, "Specifically, the democratic principle states that only those statutes may claim legitimacy that can meet with the assent [*Zustimmung*] of all citizens in a discursive process of legislation that in turn has been legally constituted."[17] This does not imply that individuals must make actual decisions unanimously. Habermas recognizes that such a requirement would be unworkable at the legislative level. Instead, he suggests that democratic legitimacy rests on an ideal of unanimity within an ideal procedure, a procedure defined in part by what he calls "ideal speech" conditions.[18] In Habermas's view, legitimate democratic decisions should be made in the context of an ideal environment where all citizens are free to deliberate and reason with each other about policy. In part, such an ideal procedure is defined by citizens' willingness to reason about policy by appeal to reasons that acknowledge each participant's status as an equal. Moreover, the theory requires that citizens would be assured a variety of preconditional rights, such as a right to basic material welfare, to ensure that they can function within the procedure as autonomous and equal. Since decisions within the ideal procedure

[17] Jürgen Habermas, *Between Facts and Norms: Contributions to a Discourse Theory of Law and Democracy*, trans. William Rehg (Cambridge, Mass.: MIT Press, 1996), 110.
[18] Ibid., 322–23.

must be unanimous and acceptable to all, each citizen is assured that his interests cannot be neglected. According to Habermas, the view is purely procedural in that the decisions of individuals within the ideal procedure provide the sole basis for democratic legitimacy.

Although Habermas's view is not majoritarian, the same challenge I presented against the preconditional view is appropriate here. What if those in the ideal speech situation wished to alter the preconditions that Habermas believes define it?[19] This problem would arise if, for instance, participants in the ideal procedure unanimously decided to jettison welfare rights. One response is that such an instance simply violates the requirements of the ideal procedure necessary for legitimacy. Yet to make this argument coherently, Habermas would have to claim that the ideal procedure is more fundamental than the actual decisions of deliberators.

Habermas seems to reject this suggestion. He argues that a theory of democracy must ground any account of rights in an account of democratic procedure or risk collapsing into a liberal theory of justice. For Habermas, any nonprocedural approach to democratic accounts of rights is problematic because on such accounts, rights would then be "possessed like things."[20] For the citizens in Habermas's ideal environment, such a view could not "reignite the radical democratic embers . . . in the civic life of their society, for from their perspective all of the *essential* discourses of legitimation have already taken place within the theory; and they find the results of the theory already sedimented in the constitution."[21] Habermas suggests that the legitimacy of even the basic rights essential to the ideal procedure must rest on affirmation by citizens. As I read him here, Habermas is suggesting that any attempt to justify rights with reference to an ideal standard, independent of actual affirmation, is unacceptable be-

---

[19] Samuel Freeman has raised a similar question about Joshua Cohen's work in "Deliberative Democracy: A Sympathetic Comment," *Philosophy and Public Affairs* 29, no. 4 (Autumn 2000): 392. Specifically Freeman argues that the "ideal procedure" Cohen posits as the basis for democratic legitimacy could undermine the preconditions of such a procedure that legitimacy also demands. Cohen, however, has an advantage over Habermas in that he recognizes that rights such as minimal income and welfare are in fact substantive. Yet a question could still arise as to why these rights are more fundamental than democratic procedures if the two conflict. In later work, Cohen defends substantive rights such as freedom of religion on the basis that they are necessary to reflect background conditions of "reasonable pluralism"; see Joshua Cohen, "Procedure and Substance in Deliberative Democracy," in *Democracy and Difference: Contesting the Boundaries of the Political,* ed. Seyla Benhabib (Princeton: Princeton University Press, 1996), 95–119.

[20] Habermas's contribution to his exchange with Rawls is reprinted in Habermas, *The Inclusion of the Other: Studies in Political Theory,* ed. Ciaran Cronin and Pablo De Greif (Cambridge, Mass.: M.I.T. Press, 1998), 54.

[21] Ibid., 69.

cause it introduces the problem of constraint and thus undermines his aim of having coercion be based entirely on a theory of self-government. While claiming to endorse the "co-original" status of rights and democracy, therefore, Habermas has not answered the challenge that a purely procedural theory can be self-defeating when it comes to preconditional rights. Because he emphasizes that the decisions of citizens within his ideal procedure are the sole basis for democratic legitimacy, Habermas cannot explain why rights are not vulnerable to revocation by those participants within democratic procedure.

To summarize, a coherent version of majoritarianism would have to recognize that a tension exists between majority voting and the reasons for such voting. Sophisticated theories respond by putting forward a variety of rights as preconditions of democratic procedures. But these theories cannot successfully defend preconditions in a noncontingent way without abandoning the idea that procedure serves as the fundamental locus of democracy.

In the following section, I argue that democratic theorists should abandon what has been an excessive fixation on procedures and acknowledge that substantive values lie at the core of the ideal of democracy. I do not deny that procedures such as majority rule play a central role within democratic theory.[22] I argue, however, that a set of procedure-independent core values constitute the democratic ideal, properly understood. Although these values are not acknowledged by proceduralists, they underlie all democratic procedures. I will show that proceduralists such as Habermas are mistaken to think an embrace of procedure independence means a reintroduction of the problem of constraint and an abandonment of self-government as the central basis for legitimacy.

III. PROCEDURE-INDEPENDENT THEORIES: EPISTEMIC AND DEMOCRATIC

In the previous section, I demonstrated the weakness of procedural theories that fail to recognize their reliance on procedure-independent standards. In this section, I propose an alternative theory: the *value theory of democracy*. This theory relies on a procedure-independent standard comprised of what I call the *core values* of democracy. According to the value theory, this core values standard serves as the basis for both justifying democratic procedures and constraining them.

Establishing the core values as central to the meaning of democracy first requires distinguishing them from theories that seek to ground democratic

---

[22] For instance, the abolition of elections is clear evidence that a polity is no longer democratic. For a wider discussion of the role of procedures in a value theory of democracy see Brettschneider, "Balancing Procedures and Outcomes Within Democratic Theory."

procedure in a standard that is just or legitimate, but not necessarily democratic. I undertake this task in the next part of this section. I begin with a discussion of epistemic theories and their nondemocratic procedure-independent standards. Then I outline my contrasting approach: a theory that rests on a democratic procedure-independent standard. Finally, I describe the core values that compose this standard: *equality of interests, political autonomy,* and *reciprocity*.

Epistemic Theories and Nondemocratic Procedure-Independent Standards

Many traditional liberal theorists have identified the need to defend democratic procedures by appealing to values external to these procedures. They judge a particular procedure based on whether it tends to produce outcomes that are just, true, or good, thus assigning democracy a subordinate, instrumental role within a specific theory of truth or justice. For instance, epistemic theories of democracy defend majoritarian procedures as valid means of lawmaking because they tend toward the promotion of truth; when these procedures fail to promote truth, epistemic theorists believe that they should be overridden.[23] According to these theorists, democracy itself is only justifiable because it promotes substantive outcomes that are closer to an ideal of justice than any other alternative. In the absence of any one expert authorized to decide what constitutes the truth, epistemic theories suggest that majorities offer the best means of advancing policies that are likely to be close to the truth.

Epistemic theories are attractive because they explain why the principles that underlie democratic procedure can also justify overriding that procedure if it produces outcomes that threaten its own justification. This provides an answer to the problem I noted with Habermas's account of democracy: his inability to explain why legitimacy would require an override when participants in the ideal procedure decided to revoke preconditional rights. Although the epistemic theorist's answer is an improvement over Habermas's, a serious difficulty remains. The problem is that once the theorist appeals to values beyond procedure, there is a danger that she will reintroduce, rather than resolve, the problem of con-

---

[23] Although this structure characterizes epistemic theories in general, David Estlund's account stresses why "truth" in political matters rightly focuses on the question of legitimacy, or rightful rule. Rightful rule in conditions of pluralism cannot be based on one comprehensive theory; thus, a theory which looks to truth cannot itself be comprehensive. My own view attempts to define legitimacy in a manner consistent with the ideal of democracy. While I avoid the term "truth," I share Estlund's belief that political legitimacy should not rest on one comprehensive theory and should be compatible with a plurality of comprehensive doctrines. See, for instance, idem, "Democratic Theory," and idem, "The Insularity of the Reasonable: Why Political Liberalism Must Admit the Truth," *Ethics* 108, no. 2 (January 1998): 252–75.

straint. In other words, because the epistemic theorist has appealed to a non-democratic procedure-independent standard, she must demonstrate that this standard is more fundamental than democracy.

If, for instance, the ideals of truth or justice appeal to a particular comprehensive view of the good, I argue that they would rightly be dismissed as non-democratic. In any society, citizens have an abundance of reasonable beliefs about what truth is, or indeed about whether there is such a thing as truth. Conceptions of justice are similarly wide-ranging. For example, some notions of divine justice might conflict with comprehensive Kantian theories, yet both might still be reasonable. The imposition of one comprehensive view would therefore be especially problematic if it were done in the name of democracy. The ideal of democracy, I argue, is self-rule, and subordinating democratic institutions to one particular comprehensive view would impose external rule on citizens who, reasonably, did not share that view.

The Value Theory of Democracy

To avoid the logical flaws of procedural and epistemic theories, we have established that our alternative theory cannot adhere unflinchingly to the outcomes of democratic procedures, nor can it rely on a comprehensive standard of justice that constrains those procedures. How, then, can we ground this alternative theory? I propose that a truly democratic theory must be grounded in the fundamental, or "core," values of democracy itself.[24] These values are implicit in commonly accepted democratic institutions, such as the rule of law and free speech.[25] They also compose the key elements of an ideal democracy: "government of the people, by the people, for the people."[26] In the discussion that follows, I will demonstrate that the value theory of democracy—and its core values—rest on the respect of all citizens as rulers. This conception is importantly different from procedural theories in that it emphasizes the status of citizens as more fundamental than their role in democratic procedures.

In breaking from the proceduralist tradition to develop a substantive theory of democratic values, my approach risks losing an uncontroversial definition of

---

[24] The argument that follows draws heavily from my interpretation of Rawls's overall theory. On my view, it is Rawls's political conception of the person—in particular the idea of free and equal citizenship, and the values this entails—that can serve as the basis for a theory of democracy. Unlike traditional contractualist readings, my reading sees Rawls as fundamentally concerned with core values. The view at stake is most clearly articulated in John Rawls, *Justice as Fairness: A Restatement,* ed. Erin Kelly (Cambridge, Mass.: Harvard University Press, 2001).

[25] I discuss the relevance of the rule of law and free speech to the value theory in chapter 2.

[26] Etymologically, the root "demos" refers to "people," while "kratos" means "rule" or "power."

democracy, namely, citizens authorizing legitimate law through their participation in democratic procedures.[27] The argument of the previous section illustrates, however, that there is theoretical controversy over which procedures are most legitimate in a democracy, and that the best way of evaluating these differences is to look to the underlying values implicit in the various theories of democracy. Thus, the shift to a focus on values makes the issues in these debates more transparent.

This emphasis on values does not deny that certain procedures are a necessary condition of legitimate democracies. I merely contend that democratic procedures should be grounded in a broader theory of democracy with explicitly articulated values, values focused on citizens' status as self-rulers, or what might be called their "sovereign status." Once the content of these values is understood, I will elaborate on how the values not only justify democratic procedures but also can be used to evaluate the policy outcomes produced by these procedures from the standpoint of the democratic ideal. I contend that certain democratic outcomes consistent with these fundamental values are also necessary conditions of legitimate democracies.

Let us return now to the discussion of citizens' status as rulers, the central concern that must be reflected in the value theory of democracy. In order to understand why the sovereign status of the citizen is more fundamental than the specific capacity of democratic citizens to participate in self-rule, consider in greater depth the phrase "rule by the people." Democratic theorists' understanding of this phrase traditionally has emphasized the verb "rule." Theorists from majoritarians to sophisticated proceduralists have sought to center their theories on a procedural action taken by a group of the people. Before we can discuss what it means for a democratic people to rule, however, we must express what it means for them to be constituted as a people. This requires a discussion of the proper treatment of citizen rulers.

In part, individuals' status as rulers implies their capacity as citizens to participate in procedures for political decision making. Respecting a citizen's status as a ruler also requires, however, that policy outcomes that result from democratic procedures do not undermine this status. That the core values of democracy have procedural implications while limiting what counts as a legitimate democratic outcome can be illustrated by considering the famous definition of democracy articulated by Lincoln in the Gettysburg Address: "government of the people, by the people, for the people."[28] The notion that

[27] This concern was raised by Henry S. Richardson at the Cornell Young Scholar's Conference, May 1, 2004.

[28] The full quotation reads: "It is rather for us to be here dedicated to the great task remaining before us; that from these honored dead we take increased devotion to that cause for which they

government is *of* the people can be understood as a claim about authority. Coercion is justified best by an appeal to its origin in, or authorization by, the people who are coerced. The notion of rule *by* the people indicates that this coercion must respect, with proper procedures, the importance of the people's role in decision making. Procedure alone, however, cannot protect citizens' status as rulers. Government also must be *for* the people—government policies themselves must reflect the status of citizens as the ultimate source of authority by respecting their interests and by ensuring that state coercion does not treat them in a manner that undermines that status.

To highlight the contrast between the value theory and a proceduralist approach to theorizing democracy, consider two instances in which an aggregate of persons is not a democratic people. As a preliminary definition, I use the phrase "democratic people" to mean that those within a polity are treated in the manner required by democratic legitimacy. Our first instance is rule by an unelected colonial power. This is obviously undemocratic because it involves government not "by the people" but by a potentially hostile external force. No colonists are involved in the process of governing, so they are granted no procedural rights. The second instance is a colonial political system in which an indigenous group *does* retain procedural rights as subjects of an empire but still might argue justifiably that the principle of self-rule has been violated. This instance is exemplified by the American colonists. For all of what we might call their "proceduralist" arguments against British "taxation without representation," it is important that the colonists also refused representation in Parliament on the grounds that their fundamental interests as colonists would be neglected even if they enjoyed procedural equality with Englishmen.[29] In other words,

---

here gave the last full measure of devotion; that we here highly resolve that these dead shall not have died in vain; that the nation shall, under God, have a new birth of freedom, and that government of the people, by the people, for the people, shall not perish from the earth" ([Abraham Lincoln's] "Gettysburg Address," in Lois J. Einhorn, *Abraham Lincoln the Orator: Penetrating the Lincoln Legend* [Westport, Conn.: Greenwood, 1992], 177). I read Lincoln's argument here to be about what it means to be a democratic people. A separate question concerns the idea of a people. To claim that a people is nondemocratic does not mean that it in no sense is a people. A people ruled by a despot or a dictator could certainly have an identity as a national or ethnic people. But sociologically these terms are not normative. My point regards what is required to be a democratic people, which I believe has implications for democratic legitimacy. For a discussion of this issue see, Rogers M. Smith, *Stories of Peoplehood: The Politics and Morals of Political Membership* (Cambridge: Cambridge University Press, 2003).

[29] See "The Official Colonial Protest: The Declaration of the Stamp Act Congress (October 19, 1765)," in *Colonies to Nation 1763–1789: A Documentary History of the American Revolution*, ed. Jack P. Greene (New York: Norton, 1975), 63. I would like to thank Nate Goralnik and Gordon Wood for directing me to this document and for this point.

even had their democratic rights to participation been honored, they were concerned that Parliament's procedure would lead to unfair economic policy.

I take this to suggest that democracy entails not only procedural rights to rule by the people but also government *for* the people.[30] Even when colonists are granted procedural rights, colonialism is undemocratic when the governing power fails to serve the legitimate interests of the governed. If the American colonists had accepted representation in Parliament but its colonial tax policy had remained the same, they still would have been the victims of undemocratic treatment. This policy allowed Englishmen to use the colonies as mere means to enrich themselves, a practice that patently implied the unequal status of the colonists. Such a practice would have undermined the colonists' status as rulers, regardless of whether they had actually participated in a vote about it in Parliament.

The requirement that democracy be both by and for the people cannot be accounted for in purely procedural terms. Procedural theories address the actions that a people take in authorizing law, but they neglect to provide guarantees that the outcomes of the democratic process will also respect citizens' fundamental interests. Democracy's dual commitments to rule by and for the people suggest a more fundamental grounding of both of these components in the status of a democratic people as self-ruling. In turn, this collective notion of the status of a democratic people entails a respect for individual citizens and their status as individual rulers. This status underlies both the procedural guarantees ensuring that members of a democracy can participate in lawmaking and the limits that must be placed on nondemocratic outcomes. These limits are substantive, not procedural; they ensure against policy that undermines citizens' fundamental interest in being treated as rulers and thereby support what I will argue in the following chapter is a democratic entitlement to reasonable treatment.

The view that democratic authority comes from the people but must also respect the status of the people as citizens opens democratic theory to a realm of inquiry traditionally limited to moral philosophy and accounts of justice. Democratic theory has often been confined to procedural discussions of democratic politics in the narrow sense or to democratic "culture" in a very broad sense. However, understanding the democratic ideal as centrally defined by values introduces democratic theory to examinations of the justification and limits of legitimate coercion in political society. The core democratic values should play a central role in discussing these aspects of coercion.

Now that we have elaborated on why the value theory of democracy respects

[30] For a useful discussion of this phrase in the context of Rawls's work, see Joshua Cohen, "For a Democratic Society," in *The Cambridge Companion to Rawls,* ed. Samuel Freeman (Cambridge: Cambridge University Press, 2003), 86–138.

citizens' status in the sense of rule both by and for the people, we are in a position to define explicitly the core values of this theory and their procedural and substantive implications.

The Three Core Values of Democracy

The values I invoke as components of the value theory of democracy—equality of interests, political autonomy, and reciprocity—could, standing alone, underlie a whole range of political ideals that are not clearly democratic. My aim, however, is to develop a collective understanding of these values that focuses on their specifically democratic meaning. Each of the values is interpreted so as to avoid an appeal to a comprehensive notion of truth and to articulate aspects of the shared ideal of democratic citizenship. I elaborate on both the procedural and substantive democratic implications of each of the values in turn.

The first core value I call "equality of interests." Equality of interests does not provide a comprehensive statement about the nature of humans. It does not, for instance, rely on a conception of equality before God. Rather, as a standard for evaluating democratic procedures and democratic outcomes, it requires that all reasonable interests of citizens be respected as having equal weight. No one person should have his interests counted more than those of any other person by virtue of his social position or class. Equality of interests is implicit in most procedures regarded as democratic; it is expressed in the general principle of "one person, one vote."[31] Moreover, procedures that violate this value by counting one person's interests as intrinsically more valuable than another's are intuitively regarded as undemocratic.

Famously, John Stuart Mill once proposed that those who were educated at Oxford or Cambridge should have two votes, while those without such an education should have one.[32] On Mill's account, since voting primarily is meant to produce the best outcome, it would be sensible to allow those with more education more voting power. This proposal brings out the intuitive problem with solely instrumental accounts of democratic procedure; more importantly, it demonstrates why equality of interests is an intrinsically valuable part of the democratic ideal, not defensible merely with reference to its good consequences. Allowing some citizens more votes than their fellows, whether because of education or noble birth, undermines the sense of democracy as

---

[31] In *Reynolds v. Sims*, 377 U.S. 533 (1964), the Supreme Court identified this principle at the heart of the Fourteenth Amendment's "Equal Protection" Clause. See also *Baker v. Carr*, 369 U.S. 186 (1962).

[32] John Stuart Mill, "Considerations on Representative Government," in *On Liberty and Considerations on Representative Government*, ed. R. B. McCallum (Oxford: Basil Blackwell, 1948), 218.

government by all the people and the democratic idea that all citizens have equal status.

While there are important procedural implications of democratic equality as a value based on government "by" the people, this value also serves as a democratic limit on procedure. In other words, equality of interests also ensures rule *for* the people. As I suggested in section II, above, structuring a procedure to reflect equality of interests does not guarantee that the law ultimately will respect this value in its substance. Thus, I argue in the following chapters that law in a legitimate democracy should be formulated and coercive institutions arranged to ensure that all citizens are *treated* as having equal interests.

The second core value I call "political autonomy." Broadly, it entails the treatment of citizens as individual rulers in a society characterized by collective self-rule. Part of the requirement of political autonomy is a role for citizens in deciding through democratic procedures how policy should be formulated. In elaborating this concept, it again is helpful to look at the standard implicit in common distinctions between democratic and nondemocratic procedures. Imagine that in a majoritarian procedure a majority would, free from outside intervention, vote in a manner that undermined the overall good. If the value of citizens' participation in these procedures were merely instrumental, we might conclude that there was nothing wrong with forcing citizens to vote for the proposal that would bring about the most overall good. Our intuitions about democracy tell us, however, that even if such forced voting might result in more overall good, it would be undemocratic to force citizens to vote in a particular way. Similarly, for certain citizens to purchase the votes of other citizens would rightly be regarded as a violation of democratic values. Such procedures would be undemocratic because they would not allow individuals to make their own autonomous decisions about politics.

Just as democratic equality should be understood as a value based on rule both by and for the people, so, too, the democratic meaning of political autonomy does not merely protect individual rights to participate in collective decision making. Political autonomy also has substantive implications for the democratic treatment of citizens as rulers. For instance, I argue in the next chapter that part of the distinctly nonprocedural harm that comes from ex post facto laws is their failure to give citizens fair warning about possible punishments. Subject to coercion without fair warning, citizens could not plan their lives without fearing arbitrary mistreatment.[33] This restriction, I argue, violates a fundamental aspect of democratic autonomy.

[33] Compare this meaning with Rawls's understanding of how citizens are "autonomous, politically speaking" (Rawls, *Political Liberalism* [New York: Columbia University Press, 2005], 98). Also, compare it with the definition of liberal legitimacy, ibid., 137.

A third value, reciprocity, is a commitment to reason giving as a central obligation and entitlement of citizens in a legitimate democracy. Reciprocity is the notion that policies governing citizens' treatment must be defensible by appeal to arguments that reasonable citizens can accept.[34] At times the phrase "mutual justification" is used in the literature of democratic theory to capture the type of reasoning that reflects reciprocity. On my view, mutual or reciprocal justification should appeal to citizens' common values of autonomy and equality to discern the limits of coercion. Reciprocity thus might be referred to as an organizing value because it suggests how to apply the other two core values. Reciprocal reason giving can be distinguished from bargaining based on self-interest. While bargainers attempt to promote their own interests and secure for themselves the best "deal" possible, citizens who engage in mutual justification seek to justify particular public policies and the coercion these policies entail by appealing to the core values of equality and autonomy.

The ideal of reciprocity is sometimes associated with the vast literature on deliberative democracy, in particular with the formation of procedures of deliberation. Habermas, for instance, makes reciprocity central to his theory of ideal deliberation. Other thinkers, such as James S. Fishkin and Bruce Ackerman, have attempted to incorporate reciprocity and democratic deliberation into public forums and methods of polling.[35] Even procedures that reflect reciprocity could, however, produce outcomes that fail to embody it in the fully democratic sense. For instance, I stress in the next chapter why, even if they were passed by a democratic procedure, ex post facto laws still do substantive harm to a democracy because of their arbitrariness. The problem here, beyond the impact I have mentioned on autonomy, is that such laws undermine a central tenet of reciprocity developed in the next chapter: that citizens are entitled to reasonable (and thus nonarbitrary) treatment.[36] In chapter 3, I develop this

---

[34] Amy Gutmann and Dennis Thompson offer a similar view. They explain that reciprocity requires that "citizens try to offer reasons that other similarly motivated citizens can accept even though they recognize that they share only some of one another's values" (Gutmann and Thompson, *Democracy and Disagreement* [Cambridge, Mass.: Harvard University Press, 1996], 14).

[35] Bruce Ackerman and James S. Fishkin, *Deliberation Day* (New Haven: Yale University Press, 2004).

[36] My emphasis on the substantive implications of reciprocity draws in part from procedural theories such as Habermas's but it also refocuses democratic theory on Rawls's notion of reciprocity. Although Rawls does not fully develop the ideal of reciprocity as a democratic principle, he does emphasize that his account of legitimacy is one "for a democratic society" (John Rawls, *A Theory of Justice*, rev. ed. [Cambridge, Mass.: Harvard University Press, 1999], xviii). References to democracy also pervade his other work. See, for instance, Rawls, "The Idea of Public Reason Revisited," in *The Law of Peoples, with "The Idea of Public Reason Revisited"* (Cambridge, Mass.: Harvard University Press, 1999), 131; idem, *Justice as Fairness: A Restatement,* 5; and idem, *Political Liberalism,*

idea of reasonable treatment into a theoretical framework that I use in later chapters to reformulate substantive-rights controversies about privacy, property, welfare, and punishment.

We are now in a position further to contrast my view, the value theory of democracy, with both procedural and epistemic views. Unlike proceduralists, I have provided an independent standard for assessing democratic legitimacy: the core values. Consequently, I can account for the role of substantive values in democratic theory, and thus the importance of substantive limits on democratic procedure (a role proceduralists deny). I argue in the next chapter that these substantive limits are properly understood as democratic rights. We can already see this argument take shape here because these limits, like the democratic process, are justified by the core values. While democratic procedures provide for rule *by* the people, substantive rights ensure that these procedures function *for* the people.

Epistemic theories are vulnerable to charges of sectarianism because they appeal to a comprehensive truth. The standard provided by the core values does not, however, subordinate democracy to truth; instead, it suggests how to recognize the status of a democratic people and its citizens. The three core values are formulated to be sufficiently narrow to capture the meaning of rule by and for the people. The values are *of* a people rather than imposed upon them, because they are a way of respecting the common ruling status of all persons subject to coercion. The values draw neither from a particular theory of truth nor from a comprehensive morality; in Rawls's terms, they are not "metaphysical."[37] The core value of political autonomy, for instance, brackets questions regarding free will. Likewise, the core value of equality is not derived from the concepts of metaphysical equality or equal abilities. The core values thus are compatible with a wide range of reasonable comprehensive conceptions and avoid the charge of sectarianism because they address only the specific question of legitimate rule by appeal to the common ruling status of those subject to coercion.

IV. Conclusion

Democratic theory traditionally has emphasized the importance of procedure in contrast to individual rights. I have argued, however, that this exclusive focus

---

11. Gutmann and Thompson, as well as Joshua Cohen, are among the major theorists of deliberative democracy who acknowledge Rawls's influence on their theories. In particular Rawls has influenced their view that democracy has substantive as well as procedural dimensions. See in particular Gutmann and Thompson, *Why Deliberative Democracy?* (Princeton: Princeton University Press, 2004), 102, and Cohen, "For a Democratic Society."

[37] John Rawls, "Justice as Fairness: Political not Metaphysical," *Philosophy and Public Affairs* 14, no. 3 (Summer 1985): 223–51.

on procedure neglects a more fundamental justification at the heart of the concept of self-government. The values of equality of interests, political autonomy, and reciprocity provide an underlying justification of democratic procedure and are rightly regarded as the core values of democracy. This thesis proposes a general shift in democratic theory from an emphasis on value-neutral procedure to a moral account of democratic values. The best defense for thinking of these values as democratic is that they are founded upon respect for the self-ruling status of the citizens who compose a democratic people. A state can best respect this status by honoring the right of citizens to participate in democratic procedures *and* by limiting those policy outcomes that would fail to respect citizens as rulers.[38]

In the next chapter, I begin the argument that these limits are properly regarded as democratic rights. I also continue elaborating on the democratic meaning of the core values, which serve as a way to delineate these rights.

[38] Like any ideal of politics, actual polities will realize the requirements of the value theory of democracy to varying degrees. To the extent that polities claim to be democratic, they should strive to implement, as effectively as possible, the institutions and policies that the core values require. This entails not only that democracies have a set of procedures reflecting the core values, but also that the outcomes of these procedures demonstrate the core values. Held up to such a standard, many societies that consider themselves democratic may well fall short. The standard, however, is not all-or-nothing. Rather, the realization of the democratic ideal as it is articulated by the core values is a matter of degree. It may be true that the United States, Great Britain, or ancient Athens lack some of the democratic characteristics I argue for throughout this book, but this is not a valid reason to challenge my conception of the core values. Such a criticism would invoke a non-normative sense of democracy.

Chapter 2

Paradigmatic Democratic Rights and Citizens as Addressees of Law

Free men talk about their government, not in terms
of its "favors" but in terms of their "rights."
They do not bargain. They reason.
—*Alexander Meiklejohn,* Free Speech and
Its Relation to Self-Government

I. Introduction

In the previous chapter, I argued that democratic theorists have been mistaken
to locate the basis for democratic legitimacy in democratic procedure itself. Instead, I suggested that democratic institutions derive their justification—and
their constraint—from the ideal of rule by, for, and of the people, and from the
related core values of equality of interests, political autonomy, and reciprocity.
In this chapter, I extend my critique of proceduralism and continue to develop
the value theory of democracy by demonstrating why citizens' status as rulers
in a legitimate democratic society entitles them to individual rights based on
the core values. Although I speak to the importance of granting procedural individual rights in a democracy, my primary focus is on developing a justification
of substantive individual rights.

I begin this justification by drawing on Habermas's proposition that citizens
should be understood both as "authors," or makers of law and as "addressees"
impacted by law. In contrast to procedural accounts like that of Habermas, I
propose that the rights of addressees are substantive and are best justified by appeal to the core value of reciprocity, a procedure-independent standard. I then
elaborate on the meaning of reciprocity proposed in chapter 1 by arguing that
it should be understood to entitle addressees of law to treatment that is *reasonably justifiable* to them and respects the core values of political autonomy and
equality of interests. The value theory thus breaks sharply with Habermas's account of the ideal procedure as the source of democratic rights by positing an
independent basis for rights.

In the last two sections of the chapter, I contend that this account of democratic reciprocity as requiring reasonable treatment justifies our intuition that legitimate democracies must protect paradigmatic rights such as the rule of law and free speech. Democracy's principled commitment to the rule of law requires rights such as prohibitions on ex post facto laws and bills of attainder.[1] The crucial role of these rights in a democracy cannot be explained fully without reference to the entitlement of addressees to reasonable treatment consistent with the core values. Similarly, I argue that rights of free speech ensure guarantees for citizens as addressees, guarantees that extend beyond their role as participants in procedures of lawmaking. I focus in this chapter on developing the value theory's account of the rights of addressees by illustrating it with paradigmatic cases. This lays the groundwork for an inquiry into more controversial debates about rights in the chapters to come.

II. Citizens as Authors and Addressees: Co-Originality and Citizens' Status

A central insight of democratic thinkers such as Habermas and Dworkin is that the democratic ideal requires the protection of individual rights. Habermas's theory of the co-originality of democracy and rights, for instance, distinguishes between two sovereign capacities in which citizens retain rights. As "authors" of law, citizens have the rights of political participation recognized by procedural theories: the rights to propose, deliberate about, argue over, and vote on legislation. These participatory rights of authors ensure that rule is *by* citizens. Habermas, however, stresses that citizens do not only make law as "authors," but also "submit to" law as "addressees."[2] As addressees, citizens are owed rights to legitimate treatment, guaranteeing what I have described as rule *for* citizens. For instance, Habermas suggests that to respect citizens' status as addressees, laws must be generally applicable. Moreover, legislatures also should not pass ex post facto laws, allow for double jeopardy, or establish ad hoc courts.[3]

Habermas's recognition of the rights of addressees and authors of law im-

---

[1] Ex post facto laws criminalize actions retroactively, prescribing punishment for actions that were legal at the time they were committed. Although bills of attainder traditionally refer only to legislative acts that sentence persons to death, I use the phrase here to refer to any legislation that declares individuals guilty of crimes and punishes them without the benefit of trial. Article I, Section 9, of the United States Constitution explicitly prohibits Congress from enacting both ex post facto laws and bills of attainder, understood in their wider meaning.

[2] Habermas, *Between Facts and Norms,* 126.

[3] Ibid., 126.

portantly acknowledges that the democratic ideal has implications for individual citizens, not just for a polity as a whole. By invoking the concept of rights, he suggests that individuals' interests as authors and addressees should be treated as distinct from the overall interests of society and should not be subject to sacrifice for the common good. The recognition of the individual interests of citizens is defensible because coercion does not impact a "people" as a collective; it impacts individuals, and thus individuals should be regarded as rights-holders.

Habermas attempts to ground the protection of the addressee's rights in his wider procedural theory. I will argue, however, that this protection requires substantive limits on democratic procedures. Throughout his discussion of the capacity of citizens as addressees of law, Habermas suggests that the democratic entitlements linked to this capacity are rooted in his conception of an ideal procedure. As *authors* of law, Habermas argues, citizens in the ideal procedure would only endorse legislation that they could imagine themselves legitimately being affected by as *addressees* of law. Consideration of the law's impact on others thus would constrain democratic decisions, so the ideal procedure could be said to require reciprocity. Ultimately, however, Habermas's proceduralism grounds the "co-originality" of democracy and rights.[4] He is clear that as "legal subjects," citizens "achieve autonomy only by both understanding themselves as, and acting as, authors of the rights they submit to as addressees."[5] Although Habermas does suggest some basic rights of addressees, he hesitates to specify them in too much detail because he believes that the ideal procedure ultimately grounds these rights and makes them democratic. Articulating rights, then, is best left to those participating in the procedure, not to theorists.

I believe Habermas's notion of the addressee of law has important implications for democratic theory and, specifically, for democratic rights. However, unlike Habermas, I think it is a mistake to subordinate the normative concerns of citizens qua addressees to the process that citizens engage in as authors in the ideal procedure. My view is that citizens' status as rulers is the most fundamental basis for their protection from illegitimate coercion. Democratic citizens are also entitled to protections as makers or authors of law, but these focus on enabling their equal participation in political decision making. It is important not to conflate the substantive rights of addressees with procedural rights enjoyed by citizens as authors of law. In Habermas's own terms, citizens as ad-

---

[4] Habermas stresses that his theory of rights is procedural as opposed to moral: "The system of rights can be reduced neither to a moral reading of human rights nor to an ethical reading of popular sovereignty, because the private autonomy of citizens must neither be set above, nor made subordinate to, their political autonomy" (ibid., 104).

[5] Ibid., 126.

dressees no longer "choose the medium in which they can actualize their autonomy."[6] In this postprocedural position, however, I maintain that citizens retain rights against coercion, rights based in the core values, not democratic procedures.

To illustrate the importance of grounding the rights of addressees outside of democratic procedure, consider the following hypothetical. Larry Legislator is a democratically elected representative in a regime that, due to an ancient tradition, requires its representatives to be locked in a cell during their term in office. The representatives, however, are still entitled to govern from confinement. Imagine that Larry is provided with a sophisticated communication system to receive information from the outside world so he can make well-informed policy decisions. He can participate in democratic debate and place his votes by telephone, and he receives a furlough to allow him to campaign in election years.

If we were to define the democratic ideal solely in terms of participatory freedoms that citizens enjoy as makers of law, we might conclude that there is nothing undemocratic about Larry's confinement. He retains a set of political rights as a maker of law. But are the conditions that coerce Larry in every other area of his personal life consistent with his status as a citizen? Our intuition tells us that, despite his freedom to participate in making laws, Larry is not living the democratic ideal. If citizens are deemed capable of making decisions for others on the basis of rights of political rule, it should follow that they are capable of making decisions for themselves in the most important matters of their own personal lives. When the state coerces citizens arbitrarily, it trivializes political rights such as participation by denying their competence as decision makers.[7] Larry serves as an extreme example of why a society that does not value the rights of addressees of law enough to guard against arbitrary coercion would violate the ideal of citizens as rulers. This example suggests the importance of a procedure-independent standard in discerning the democratic rights of addressees.

The proceduralist might contend here that Larry does retain his rights as an addressee because he has the ability, through the democratic process, to lobby for and perhaps ultimately gain guarantees of these rights. This objection, however, ignores the fact that even if Larry were to attempt to win these rights through the democratic process, he might be unsuccessful. More importantly,

---

[6] Ibid.

[7] This example foreshadows my argument in chapter 4 that citizens' rights to make personal as well as public decisions are essential in a democracy. I will contend that these rights are part of citizens' democratic rights to privacy, which in turn are a subset of the substantive democratic rights of addressees of law.

if rights of addressees can be reduced simply to citizens' rights as authors of law, it becomes difficult to explain how citizens who are unable or unwilling to participate in the political process retain rights against illegitimate coercion. For example, many individuals who are eligible to participate in democratic procedures choose not to, whether out of indifference or conscientious refusal. Yet it would clearly violate the democratic ideal to use their lack of participation as a pretext for denying them rights as addressees. Equally mistaken would be the approach Habermas takes: to rely so heavily on the notion of an ideal democratic procedure that he ignores the reality that some addressees simply will not participate. Habermas merely treats nonparticipants *as if* they were participants, basing their rights to democratic treatment on the erroneous assumption of universal participation in the ideal procedure.

The proceduralist might also argue here that we guarantee nonparticipants rights as addressees to ensure that they might have the ability to participate in the future, should they choose to do so. But, as I will argue in the second half of this chapter, the rights of addressees are distinct from, and often irrelevant to, political participation, so it would be a mistake to ground these rights in one's willingness to participate in lawmaking in the present or the future. Second, those who are ineligible to participate in democratic procedures should still be entitled to democratic treatment as addressees of law. For example, minors and resident aliens are not eligible to vote in the United States, yet they are still rightly entitled to protections against arbitrary coercion. Such persons retain rights to democratic treatment in spite of the fact that they are legally barred from participation.[8] Although resident aliens are not legal citizens, I argue in the next chapter that they retain a right to be treated as democratic citizens in a moral sense because of their status as addressees of law.

These examples suggest that there is a principled basis for citizens' rights as addressees of law not rooted in an account of citizens as authors of law. It is important, therefore, not to collapse either of these capacities into the other. The fact that citizens subject to coercion are not "choosing" how law should govern them and are not equals, in the sense of having equal power to deliberate or influence the legislative process, does not mean that they are no longer citizens in their capacity as addressees or that they lose their entitlement to be treated as the core values demand. Rather, the core values suggest a guiding principle for policy that impacts any addressee: laws must be constructed such that citizens who choose to obey them do so not merely because of the threat of sanction, but because the laws treat them in a way consistent with their status as free and equal rulers. Because it extends to all addressees of law, including minors

[8] I owe this formulation to a discussion with Nan Keohane.

and resident aliens, this status is not synonymous with the simple act of voting or participating in some other aspect of democratic procedure. It entails a more fundamental entitlement to reasonable treatment demanded by the value of reciprocity.

Habermas himself describes a distinctly nonprocedural meaning of what is required to treat citizens as rulers. In his words: "Legitimate law is compatible only with a mode of legal coercion that does not destroy the rational motives for obeying the law: it must remain possible for everyone to obey legal norms on the basis of insight."[9] Despite Habermas's own proceduralist context, the principle itself seems to acknowledge that law should be justifiable "on the basis of insight" rather than imposed arbitrarily by brute force, not only in its making but also, crucially, in its impact. To extend Habermas's principle, we might say that citizens' capacity as addressees entitles them to reasons for the coercion that affects them, reasons that enable them to obey "on the basis of insight." Granting citizens this entitlement ensures that coercive laws will not violate the basic ideals of democracy, a risk procedural theories are unable to guard against.

Protecting the rights of citizens as addressees ensures that they are treated in a manner consistent with their status as members of a sovereign democratic people. The state can exceed the limits imposed by the democratic ideal not only by failing to abide by democratic procedures, but also by treating citizens in a manner inconsistent with their sovereign status as the addressees of law. Aristotle famously defined citizenship as taking turns "ruling and being ruled." The value theory conceives of citizenship so as to recognize the rights that come from both aspects of this definition. When a citizen is not the author of a law—when it is his turn to be ruled, so to speak—he does not cease to be a citizen. Citizens retain their sovereign status even in their seemingly passive role as addressees of law, and this status remains fundamental to defining the limits of legitimate law. Some of these rights, as proceduralists argue, are necessary to democratic participation. Others, however, are rightly invoked by citizens when the state undermines their sovereignty in their capacity as addressees.

In *Freedom's Law,* Ronald Dworkin articulates a distinctly nonprocedural, status-based notion of a democratic people and of democratic individual rights. Dworkin is concerned to articulate what conditions are necessary for state authority to be consistent with individuals' status as rulers. "Why am I *free*—how could I be thought to be governing *myself*—when I must obey what other people decide even if I think it wrong . . . ?" he asks.[10] It is not enough, he

[9] Habermas, *Between Facts and Norms,* 121.

[10] Ronald Dworkin, *Freedom's Law: The Moral Reading of the American Constitution* (Cambridge, Mass.: Harvard University Press, 1996), 22.

points out, that persons consider themselves part of the national community, or that they enjoy procedural rights in a democracy. Invoking a dramatic example, Dworkin explains: "German Jews were not moral members of the political community that tried to exterminate them, though they had votes in the elections that led to Hitler's Chancellorship, and the Holocaust was therefore not part of their self-government, even if a majority of Germans would have approved it."[11] The test of whether state authority truly is consistent with the ideal of self-government, Dworkin concludes, is thus not procedural but "moral."[12] For state authority to be consistent with citizens' self-government, citizens must be entitled to certain substantive guarantees that protect their sovereign status, and thus the "moral membership" that Dworkin suggests legitimizes state coercion. In particular, while citizens must enjoy rights of participation in democratic procedures, their "moral membership" requires substantive rights to legitimate treatment, even if they contradict laws passed by those procedures. Unlike Habermas, who develops the concept of the addressee in the context of a procedural theory, Dworkin believes that democratic procedures can so violate the sovereignty of an individual as to undermine their legitimacy altogether. Dworkin's conception of status as the basis for rights thus is more stable than Habermas's procedural conception of democratic rights.

We are now in a position to articulate how the argument of this chapter so far helps elucidate the core values of democracy. Drawing on Dworkin's move to ground individual rights in status rather than procedure, we can posit that the addressee of a law has rights guaranteeing that the law will not undermine her sovereign status. The contours of these rights of addressees are shaped with reference to the core values: equality of interests, political autonomy, and reciprocity. Fundamentally, I have shown that citizens should be treated as equals, not just in the establishment of democratic procedures, but also through the assurance that the laws produced through those procedures embody the equal consideration of their distinct interests. I also have argued that citizens are entitled to be treated as autonomous not just through rights to participate in the procedures of self-rule, but also through the requirement that laws be justifiable to them. Rights protections suggest when the state has crossed these boundaries and highlight when the resulting treatment undermines the value of autonomy. As rulers, citizens should seek not to dominate each other but to uphold the value of reciprocity by respecting their fellows as autonomous and equal.

There remains the problem of articulating a standard of reciprocity based on the status of citizens, rather than on an account of procedure. For Habermas,

[11] Ibid., 23.

[12] Ibid. Dworkin distinguishes helpfully between an aggregative view of democracy, such as majoritarianism, and the substantive requirements of moral membership.

requirements of reciprocal reasoning are relevant only for participants in the ideal procedure. Our charge, however, is to apply the standard of reciprocity to the substantive treatment of addressees of law. Given the pitfalls of procedural accounts, which I discussed in chapter 1, I believe a more promising approach is to pose a standard dictated not by the decisions of actual persons but by an inquiry into what types of coercion are *justifiable* to citizens in virtue of their sovereign status.

Such a standard is present in Rawls's "principle of reciprocity":

> Citizens are reasonable when, viewing one another as free and equal in a system of social cooperation over generations, they are prepared to offer one another fair terms of social cooperation (defined by principles and ideals) and they agree to act on those terms, even at the cost of their own interests in particular situations, provided that others also accept those terms. For these terms to be fair terms, citizens offering them must reasonably think that those citizens to whom such terms are offered might also reasonably accept them.[13]

For Rawls, coercive law not only should bind all citizens, including those who have proposed it, but also should respect the interests of all citizens as *reasonable*. The idea of reasonable treatment can be incorporated into the value theory as a procedure-independent standard for thinking about the rights of addressees. Rather than relying on those within the democratic procedure to reason reciprocally, Rawls's standard of reasonableness grounds the rights of addressees in a way that does not depend on procedural decisions. This standard respects individual citizens' interests in that it looks to the particular social position, perspective, and point of view of those citizens "to whom such terms are offered," and whom the law coerces.[14] But unlike Habermas's account, the

---

[13] John Rawls, *Political Liberalism*, xlii.

[14] The Rawlsian standard of the reasonable, prominent in contemporary theories of political liberalism, has been much criticized on the grounds that arguments about reasonableness are circular, referring only to reasonableness in matters of justification. A related criticism is that the notion of the reasonable itself is taken as a sufficient argument for or against a given policy matter. Leif Wenar, among others, suggests one way out of this potentially circular argument: to stipulate criteria for reasonableness by appealing to the notion of a reasonable person, constituted in part by a sense of the good and a sense of justice. See Wenar, "Political Liberalism: An Internal Critique," *Ethics* 106, no. 1 (October 1995): 36. Such persons would have to seek common ground on "principles and standards as fair terms of cooperation" in exchange for their interlocutors' same commitment (Rawls, *Political Liberalism*, 49). In the text, I discuss a related Rawlsian response to the charge of circularity: the notion of reflective equilibrium. For a variation on this point, see Eamonn Callan's elaboration of reciprocity that stresses a noncircular notion of reasoned reciprocity: "In exhibiting reciprocity, I begin by putting before you what I take to be fair. But I must also be ready

standard of the reasonable is formulated as a way of evaluating law's effects, not just the process of its creation. The standard thus serves to evaluate the impact of coercion on addressees of law, not only the constraints on authors.

Proceduralists might object to the interpretation of democratic reciprocity as a standard of reasonableness on the grounds that any account that specifies rights independent of procedure risks deemphasizing the importance of citizens authoring law.[15] This concern, however, conflates the elaboration of the rights of the addressees of law with an abandonment of the procedural aspects of democracy. In an ideal democracy, citizens certainly would affirm the rights of addressees through democratic procedures. In such an ideal, democratic procedures enhance the legitimacy of democratic rights. But the introduction of the rights of addressees as democratic in a distinctly nonprocedural sense only adds another means by which to elaborate rights. This move does not detract from the added legitimacy that comes when rights are affirmed within democratic procedures. One central question for democratic theorists, given a clear distinction between rights of addressees and rights of authors of law, is what the most democratic resolution is when these rights conflict. I turn to this question in chapter 7.

In sum, the value theory's conception of democratic rights draws on the insight of procedural theories that the entitlement of a people to democracy fundamentally entails rights of each of its citizens. Habermas's contribution to the value theory's account of rights lies in his recognition that the sovereignty of individual citizens requires respecting their distinct interests as both addressees and authors of law. Yet unlike Habermas, I have suggested that the rights of addressees are best understood as grounded in their status as rulers, which entitles them to treatment that is reasonably justifiable with reference to the core values of democracy. In the next chapter I will develop this standard of reciprocity into a framework that can be used to argue for a set of substantive dem-

---

seriously to discuss the opposing proposals that you make in the hope of moving, through the discipline of dialogue, toward a common perspective that each of us could adhere to in good conscience. Your viewpoint is as important as mine to the fulfillment of that hope, and only through empathic identification with your viewpoint can I appreciate what reason might commend in what you say" (Callan, *Creating Citizens: Political Education and Liberal Democracy* [Oxford: Clarendon, 1997], 26).

[15] The turn to Rawls's standard of reasonableness in theorizing democratic reciprocity abandons Habermas's insistence that any account of democratic rights should not stray from a procedural ideal. In his exchange with Rawls, Habermas argues that while he and Rawls share Rousseau's concern to merge the liberties of the ancients and the moderns, Rawls's refusal to ground rights in procedure "contradicts the republican intuition that popular sovereignty and human rights are nourished by the same root," and "sediments" rights in a theory that abandons democratic justification (Habermas, *Inclusion of the Other*, 71).

ocratic rights. Some of these rights, such as the privacy rights I discuss in chapter 4 and the rights of convicted criminals, taken up in chapter 5, are "negative" rights to be free from state coercion. Other rights, such as the welfare rights I argue for in chapter 6, are positive rights to be given goods by the state. While these positive and negative rights are similar in content to liberal accounts, they are fundamentally democratic in justification. These chapters take us into some of the most contested rights controversies facing polities today.

Rather than begin by exploring the implications of the value theory for these controversies, however, it is important first to illustrate the fit between the idea of the rights of citizens as addressees and relatively uncontroversial examples of democratic rights: those associated with the rule of law and free speech. Before I proceed to explore and analyze these paradigmatic rights, I want to clarify the role of the following two sections in the overall justificatory structure of the book. I do not aim merely to apply the core values of democracy across a range of controversies. Instead, in the following two sections and in the chapters to come, I draw on the methodological ideal of reflective equilibrium introduced by John Rawls. For Rawls the reasonableness of an argument is established not only by applying abstract ideals to concrete cases, but also by allowing intuitions and "considered judgments" to revise and clarify general principles. Thus, reflective equilibrium requires that citizens reason about politics in both a top-down and a bottom-up manner. From the top, they should ask what policies are required by their general working theory of justice and the broad values they think just. From the bottom, they should look to what, on reflection, their basic intuitions or "considered judgments" about justice tell them when they are confronted with specific instances of injustice. These judgments, in turn, suggest ways in which the general theory of justice should be refined.[16]

In the rest of this chapter and in subsequent chapters, my method of argumentation draws on reflective equilibrium. But instead of using the method to develop a theory of justice, I invoke both bottom-up and top-down thinking to theorize about democracy and specifically to clarify the meaning of the core values of democracy.[17] My method is bottom-up in that it begins by examining several institutions that are commonly thought to be paradigmatically democratic. I draw on considered judgments about these institutions to develop and clarify the democratic meaning of the core values. I then adopt a generally top-down method, extending these core values to more controversial cases.

An analogy to the bottom-up and top-down aspects of my method lies in the techniques of textual interpretation. Imagine that there are two rival theories

[16] John Rawls, *A Theory of Justice,* 42–43.

[17] This more narrow concern fits Rawls's stated ambition of formulating a theory of legitimacy "for a democratic society." See note 33, chapter 1.

about how best to interpret Plato's *The Laws* and *The Republic*.[18] My method would begin by using a bottom-up approach, taking a certain set of clear conclusions reached by Plato and then asking which of the theories best explained those conclusions. With our chosen theory in place, we would then adopt a top-down approach, extending the theory to inquire into more controversial and less clear areas of interpretation. In the present case (analogizing democratic institutions with conclusions reached by Plato), we can say the following: beginning with a bottom-up approach, we should seek to clarify the core values by appeal to their fit with and justification of paradigmatic democratic institutions. After this clarification, we should use a top-down approach to apply the core values to more controversial terrain.

In the following two sections I use relatively uncontroversial cases to draw out our considered judgments about the importance of rights associated with democratic rule of law and free speech. These cases and our considered judgments about them emphasize the importance of rights in a democracy and develop the meaning of the core values. In chapter 3, I incorporate these values into a framework for evaluating the scope and content of democratic rights. In chapters 4 through 6, I draw on this framework to develop arguments for several democratic rights more controversial than those examined in this chapter. My inquiry in these chapters will clarify further the meaning of the core values and their implications for democratic legitimacy.

One issue I postpone until I consider these harder cases concerns what to do when the core values conflict with one another. Fundamental among conflicts within the core values is the potential tension between values of equality and autonomy. I explore this tension in chapter 4 when considering hard cases involving issues of sexual privacy and marriage.

III. Rule of Law

It is a settled judgment, so much so that it is simply assumed in almost all of the literature of democratic theory, that no regime can properly be regarded as democratic without the rule of law. If an elected legislature habitually jailed political opponents without charge, for instance, we might have a majoritarian institution, but it would be wrong to call it democratic. This is true, I will contend, even if such a legislature were to incarcerate its citizens in this fashion in a good-faith attempt at just rule. After all, legislatures are, by definition, "law-

[18] I owe this example to David Estlund. For more on a similar method see Gopal Sreenivasan, "Interpretation and Reason," *Philosophy and Public Affairs* 27, no. 2 (Spring 1998): 142–71. This article also seeks to clarify why interpretivism is not relativistic.

makers." Even in direct democracy, plebiscites do not deal out justice ad hoc; they are a process of popular lawmaking.

My point is not that the rule of law itself requires democracy. We can imagine regimes that are quite undemocratic yet adhere to the rule of law. Hobbes, for instance, thought the rule of law instrumentally valuable to the stability of a nondemocratic sovereign. Constitutional monarchy is an attempt to merge rule by a king with the guarantees of the rule of law. But while we can imagine a Hobbesian ruler or a constitutional monarch at times employing the rule of law and at times discarding it, I want to suggest that it is a principled requirement of a democracy to respect the rule of law in all cases, not merely when it proves instrumental. This requirement is based in democracy's commitment to the generality of law, a commitment that serves the two capacities of citizens as authors and addressees of law. The rule of law is in part a procedural restraint on lawmakers who otherwise might place themselves above the people by making laws that aggrandize their power. But proceduralist justifications alone do not explain the necessity of the rule of law in a democracy. Rights against ex post facto laws and bills of attainder, for instance, are also necessary to respect citizens' status as addressees of law, in particular to prevent arbitrary coercion and to ensure that laws do not degrade their status as equals. Thus, an account of democratic values capable of explaining the necessity of the rule of law must respect citizens' sovereign status in their capacities as political participants *and* as addressees of state coercion. My aim in this section is to explore the rationale for the settled judgment that democracy requires the rule of law, as well as to argue that our intuitions about this basic democratic institution help to elaborate on why democracy requires both procedural rights and rights to limits on citizens' treatment.

To unpack our intuitions about why democracy requires the rule of law for principled and noninstrumental reasons, consider a democratically elected body disregarding the requirement that laws be generally applicable and instead passing legislation singling out individuals for special treatment. For example, such a legislature might decide to incarcerate individuals ad hoc for actions not previously considered crimes. If the democratic justification for the rule of law were solely instrumental, we could imagine why such a "special law" would be justifiable. Though the rule of law might normally promote stability, say, by using clear, generally applicable criminal sanctions to deter individuals from antisocial behavior, it is conceivable that the rule of law might at times fail to serve its purpose. Thus, cases might arise when expediency would justify violating individual rights. For example, state prosecutors unable to achieve a "guilty" verdict against a known murderer might want to define new crimes ex post facto so that the defendant could still be convicted. I believe that the intuition that it would be wrong to stray from prohibitions on ex post facto and special laws, even when they serve some "higher" purpose, can be explained with reference both to accounts of justice and to the principled role the rule of law plays in establishing rights in a democracy. Instrumental justifications might explain why the rule of law is sometimes helpful, but they cannot explain why protections against arbitrary treatment are fundamental rights in a democracy.

In the *Federalist Papers,* James Madison offers the classic explanation for why bills of attainder and ex post facto laws are contrary to democracy's basic principles and suggests an argument for democratic rights against such violations of the rule of law:

> Bills of attainder, [and] *ex post facto* laws . . . are contrary to the first principles of the social compact, and to every principle of sound legislation. . . . Our own experience has taught us . . . that additional fences against these dangers ought not to be omitted. . . . The sober people of America are weary of the fluctuating policy which has directed the public councils. They have seen with regret and with indignation, that sudden changes, and legislative interferences, in cases affecting personal rights, become jobs in the hands of enterprising and influential speculators; and snares to the more industrious and less informed part of the community.[19]

Madison's concern about the conduct of "enterprising and influential speculators" toward those citizens who are "more industrious" but "less informed" suggests a proceduralist justification for rights against bills of attainder and ex post facto laws. While a general concern about the "capture" of any law by special interests without regard for the common good is always present in democracy, bills of attainder and ex post facto laws seem specifically geared to allow some citizens to aggrandize their power at the expense of others. A classic concern is that a parliament will use the power of criminal punishment against political opponents, as with "special laws" that have been used in modern times to bar members of unpopular political parties from certain positions in society or otherwise to single them out for undemocratic treatment.[20] However, the justification for such prohibitions is not solely that "special laws" risk abusing

[19] James Madison, Federalist 44, in "The Bounds of Legislative Specification: A Suggested Approach to the Bill of Attainder Clause (in Notes and Comments)," *Yale Law Journal* 72, no. 2 (December 1962): 345.

[20] For example, the Internal Security Act of 1950, commonly known as the McCarran Act, required members of the Communist Party and communist organizations to register with the government in what was recognized widely as an attempt to scare people out of joining those unpopular political groups. See Ellen Schrecker, *The Age of McCarthyism: A Brief History with Documents* (Boston: St. Martin's, 1994), 47.

minorities' lack of political power or that they can be used as a weapon against political opponents. More fundamentally, the problem with such laws is that they violate the core values of equality, political autonomy, and reciprocity that define how to treat the individual citizen as a part of a sovereign people. In the following paragraphs, I appeal to our intuitions about these laws to help establish the democratic requirement that law respect citizens' status as addressees. I also elaborate on how each core value follows from this status to demand protection of individual rights.

First, bills of attainder and ex post facto laws degrade individuals to such an extent that they undermine their status as equals and their entitlement to have their interests treated equally in matters of coercion. In a democracy, what Habermas calls "the rational character of the legal form as such" demands that laws be generally applicable, which in turn means that they must affect all citizens equally.[21] Law's generality is partly a protection against a violation of equality of interests tied to political participation. Bills of attainder and ex post facto laws enable the state selectively to expose citizens to punishment at the hands of an unpredictable and politically motivated legislature. Such legislation could be used, for instance, arbitrarily to incarcerate politically unpopular individuals who have not been found guilty of any crime in a fair judicial procedure, thereby denying them the equal protection afforded by generally applicable laws. But the prohibition also ensures against degradations of democratic equality not tied to political participation. Here, a contrast between bills of attainder and ex post facto laws is helpful. While ex post facto laws can undermine the autonomy of all citizens by subjecting them to laws they could not predict (a point I will elaborate in the next paragraph), bills of attainder undermine both autonomy and equality by singling out an individual for different treatment from her fellow citizens. This harm clearly violates citizens' right to equal treatment as the addressees of law. Bills of attainder violate this right by intentionally degrading one particular citizen, who is thereby denied his basic entitlements as a ruler.

Second, even when individuals singled out by "special laws" do not suffer disenfranchisement as a result, such laws still undermine their status as autonomous self-rulers by abridging their ability to foresee when the state will and will not coerce them. If democratic autonomy entails the ability to make choices about one's life within the limits of the law, then knowing in advance what these limits are is crucial to the ability to make such choices. A citizen who could be

---

[21] "Finally, the guarantees of equal protection and legal remedies are interpreted through procedural guarantees and basic legal standards. These include the prohibitions against retroactive punishment, double jeopardy, and ad hoc courts, as well as the guarantee of an independent judiciary, and so on" (Habermas, *Between Facts and Norms*, 126).

jailed unexpectedly under an ex post facto law passed through democratic procedure would suffer a similar fate to those subject to sudden punishment at the whim of an unaccountable dictator. Her procedural right to vote on ex post facto legislation would not compensate for the loss to her right, as an addressee, to be free from punishments for actions she had previously been assured were legal. Prohibitions against such arbitrary treatment thus help us to elaborate what it means to respect the autonomy of citizens as addressees in a democracy and to distinguish democratic treatment from dictatorial treatment. Citizens' democratic status not only implies a procedural entitlement to autonomy conceived as a right to political participation, but also implies important rights against arbitrary coercion by the state. Even if citizens enjoy rights to participation, their autonomy is abridged fundamentally if they are incarcerated for reasons that they could not reasonably foresee. If citizens are to be rulers in a polity, the law must not coerce them arbitrarily but rather must serve their interests in a reasonable and relatively predictable manner.

Finally, our intuitions about the importance of the rule of law in a democracy also help to clarify the significance of reciprocity as a core democratic value. Bills of attainder and ex post facto laws harm citizens' status as rulers partly because they violate the ideal of reciprocity, which entitles citizens as addressees to reasonable treatment. Through bills of attainder, for instance, the government simply enacts the punishment of specific individuals without allowing them to contest the reasons for their punishment in a fair, impartial judicial proceeding. Justice Story of the Supreme Court usefully distinguished bills of attainder from sentences issued by courts of law, in which authorities explain charges against individuals based on established and explicit criminal sanctions and give defendants the opportunity to contest these charges to ensure their treatment is not arbitrary. With bills of attainder, he argued, "the legislature assumes judicial magistracy, pronouncing upon the guilt of the party without any of the common forms and guards of trial, and satisfying itself with proofs . . . whether they are conformable to the rules of evidence or not." Bills of attainder and ex post facto laws, in other words, subject individuals to potentially arbitrary coercion based not on reasons that can be predicted, explained, and contested, but that may well be "governed solely by . . . political necessity or expediency."[22] While democracies punish citizens based on their guilt or innocence in violating legitimate and widely known laws, bills of attainder and ex post facto laws facilitate punishment that is selectively imposed rather than justified by rules that citizens can

[22] Joseph Story, *Commentaries on the Constitution of the United States* 21 (4th ed., 1873), in "The Bounds of Legislative Specification: A Suggested Approach to the Bill of Attainder Clause (in Notes and Comments)," *Yale Law Journal*, 72, no. 2 (December 1962): 330–67, quote on 345.

reasonably be expected to follow.[23] Such laws thus are paradigmatic violations of citizens' sovereignty as addressees and their entitlement to reasonable treatment, even when they retain procedural rights of participation.

We can understand why the widely accepted democratic guarantee of the rule of law reinforces the democratic meaning of reciprocity by imagining a legislature that relies on bills of attainder, rather than on an adversarial judicial system, to administer punishment to criminals. Imagine that the results of this process tend to be just: individuals receive punishments appropriate to their behavior, and no individual is treated especially harshly or gently. In this system, however, individuals cannot contest charges against them because there are no formal charges, and the legislature simply incarcerates them ad hoc. Murderers, for example, are not sentenced according to any legal definition of murder. Instead, they simply are sentenced to life in prison because a majority of legislators voted as such. Even if, as I have stipulated, the results of such a process were just, such a system is inconsistent with the democratic ideal because citizens as rulers must be given reasons for state coercion. The ideal of rule by the people is not satisfied if the government does not explain its actions to the people. These explanations need not provide reasons that citizens *actually* accept. Many of the guilty, of course, would likely refuse any punishment, no matter how legitimate its justification. Rather, coercion should be justifiable by appeal to some standard of reasonableness and nonarbitrariness, out of respect for citizens' free and equal status. The idea that citizens should be given reasons for coercion, which I see as implicit in the institution of the rule of law, forms the basis of the core value of reciprocity. Treating citizens as sovereign requires not only that they enjoy procedural rights of participation in lawmaking, but also that the government's actions can be reasonably justified to them, especially when the citizens in question are those most affected by state coercion.

In sum, it is a settled judgment that democratic societies must respect the rule of law. This judgment, in turn, requires democratic rights of citizens against bills of attainder and ex post facto laws. These rights are partly based in the concern to ensure fair political procedures. But their fundamental importance lies in the entitlement of citizens as addressees of law to treatment in accordance with the core values of autonomy, equality, and reciprocity. Ex post facto laws and bills of attainder violate democratic rights because they undermine aspects of each of the core values: they do not respect the generality of law (an issue of equality); they do not give citizens fair warning about coercion (an

---

[23] The most prominent argument tying the prohibition of ex post facto laws and bills of attainder to the rule of law itself is found in Lon Fuller, *The Morality of Law* (New Haven: Yale University Press, 1965).

issue of autonomy); and they fail to give citizens principled reasons for this coercion (an issue of reciprocity). Democratic rights against bills of attainder are
further necessary because such laws single out individual citizens for special
treatment and thus violate the core value of equality.

IV. Freedom of Expression and Conscience

Legislation that restricts the freedom of conscience—especially regarding private or public expressions of political views—is another paradigmatic violation
of democratic rights. The large number of political dissenters in the prisons of
many nondemocratic societies seems to support this claim. What is the best explanation for the commonly accepted link between democracy and freedom of
conscience and expression? In this section, I will argue that the best defense of
free speech is not that it enables citizens as the makers of law to participate in
democratic discussions, furthering the ability of their fellows to make decisions.
Even more fundamental is what this right provides citizens as addressees of
law: the ability to be informed and to make up their own minds about government policies, including a procedure-independent right to listen to and hear
the arguments of fellow citizens. The right to free speech thus is not subject to
merely instrumental or proceduralist justification. Rather, freedom of speech,
and the freedom of conscience that underlies it, are core elements of how the
state treats its citizens as sovereign.

If freedom of speech and conscience are indeed rights in a democratic society, it is necessary first to dispense with those justifications of free speech that
are merely instrumental. Such justifications cannot explain why free speech is a
right retained by citizens when jettisoning it would serve some general societal
interest. A prominent instrumental defense of free speech is epistemic; recall
how I argued in the previous chapter that the general epistemic theory of democracy is incompatible with the value theory of democracy because of its sec-
tarian embrace of "truth." In *On Liberty*, Mill famously argued that the purpose
of free expression is that it allows for an open discourse ultimately resulting in
"truth."[24] On this view, we should allow all voices to be heard because doing so
contributes to a marketplace of ideas that tends to promote both knowledge of
truth and enactment of this knowledge. However, a simple thought experiment
reveals the flaw with this view. Suppose an empirical study found that free expression in fact led to more distortion than truth. Though purely instrumental
views would conclude that freedom of speech is not justified, our most basic in-

[24]John Stuart Mill, "On Liberty," in *On Liberty and Considerations on Representative Government*, 1–104.

tuitions about democracy suggest that a democratic government still would need to guarantee the right to free speech.

An inquiry into whether rights to free speech are solely instrumental in democracy can usefully begin by examining an underlying right, the freedom of conscience. Rights to express and to listen to ideas are justified by the more basic right of citizens to make up their own minds about politics. To demonstrate why freedom of conscience is not merely instrumental to the promotion of truth but is an inherently valuable right in democracy, imagine a society in which it were known that, left to their own conscience, citizens would vote wrongly in an election and so would undermine what an epistemic theorist might regard as "true" justice. In such a case, would it be democratically justifiable to force citizens to change their votes to ensure the right outcome?[25] It is clear that any attempt to force citizens to vote a particular way would be a paradigmatic violation of the democratic right to freedom of conscience. The reasons why such a forced vote is unacceptable in a democracy are not merely instrumental; they go to the heart of what it means to treat citizens as sovereign. The ability to decide wrongly is itself a fundamental democratic right. In no sense can citizens be regarded as rulers if restrictions are placed on how they can think about politics, especially when it comes to how they vote. Freedom of conscience is essential to democracy—particularly to the core value of political autonomy—because it ensures that self-rulers will be able to think for themselves about political problems without being subject to external coercion.

These fundamental intuitions about democratic rights to freedom of conscience can be extended to an argument for democratic rights to free speech. The ability to make up one's own mind should, in a democracy, include the freedom to develop one's opinions in consultation with others. Alexander Meiklejohn makes this point through a metaphor that asks us to imagine citizens as participants in a town meeting. In such a setting, Meiklejohn argues, it would be unacceptable from the standpoint of democracy for a moderator to limit the content of any one person's argument about a particular policy. Such an intervention would violate not only the speaker's autonomy, but also the autonomy of those in the audience who have a fundamental right to listen to and hear the arguments of others:

> In the town meeting the people of a community assemble to discuss and to act upon matters of public interest—roads, schools, poorhouses, health, external defense, and the like. Every man is free to come. They meet as

[25] This question is quite different from the issue of whether citizens can vote in a way that undermines the core values. I deal with the distinct question of whether judicial review is democratically legitimate in chapter 7.

political equals. Each has a right and a duty to think his own thoughts, to express them, and to *listen to* the arguments of others. The basic principle is that the freedom of speech shall be unabridged.[26]

Although Meiklejohn's emphasis is on the rights of speakers, his argument that citizens have a right "to listen to the arguments of others" suggests that if it is to be meaningful, the right to free speech should not just encompass the ability to express one's opinions. Rather, free speech requires the ability to hear the views of others.

In chapter 1, I suggested why Meiklejohn can be read as a proceduralist who views speech as a precondition to full participation. That said, his articulation of the right to listen nonetheless is helpful in developing a nonprocedural account of free speech. Rights to listen do not just protect citizens' capacity as authors of law; they also concern citizens' capacity as addressees. As I have argued, citizens who do not actively participate in the making of law are still entitled, as self-rulers, to understand the impact of the law and to know what is being done in their name. To return to Meiklejohn's metaphor, we can imagine that some in the town meeting are generally silent in matters of public policy, and might abstain from voting. But these citizens, despite their lack of active participation, still should be treated as sovereign. It would not be democratic to revoke their rights to sit in the meeting, or to listen to the arguments of others, merely because they have chosen to remain silent. Thus, although the metaphor of a town meeting in which all citizens directly vote on the law suggests a proceduralist justification for the right to free speech, the importance of the rights of listeners extends beyond citizens' capacity to decide in direct democracy. It is important to emphasize that the town meeting is a metaphor not to be limited to a literal interpretation, especially given that most democratic societies do not have a direct democracy. The point is particularly important in representative democracy, in which citizens retain rights to make and to hear arguments about politics although they are not active in day-to-day lawmaking. The rights to listen that Mieklejohn mentions should extend to all citizens, regardless of their willingness to participate in democratic procedure. They hold for those whose views are expressed at dinner tables or in cafés, even when these citizens do not participate in the making of law.

Central to the free speech rights of citizens as both authors and addressees of law is the ability to know how the law impacts them. This point is illustrated in the Pentagon Papers case, in which the Supreme Court asked whether the First Amendment guaranteed the *New York Times* the right to publish secret information regarding the war in Vietnam although it risked harming national secu-

---

[26] Alexander Meiklejohn, *Free Speech and its Relation to Self-Government*, 22; my emphasis.

rity.[27] In his majority opinion, Justice Black invoked a Meiklejohn-like argument, suggesting that freedom of the press is fundamentally guaranteed to ensure that a democratic people is aware of the variety of ways by which the state coerces them. The idea here is that those who are *not* active in making law but remain the source of sovereignty have a right to know what is being done in their name, even if such knowledge might adversely affect the ability of those who actively govern to carry out policy. In Black's words, the point of a free press is "to serve the governed, not the governors." Moreover, it is the duty of a free press to "prevent any part of the government from deceiving the people and sending them off to distant lands to die of foreign fevers and foreign shot and shell."[28]

Black's argument here calls to mind some traditional proceduralist justifications. Forcing the government to make its policy known allows for a more informed electorate who might act on their new knowledge in the next election by voting the administration out of office. Thus, Black's decision inherently limits the government's power and increases citizens' power through their potential participation in a political procedure. But the point about the electorate's right to know is more fundamental than this merely proceduralist justification. It concerns the basic right of citizens, regardless of what they do with this information, to understand law's impact. In particular, the idea that this information is important to citizens as "governed" rather than governors emphasizes the importance of democratic treatment distinct from procedure. A democratic state acts in the name of the people, and for this to have any meaning the people must have a basic awareness of the policies the state is carrying out.

The right of free speech, therefore, concerns not merely citizens' capacity as rulers, but also their fundamental status as addressees of law.[29] Specifically, the idea of free speech as a right to "listen" emphasizes the importance of the core values for citizens in this nonprocedural capacity. Like the rule of law, the right to listen fundamentally concerns citizens' entitlement to be given reasons for government coercion. As the Pentagon Papers decision illustrates, citizens are entitled to know what is being done in their name and the nature of the coercion that they might face, especially during war. Even for those who do not vote, or in the case of seventeen-year-olds who cannot vote but might join the armed forces, the ability to discuss and to learn about government policy is essential to the ideal of democratic self-government and does not merely serve the instrumental purpose of enhancing democratic procedures.

The rights of addressees, however, extend beyond rights to know facts; they

---

[27] *New York Times Co. v. United States,* 403 U.S. 713 (1971).

[28] Ibid.

[29] For another status-based account of free speech, see Thomas Nagel, "Personal Rights and Public Space," in *"Concealment and Exposure" and Other Essays* (Oxford: Oxford University Press, 2002), 43.

include rights to hear arguments considered "wrong" and "subversive." The Communist Scare cases of the early twentieth century help to demonstrate why the rights of citizens as addressees of law to hear arguments from across the political spectrum are fundamental to what it means to treat citizens as rulers. In these rulings, the Supreme Court refused to extend First Amendment protection to "subversive" speech that, it was argued, posed a "clear and present danger" to the security of the nation. Today, however, it is a settled judgment that these cases were decided wrongly, and the Court has since abandoned this doctrine in favor of strict protection of political speech. By using these cases to examine further our intuitions about the importance of free speech, I believe we can emphasize why in a democracy the core values should protect the rights of citizens in their capacity as addressees.

The Supreme Court's most famous decisions regarding political speech are often framed in terms of the right of dissidents to criticize the state balanced against the right of society to security. For example, in *Gitlow v. New York,* Justice Sanford argued that there is not an absolute right to speak or publish subversive opinions and focused instead on the danger of those who advocated the overthrow of the government. But Justice Holmes, in a dissenting opinion that influenced the Court's future jurisprudence on this issue, suggested why Sanford was wrong to conceive of citizens as passive recipients of spoken or written opinions, rather than as rulers capable of reasoning:

> It is said that this manifesto was more than a theory, that it was an incitement. Every idea is an incitement. It offers itself for belief and if believed it is acted on unless some other belief outweighs it or some failure of energy stifles the movement at its birth. . . . Eloquence may set fire to reason.[30]

Holmes here shifts the focus from the rights of speakers to those of listeners. His point is that citizens should not be treated as objects impacted by ideas, but rather as thinking subjects entitled to make up their own minds and capable of reasoning about politics. For Holmes, therefore, rights to free speech concern not just citizens' procedural capacities to advocate for certain arguments, but their treatment as rulers rather than as mere objects of rule. Treating citizens as autonomous reasoners is so central to the democratic ideal that, in Holmes's words, "If in the long run the beliefs expressed in proletarian dictatorship are destined to be accepted by the dominant forces of the community, the only meaning of free speech is that they should be given their chance and have their way."[31] Although for Holmes a proletarian revolution is the essence of a bad

---

[30] *Gitlow v. People of the State of New York,* 268 U.S. 652 (1925).
[31] Ibid.

consequence, he recognizes that a polity that seeks to protect its citizens from their own ideas fundamentally violates the ideal of citizens as rulers.

Holmes's eloquent defense of the rights of listeners, even when certain opinions might pose a danger to democracy, has broad implications for democratic theory. His contribution is to help delineate why a democratic account of reasonable treatment that sees citizens as autonomous and equal entails treating them as reasoners. A polity that treats citizens as reasonable will respect their autonomy as deliberators and listeners, and will not seek to manage their opinions or protect them from "subversion." This also implies a respect for citizens' equality. No citizen should be judged less capable of withstanding and evaluating arguments than a Supreme Court justice, an executive administrator, or a censor. An overarching substantive implication of these principles concerns the core value of reciprocity. The right to free speech is in part a right of citizens to have access to reasons for coercion, both moral and factual, and to be respected as reasoners. Rights to free speech thus elaborate one fundamental requirement of treating citizens reciprocally, or as entitled to reasons for coercion. But this entitlement is broader than mere access to reasons. It requires that citizens generally be treated not as causal objects, but as active thinkers capable of engaging with these reasons and determining whether the coercion they support is respectful of their status as autonomous and equal citizens. Therefore, the entitlements of listeners are aspects of the broader entitlement of citizens as addressees of law that coercion be justifiable to them rather than merely imposed by the state.

Thus far I have sought to clarify the importance and meaning of the core values by examining paradigmatic democratic rights associated with free speech and the rule of law. While the core values are fundamental to legitimacy in democratic polities, I do not want to suggest that they are the only legitimate values in a democracy. For example, the value of citizens' basic security is important to all politics. Often measures to protect this value do not conflict with the core values or with paradigmatic rights, such as those associated with the rule of law and free speech. Indeed, the point of democratic rights associated with the rule of law is that they provide a constraint, not a prohibition, on public policy meant to ensure safety. For instance, I argue in chapter 5 that criminal punishment is justifiable on democratic grounds but that legitimate punishment must be balanced against the democratic rights of those found to be guilty of crimes. The core values of democracy thus are not meant to serve as an exclusive set of values to appeal to in justification. Rather, they set the minimum requirements for treatment of democratic citizens and are entirely consistent with a wide range of policy goals.[32]

[32]This point, of course, extends to other concerns besides security. For instance, nothing about the core values is inconsistent with the decision of a democracy to fund the arts, even though doing so might be justified entirely on aesthetic grounds rather than by reference to the core values. The

But while measures to protect security might at times be consistent with the core values, a harder set of cases concerns instances in which the three core values and the basic rights they require conflict with some other value. In a democracy citizens are entitled to have some of their rights protected even when there might be a reason—from the standpoint of the general good—to violate them. For instance, even in the absence of a particular benefit from free expression, our intuitions about democracy suggest that we need to maintain this institution whether or not it causes some loss to stability—or to another measure of the overall good. The most paradigmatic violations of freedom of speech, from the standpoint of both law and common intuitions about democracy, are those in which political speech is limited simply because it has a bad effect. For instance, no reasonable democratic argument could plausibly claim that a pamphlet advocating a particular policy should be censored because it would negatively impact the economy. Indeed, even the more controversial Court decisions to limit political speech in the tense era of World War I did not call for *any* dangerous speech to be banned, but rather only speech that posed a "clear and present danger" to national security in times of war. Thus, even a Court shaken by war deemed free speech so intrinsically valuable that only the most grave threats could justify limiting it.

If we accept the proposition that democratic rights should not be abandoned every time there is a security interest in doing so, one still might argue that certain "extreme emergencies" give a society no choice but to suspend liberties at least temporarily. This was the rationale, for instance, in the Supreme Court's "clear and present danger" test. Does this suggest that security is also a democratic value, one that might trump the three core values I have introduced so far?

Historically, even the world's most mature democracies at times have suspended the democratic rights of individuals. During war, democracies have suspended elections, revoked habeas corpus, and limited free speech. One might argue that if the courts cannot open their doors, as was the case in the Civil War, access to the rule of law is impossible. My view is that these suspensions rightly are regarded as suspensions of democracy itself regardless of whether they are justified.

The crucial intuition about democracy here comes from an evaluation of what it would mean to suspend elections in a supreme emergency. In some circumstances such measures might be unavoidable. For instance, it might be impossible to hold elections when security to vote cannot be guaranteed. However, our considered judgments about democracy must lead to the conclusion

---

core values set a minimum standard for treatment. They do not dictate or provide conclusive normative guidance for all decisions in a democracy.

that such drastic measures indicate the suspension of democracy itself. In other words, a society might understandably suspend elections for reasons of security, but such a society would not be operating as an ideal democracy. Security, while having weight as a value independent from democracy, is not rightly considered a core value within democracy to be balanced constantly against the three core values of political autonomy, equality of interests, and reciprocity. Merely to add security as a fourth core value would neglect the extraordinary nature of extreme emergencies; it would offer no way of distinguishing them from more pedestrian instances in which rights guaranteed by the core values are deemed a threat to security or some other general good. According to my account, in such minor instances the core values must trump security concerns if a society is to be regarded as democratic.[33]

The notion that certain measures to protect security in extreme emergencies rightly are regarded as suspensions of democracy is consistent with perhaps the most prominent analysis of a real "ticking time-bomb" case, popular in much contemporary political philosophy. In "Judgment on the Interrogation Methods applied by the GSS," Israeli Chief Justice Barak argued that while torture could never be consistent with democratic values such as the rule of law, "necessity" in ticking time-bomb cases might be used by an interrogator as a defense. Barak is clear, however, that while a court might be justified in excusing criminal liability for a violation of the rule of law, this does not suggest that torture in such cases is sanctioned by democracy.[34] The decision in this case illustrates how security might justify a violation of the rule of law in exceptional circumstances, while stressing why such exceptions should not be confused with either the rule of law or democracy itself.

In the next chapter, I extend insights gleaned from this discussion of our considered judgments about the rule of law and free speech to a discussion of coercion in general. Underlying the fundamental democratic rights to freedom of speech and conscience and to the rule of law should be a more generalized concern that law be justifiable to reasonable citizens rather than simply im-

---

[33] Contrast this view with that of Richard Posner, who offers a classic utilitarian argument against the view that rights should limit security in a democracy. See Posner, "Security versus Civil Liberties," *Atlantic Monthly* 288, no. 5 (December 2001): 46–48. For his general aggregative theory of democracy, see idem, *Law, Pragmatism, and Democracy* (Cambridge, Mass.: Harvard University Press, 2003). Posner suggests that deliberative conceptions of democracy are flawed because they impose an elite's values on democratic polities and fail to be sufficiently realistic in accounting for actual citizens' motivations. Arguably, however, Posner, too, relies on values, namely utilitarianism, in his account of aggregative democracy.

[34] Israeli Supreme Court, "Judgement on the Interrogation Methods applied by the GSS" (1999), published online by Derechos Human Rights, available at <http://www.derechos.org/human-rights/mena/doc/torture.html>.

posed on them. So far I have limited my discussion of free speech to the right to political speech. I have done so as a matter of exegesis, using paradigmatic examples of democratic rights to lay the groundwork for a framework that can be used to justify state coercion. In the next chapter, I develop this framework, extending the democratic idea that citizens as addressees of law are entitled to reasonable treatment.

I have sought to identify the core values of democracy both in this chapter and the last by reference to paradigmatic examples. Now that these values have been identified, we can extend them to harder cases. It is worth noting that the Supreme Court itself has followed a similar path in its free speech jurisprudence. After establishing the imperative of strong protections of "political" speech, it has recognized that the principles that support this protection extend to areas once thought neither politically relevant nor protected by the First Amendment.[35] Similarly, I suggest that the core values of democracy have implications beyond the paradigmatic democratic rights associated with the rule of law and free speech. The core values also guarantee rights of addressees in their personal sexual lives, in limiting punishments for the worst criminals, and in evaluating the legitimacy of property distribution.

V. Conclusion

Democratic theorists usually describe the democratic ideal in terms of its political procedures. To the extent that democracy requires individual rights, many of these theories suggest, they should be understood as entitlements to participate in democratic procedures, or as the preconditions of these procedures. I have argued in this chapter, drawing on the idea of the core values, that citizens of a democracy are entitled to something more fundamental than participation in procedures: respect for their status as rulers. This status entitles them not only to procedural rights in their capacity as makers of law, but also to rights as addressees as they are affected by law. By guaranteeing democratic rights in both of these respects, a polity can demonstrate its commitment to individual citizens as part of a sovereign people.

It is a considered judgment that in a democracy, the institutions of the rule of law and free speech and conscience are necessary conditions of legitimacy. I drew on this fundamental intuition in the second half of this chapter to illustrate why respect for democratic citizenship requires the protection of certain

---

[35] See, for instance, the Court's "*Miller* test," which protects works of "literary" or "artistic" value in addition to the protection of political speech. *Miller v. California*, 413 U.S. 15 (1973).

rights of addressees. Rights against ex post facto laws and bills of attainder exist to ensure that citizens are treated in a manner consistent with the core values and their status as rulers, with their assurance of equal treatment and freedom from arbitrary coercion. Rights of expression, while partly the rights of speakers, are also the rights of listeners. These rights concern citizens both as the makers of law and as its addressees. The rights of democratic citizens, including the paradigmatic rights I examined in this chapter, cannot be explained or justified within the confines of the proceduralist model. Rather, we need a broader account of justification to explain democracy's role both for democratic procedure and for the rights that citizens retain as rulers. I turn in the next chapter to harnessing the conclusions from our discussion so far into a theory that can then be extended to more controversial rights areas. Drawing on the insights of this chapter, I argue that respect for citizens requires a sharp distinction between accounts of law as authorized by will or procedure and accounts of law as justifiable to citizens based on the ideal of reasonable treatment consistent with the core values. This framework can be used to identify democratic rights in other areas in which citizens potentially are subject to the coercion of law.

CHAPTER 3

DEMOCRATIC CONTRACTUALISM:
A FRAMEWORK FOR JUSTIFIABLE COERCION

I. INTRODUCTION

In the previous chapter, I suggested why the core values—understood as a procedure-independent standard of democratic legitimacy—require recognizing that citizens retain substantive democratic rights in their capacity as addressees of law. I argued that citizens' status as rulers entitles them to protection from state coercion that undermines that status. So far, however, I have limited my discussion of substantive rights to the paradigmatic examples of the rule of law and free speech. In this chapter, I develop a democratic framework for justifying coercion that draws on the core values, especially reciprocity's requirement that citizens be treated reasonably. The framework allows me to extend the value theory's argument for substantive rights into more controversial policy areas. In chapters 4 and 5, I apply the framework to argue for substantive democratic rights that limit coercion in areas of privacy and criminal justice. In chapter 6, I use it to establish positive welfare rights that serve as necessary conditions for legitimizing the coercion inherent in private property.

The framework I develop in this chapter serves as a specific application of the value theory of democracy to justifications of coercion. I call it *democratic contractualism* to emphasize its resonance with prominent historical accounts of the social contract, such as Rousseau's, and with their modern counterparts, such as Rawls's theory of political liberalism and Scanlon's moral theory of contractualist justification.[1] Rousseau offers a helpful starting point for democratic justifications of coercion because his account of political legitimacy appeals to the values of democracy as a procedure-independent standard. Yet while Rousseau bases his defense of democratic rights in the "general will," I argue that he fails to make a crucial distinction between the idea that legitimate law should accord with citizens' will and the idea that coercion should be justifiable to citizens qua addressees of law. I offer a lexicon to help clarify this distinction. I

---

[1] Rawls, *Political Liberalism.* See also T. M. Scanlon, *What We Owe to Each Other* (Cambridge, Mass.: Harvard University Press, 1998).

then suggest two principles for ensuring that coercion is justifiable to citizens and for identifying which rights they are entitled to as addressees of law. The first is the principle of *democracy's public reason,* a requirement that coercion be justifiable to citizens generally by appeal to the core values of democracy. The second, the *inclusion principle,* requires that this general concern to justify coercion to a people be extended to each individual citizen. Together, these principles constitute democratic contractualism, a democratic framework for justifying coercion and identifying citizens' rights as addressees of law.

II. A LEXICON OF CITIZENSHIP

In developing his procedure-independent standard, Rousseau distinguishes usefully between the "sovereign people" and the "government."[2] He is careful to maintain that any government, regardless of its procedure, is legitimate only when its laws and institutions respect the sovereignty of the people. When they do not, he contends, the government loses its democratic legitimacy and rules by brute force alone. While procedures such as majority rule are useful in identifying the preferences of a sovereign people, Rousseau suggests that these procedures themselves are not to be viewed as the final arbiter of legitimacy.[3] Thus, the sovereign ideal functions as a procedure-independent standard from which we can judge the legitimacy of government action.

In elaborating how state coercion can accord with popular sovereignty, or what he calls the "general will," Rousseau is concerned to explain how the state can justify its authority over each individual citizen. It is important, on his account, that while collectively the sovereign body is called a "people," individual "citizens" make up this body.[4] Thus, the general will is not conceived of as a utilitarian-like aggregation of individual wills, the "will of all," but rather as taking into account the individual interests of every citizen.[5] To legitimize its authority over the collective, Rousseau argues in "Discourse on Political Economy," the state must respect the rights of each individual citizen that it governs:

---

[2] For Rousseau's discussion of this distinction, see Rousseau, "On the Social Contract," 173. All titles from Rousseau, *The Basic Political Writings,* (Indianapolis, Ind., Hackett, 1987).

[3] One clear piece of evidence that Rousseau views the general will as an independent standard is that procedures sometimes "err" in interpreting what is required to treat a people as sovereign, but the general will never does. Rousseau writes, "It follows from what has preceded that the general will is always right and always tends toward the public utility. However, it does not follow that the deliberations of the people always have the same rectitude" (Rousseau, "On the Social Contract," 155).

[4] Ibid., 149.

[5] Ibid., 155–56.

There is no point to believing that one can strike or cut off an arm without pain being transmitted to the head. And it is no more believable that the general will would permit a member of the state, whoever he might be, to injure or destroy another member than that the fingers of a man in his right mind would put out his eyes. Individual welfare is so closely linked to the public confederation that, were it not for the attention one should pay to human frailty, this convention would be dissolved by right if just one citizen were to perish who could have been saved, if just one citizen were wrongly held in prison, and if a single litigation were to be lost because of an obvious injustice.[6]

Rousseau's conception of the general will is useful because it illustrates how conceiving of the people as the source of sovereignty implies limits on how individuals can be treated. Namely, Rousseau requires that the social contract be unanimous because it ought to be an account of how *all* citizens can govern themselves.[7] This account thus requires protection for each individual. When the state violates the interests of any one individual, it wields illegitimate authority not consented to or willed by that individual.

Despite caricatures of him as a collectivist, Rousseau provides a starting point for understanding how the sovereign status of the individual gives rise to democratic rights independent of any procedure.[8] When it is examined closely, however, Rousseau's theory has flaws similar to those of procedural theories and suggests important pitfalls to avoid in developing a framework of justification based on the core values of democracy. Namely, Rousseau's appeal to will makes it difficult for him to distinguish between democratic justification as a normative account of the entitlements of reasonable citizens qua addressees and as a purely descriptive account of what persons actually will. I have argued that procedural theories are wrong to ground the democratic legitimacy of policy decisions in the procedures that produced them. While Rousseau avoids this specifically procedural formulation, his account of will suffers from an equally problematic flaw—conflating the voluntary decisions of citizens and the normative standards that should guide democratic societies. Rousseau recognizes that his ideal of unanimity cannot require all citizens to endorse policy in a procedural sense. Indeed, it is unlikely that procedural unanimity would be possible on even one occasion.[9] Thus, to make his

---

[6] Rousseau, "Discourse on Political Economy," 122.

[7] Rousseau, "On The Social Contract," 147.

[8] "Certainly the right to property is the most sacred of all the citizens' rights" (Rousseau, "Discourse on Political Economy," 127).

[9] Rousseau, "On The Social Contract," 147. I do not think that even the "one occasion" that Rousseau speaks of in this passage could be understood in a procedural sense.

policy conclusions and statements about rights explainable with reference to a nonprocedural notion of democracy, Rousseau opts for a deeply controversial metaphysical theory of what it means for all citizens to will the general will. Often, he claims that citizens *actually* will coercion that serves the greater good, even if it affects them adversely, because they *should* will the general interest. Thus he conflates what citizens should want or what they say they want with what they actually want. For instance, he goes so far as to say that because capital punishment is important to protect the general interest, those convicted of capital crimes consent to be executed.[10] The problem here is that Rousseau falsely attributes consent to individuals in instances in which they explicitly resist, thus subordinating individual rights to a controversial metaphysical account by which citizens "will" what is right. I call this the "problem of false attribution." Although it seems to appeal to a conception of citizens' will, Rousseau's theory denies persons' understanding of their own will and substitutes for actual consent a conception of the good that often is not transparently stated.

Democratic contractualism, as an account of legitimate coercion and the rights of citizens, draws from the concern to assure that the rights of individuals are protected because of their status as members of a sovereign people. As Rousseau emphasizes, respect for a people as self-ruling requires respect for each citizen of a polity. But it is crucial to clarify that my account of citizenship, unlike Rousseau's, is one of justifiability to citizens who are regarded as addressees of law entitled to reasonable treatment, not an account of the "real will" of citizens. I thus resist any attempt to claim to discover a "unanimous will" of the people. Specifically, I distinguish among three terms that are conflated by those who embrace "real will" theories of democracy: "persons," "people," and "citizens." With the introduction of this lexicon, I believe I can limit my own democratic conception of popular sovereignty to the question of coercion without straying into the controversial conception of will that occupied Rousseau.[11]

By "persons," I mean individuals defined by their distinct understandings of their own wills. The term is empirically descriptive and value-neutral. Persons can desire and will things that are immoral, asocial, and anticommunity. They can treat one another in ways fundamentally at odds with the values of equality and autonomy.

"People," by contrast, refers to a community whose members are treated and treat each other in accordance with the core values of democracy. A "people" is

---

[10] Ibid., 159.

[11] For Kant's discussion of the relation between "will" and "state punishment," see Immanuel Kant, *Metaphysical Elements of Justice: Part I of the Metaphysics of Morals*, 2d ed., trans. John Ladd (Indianapolis, Ind.: Hackett, 1999), 142.

a normative ideal not to be confused with any particular existing community or the beliefs that happen to be common in such a community.

I formulate the notion of a "citizen" directly from the conception of a people, so it, too, is a normative ideal.[12] Citizens are persons entitled to be treated in accordance with the three core values and obligated to treat their fellow citizens in the same way. It is not enough for a citizen merely to invoke the values. Rather, citizens must employ them in a reasonable, good-faith manner in forming their beliefs. To think as a citizen, a person should see herself as a distinct part of the whole entitled to rights that protect her against certain treatments by the state, but also subject to duties that require her to recognize the rights of her fellow citizens.

Citizenship is an ideal relevant to democratic coercion.[13] It is not, as some civic republicans have maintained, an ideal for living. Thus, to think as a citizen does not entail that one must abandon the thoughts or concepts of the good that one holds as a person. Because thinking as a citizen is limited to theorizing about politics and legitimate coercion, it is compatible with a wide range of beliefs or conceptions of the good. In this sense, to think as a citizen does not require abandoning one's identity. When reflecting as a citizen, however, one at times might find one's personal beliefs at odds with the reasonable interpretations of the democratic core values. The ideal of citizenship requires only that such personal beliefs be bracketed in thinking about how the state should act. Not to bracket such beliefs would be to respect insufficiently the status of other citizens who do not share those beliefs. The ideal of common status thus is limited to politics, as I suggested it should be, and is not a conception of the good. Citizenship functions as an ideal way of thinking about political coercion by appealing to the core values often implicitly or explicitly rejected by persons in their way of thinking about politics.

It is important to acknowledge that some human characteristics and capacities are necessary conditions for my conception of citizenship. Specifically, citizens must have the capacities that would enable them to engage in and understand their entitlement to reciprocal reason giving. Among these I include the

---

[12] Of course, some real persons embrace the ideals of citizenship when making political decisions. The presence of these ideals among actual persons shows that the concept of citizenship has appeal in a democratic culture.

[13] Although Rousseau is often guilty of false attribution, he does at one point distinguish between citizens and persons: "It is, therefore, a question of making a rigorous distinction between the respective rights of the citizens and the sovereign, and between the duties the former have to fulfill as subjects and the natural right they should enjoy as men" (Rousseau, "On the Social Contract," 157).

capacity for language and reason prerequisite for engaging in public discourse.[14] Although these conditions are necessary to a conception of citizenship, they are not sufficient. Free and equal citizenship goes beyond the recognition of human capacity, because it demands that all persons be treated in accordance with substantive democratic values.

My distinction between a "citizen" and a "person," as well as between a "people" and "persons," resolves the problem of false attribution that I identified as a fundamental flaw in Rousseau's theory. This vocabulary allows us to distinguish between acts of coercion that are justifiable to a citizen, conceived of as free and equal, and acts that are willed by a person. Many of the questions of moral philosophy revolve around what it is to be a person rather than what it means to think and deliberate as a citizen. For instance, if we want to know what a person really wills in life—what career she chooses to pursue, whom, if anyone, she chooses to marry, where she wishes to live—we should look primarily to that person's own self-understanding. If, however, we wish to pursue a narrower inquiry regarding the legitimate limits of state coercion, will is irrelevant; we should look instead to the rights one is entitled to as a citizen and an addressee of law. Of course, in their actual lives, individuals cannot live only as citizens. The value theory's definition of citizenship is not a comprehensive account of identity. It is only a statement about how persons in an ideal democracy should reason about the legitimacy of state coercion.

A fundamental question remains in developing this lexicon and in extending it: who is to be included in the ideal of democratic treatment and thus treated as a citizen? Is the conception of citizens' entitlement to democratic treatment only useful in delineating the rights of legal citizens? Or is it also of use for legal and illegal aliens as well as visitors?

In the vernacular, the term "citizen" is often associated with its legal meaning. One either has the legal status of citizenship and the full set of political rights that come with it, such as voting, or one does not. In this sense, it is all-or-nothing.[15] In contrast, the moral conception of citizenship in the sense of

---

[14] I regard all persons without severe mental impairment as having these capacities. Severely mentally impaired persons might not be able to exercise these capacities, but they are still entitled to have their interests respected. See Len Barton, "The Struggle for Citizenship: The Case of Disabled People," *Disability, Handicap and Society* 8, no. 3 (January 1993): 235–48. In this article, Barton identifies a conception of citizenship comprising both procedural rights of political participation and substantive rights to be treated as a full member of society with control over one's life.

[15] The most compelling cases for granting individuals without legal citizenship the full rights and privileges of legal citizenship are those in which the person in question has no citizenship in any democratic regime. If a state is committed to treating all citizens as the source of law, then there is an obligation, when such persons are living in a democratic regime, for their host state to extend them the full rights of citizenship.

the citizen as an addressee of law has a more subtle meaning.[16] Moral citizens are persons coerced by the law who are entitled to be treated as sovereign in a manner that accords with the core values. To treat a person subject to coercion as a sovereign addressee does not imply that he or she must be given the full range of political rights. For instance, a tourist subject to punishment for a crime committed in the country he is visiting should be treated as a citizen in his capacity as an addressee of law, though this "moral citizenship" does not entitle him to vote or to travel with a passport from the country where he committed the crime. In other words, the moral conception need not demand full political rights for all in order to be useful in determining when and how individuals rightly are coerced. Moreover, persons who are not legal but moral citizens can embrace the ideal of democratic citizenship when they think and deliberate about public policies and basic rights. In my usage, therefore, "citizenship" is an ideal of justification rather than a legal term. Any treatment that impinges upon the core values is a clear violation of moral citizenship. The sense of the citizen as addressee is relevant in delineating the limits of coercion in basic rights areas such as criminal punishment, privacy, and speech, regardless of whether a particular individual has full citizenship. To deny these rights to visitors or noncitizens would be to disrespect their moral status as citizens.

Imagine, for instance, a polity in which only those who were full citizens were allowed to speak freely. This clearly would degrade the values of democracy and inappropriately would exclude some persons from the status of moral citizenship. There also is value to legal citizens' right to listen to the views of nonlegal citizens. Indeed, those from other countries, given their varying backgrounds, might have distinct and useful contributions to make. Moreover, democratic societies should respect the basic limits of the rule of law when nonlegal citizens are accused of committing crimes. The status of citizens as addressees of law, I argued, does not depend on their "active" participation in lawmaking. Rather, this treatment stems from an ideal of coercion consistent with democratic principles. In chapter 5, I make the case for extending this ideal of treatment even to those who are guilty of the worst crimes against society. I endeavor to make the easier case here for noncitizens who have not been convicted of any

[16] This usage of the term in a moral sense is consistent with that of both Rawls and Larmore. See, for instance: Rawls, *Political Liberalism*, 29–35. This ideal is emphasized most prominently in *Justice as Fairness*, 18–24. My use of the term "citizen" is also consistent with Larmore's. He writes, "The idea is that, in this view, the individualist treatment of persons as separate from the substantial ideals they may share with others is a strictly political norm, applicable to persons in their role as citizens. . . . Political liberalism is a moral conception based on the norm of equal respect, even if its ambition is to be a minimal one" (Charles Larmore, "Political Liberalism," *Political Theory* 18, no. 3 [August 1990]: 353).

wrongdoing. In short, moral citizenship is an ideal applicable not just to citizens in the narrow legal sense. Rather, it is a principle of treatment that constrains how democratic polities can coerce all persons subject to their control.

With this definition of moral citizenship articulated, we can go on to elaborate upon the framework appropriate to justifying state coercion to citizens as addressees.

III. The Principle of Democracy's Public Reason

As we discussed in the first section of this chapter, *democratic contractualism* is a framework for justifying coercion and the rights that limit it. It consists of two principles. The first principle, *democracy's public reason,* is the focus of this section. It holds that democratically justifiable coercion must appeal to citizens' status as free and equal; however, coercion based on reasons that are either inconsistent with, or outwardly hostile to, these values is not democratically legitimate. Democracy's public reason offers one way of discerning when coercion is inconsistent with the democratic ideal, and it provides a preliminary means of sketching the contours of democratic rights.

It is helpful in clarifying the principle of democracy's public reason to begin by examining a prominent criticism of public reason that has been elaborated in liberal theory and by explaining how my own democratic conception of public reason responds to this criticism. Rawls defines public reason as "the reason of citizens," using the term "citizen" in a manner similar to the moral meaning I discussed in the previous section. Critics of Rawls have interpreted his idea of public reason to entail that citizens always should argue in the public sphere using reasons that bracket comprehensive conceptions and appeal exclusively to shared values. Critics claim that such a concept is too narrow because it excludes citizens' general moral and religious beliefs from informing public dialogue and thus robs politics of significant resources in generating public arguments. Great political leaders such as Martin Luther King Jr., for example, appealed to religious conceptions in public argument for principles of liberty and equality that theorists like Rawls deem essential.

In contrast to this interpretation, however, democracy's public reason does not function as an exclusive way for persons to speak in democratic procedures or in the public sphere. Rather, it is a standard for evaluating coercion independent of the way that citizens do, or should, express their political beliefs. When participating in political discussion, citizens very well might appeal to reasons drawn from religious and/or philosophical comprehensive conceptions rather than reasons based on the core values. Indeed, the right to free speech that I defended in the last chapter implies that citizens should be free to draw from these conceptions as they see fit. Democracy's public reason concerns not the reasons that actually are offered to justify law, but rather whether laws plausibly could be defended as consistent with the core values.

However, while this principle is compatible with various views as a matter of discerning democratic legitimacy, it still might conflict with certain comprehensive conceptions in their entirety. The purpose of democracy's public reason is not to judge whether comprehensive conceptions are correct, but rather to evaluate whether laws, including those grounded in arguments derived from comprehensive conceptions, are consistent with citizens' shared status through the core values. Many arguments, including those from outside the democratic tradition, can serve to bolster and to offer a distinct rationale for the democratic arguments that appeal to the core values. They thus should be welcome in democracy's public sphere and in public dialogue. In this sense, democracy's public reason follows Rawls' "proviso": "Reasonable comprehensive doctrines, religious or nonreligious, may be introduced in public political discussion at any time, provided that in due course proper political reasons—and not reasons given solely by comprehensive doctrines—are presented that are sufficient to support whatever the comprehensive doctrines introduced are said to support."[17]

A related point answers the criticism that public reason is too constraining of the rhetoric that makes up actual politics. Politics is not pursued exclusively through arguments and reason; citizens seek a variety of means to persuade each other, including storytelling, exaggeration, and humor.[18] But democracy's public reason does not prohibit such rhetoric when persons engage in politics or argue for the substantive rights I contend are necessary for democratic legitimacy. Thus, rhetoric is not fundamentally incompatible with this principle.

In sum, democracy's public reason is a useful principle for those theorizing about the necessary conditions for democratic legitimacy, including the basic rights necessary for democratic legitimacy. For example, citizens might argue about whether liberal property rights reflect the core values. Such examination might cause them to rethink a policy, institution, or basic right. Citizens delib-

---

[17] Rawls, "The Idea of Public Reason Revisited," 152.

[18] I owe this line of argument to an exchange with Iris Marion Young and Philip Pettit at an American Political Science Association annual meeting panel, "Reason and Rhetoric in Constitutional Democracies," organized by Mariah Zeisberg in Philadelphia, Pennsylvania, August 2003. For an elaboration on the importance of rhetoric in political discourse, see Young, "Inclusive Political Communication" in idem, *Inclusion and Democracy* (Oxford: Oxford University Press, 2000), 52–80. Another of the many helpful suggestions I find in Young's work is the notion that attention to diverse ways of speaking provides insight into reasonable claims that otherwise might be ignored from the standpoint of public reason.

erating in terms of democracy's public reason must be concerned to evaluate coercion with reference to the independent standard of the three core values.

How is it possible, however, to abstract from the influence of actual institutions and comprehensive conceptions in the midst of these deliberations? The critical distance of the critique is achieved in part by the fact that citizens should appeal to values that reflect a common status rather than their particular comprehensive views. The values are not necessarily those that persons find most important, but rather those that are appropriate to recognizing each other's status as citizens. Democracy's public reason might require bracketing those values that some persons will think most fundamental to a good life. One might think that premarital sex is a mortal sin, for instance, but at the level of democracy's public reason still recognize that the need to respect the equal status of one's fellow citizens requires privacy rights allowing for out-of-marriage sexual relations. It is a prerequisite of the core values that they are compatible with a variety of comprehensive doctrines and conceptions of the good. Given a society with pluralistic conceptions of the good, it would be unreasonable to impose any one of these conceptions on a polity. Rather, the core values are meant to be compatible with many reasonable conceptions of the good. In this sense, they reflect a common status and do not privilege one particular comprehensive doctrine as true.

At the level of democracy's public reason, three types of policy argument can be ruled out as inconsistent with the core values and thus, if reflected in legislation, in violation of democratic rights. First, arguments that are hostile to democratic values can be ruled out at the general level of democracy's public reason. Such arguments openly challenge the core values. Certain arguments for slavery, for instance, were premised on the idea that persons of African descent are unequal to those of European descent due to natural characteristics and thus should be treated unequally. This argument would be ruled out from the start. Perhaps more commonly, much political reasoning about coercion proceeds on the basis that citizens should always advance their self-interest regardless of the interests of others. Such arguments blatantly disregard the value of reciprocity because they suggest we should not reason by appeal to the interests of our fellow citizens. These arguments also would be ruled out from the start.

Second, arguments that formally cite the values but cannot be understood as reasonable interpretations of them are also ruled out. The requirement of democratic mutual justification is one of substantive evaluation, not merely a pro forma approach to styles of expression. The test of the core values is not merely whether one can transcribe arguments concerning legitimate coercion into a democratic form. It is clear that many arguments can appeal to the core values although no reasonable person could deny that they violate them. We could imagine a modified version of the slavery argument above that was made in terms of the core values—for instance, a variation of the "separate but equal" argument that justified slavery by reference to the equal interests of slaves in being enslaved—but we would still hold the argument to be inconsistent with the core values.

A third category of arguments that are ruled out at the level of democracy's public reason comprises those that rest on plausible, though undemocratic interpretations of the core values. One could make arguments from the value of equality by interpreting this value to mean equality before God. Such a conception, however, might be inconsistent with the democratic core value of equality. For instance, if one understands equality to mean that persons should subject themselves equally to God's judgment through the arm of the state, this would not treat citizens as rulers who authorize legitimate coercion.

Aggregate conceptions of equality are subject to the same claim. Utilitarian views, for instance, understand equality of interests as giving each person's interests equal weight in the calculus of the common good. Because this interpretation treats individuals' interests as interchangeable and does not guarantee that any particular individual's interests will be met, however, it is inconsistent with the democratic contractualist requirement of justification to individual citizens. The utilitarian interpretation thus violates the democratic meaning of equality. Abstracting from this example, we can see that it is not enough to appeal to commonly held interpretations of the words "equality" or "autonomy." Rather, democratic public reasons must appeal to and reflect the common status of democratic citizenship. Arguments that fail these criteria can be ruled out at the level of public reason.

In conclusion, the principle of democracy's public reason can serve as a guidepost for policymaking in legitimate democracies. Citizens who hope to honor the principle will formulate policy, and in turn legitimize coercion, by deliberating over whether this coercion respects the core values, treating citizens in general as free and equal. However, deliberation at this general level is insufficient for establishing the contours of democratic rights; for this purpose, the principle of democracy's public reason must be combined with the inclusion principle.

IV. THE INCLUSION PRINCIPLE

Democracy's public reason provides a preliminary way of evaluating whether public institutions and acts of coercion respect the core values. When examined at the general level of democracy's public reason, some violations of the core values might be defensible, however, despite violating the status of individual citizens as rulers. Such violations are only apparent when we examine the law's impact on specific individuals. In the last chapter, for instance, I argued that ex post facto laws are illegitimate because of their adverse effects on those who cannot predict their requirements. This would be true even if such laws appealed generally to the core values. For example, although I suggest in chapter 6 that taxation to fund welfare programs generally is justified on the basis of the core values, such taxation would be illegitimate if applied retroactively because it would violate persons' entitlement to know the full extent of state coercion facing them. Thus, coercion must be justifiable not only to a democratic people in general, but also specifically to individual citizens based on respect for their status as rulers. While I distinguish this notion of justifiability to citizens from procedural or will-based notions of unanimity, it does resonate with Rousseau's original formulation of rights. According to the value theory and its framework of democratic contractualism, democratic rights stem from entitlements of each citizen to justifiability. When these rights are not respected for the individual, the legitimacy of a democratic people is threatened. This conception shares Rousseau's concern to legitimize state authority over each individual citizen by emphasizing that sovereign citizens deserve to have their distinct interests protected by democratic rights.[19]

The inclusion principle is a means of ensuring that the core values are respected for particular citizens. We can ascertain whether coercion adheres to the inclusion principle by asking the following two questions: *What types of state coercion can a person reasonably accept if she embraces the core values of democracy—equality of interests, political autonomy, and reciprocity—and is motivated to find agreement with his or her fellow citizens? What types of state coercion can the same citizen reasonably reject?* These questions set a standard for evaluating law's impact on the individual and protecting citizens from illegitimate coercion.[20]

The inclusion principle has three important features, which I discuss in more detail in the following paragraphs. First, it evaluates coercion from citizens' individual "points of view," focusing on the interests of the coerced instead of the interests of society as coercer.[21] Second, it reflects the distinction made in the last chapter between "will" and "status" by looking beyond the coercion that

---

[19] Rousseau, "Discourse on Political Economy," 122.

[20] I acknowledge that there will be a wide terrain in which reasonable disagreement is possible and thus I do not claim that the inclusion principle is determinate in regard to every political controversy involving issues of coercion. For a discussion of reasonable disagreements, see Gutmann and Thompson, *Democracy and Disagreement.* Whereas Gutmann and Thompson focus their theory on how values such as reciprocity can help us to think about political issues within the side constraint of basic rights, I aim to use the core values of democracy to think about the fundamental rights essential to democratic legitimacy.

[21] The inclusion principle draws from both Scanlon's moral theory in its notion of reasonableness

persons actually *do* accept to an objective standard of justifiability that asks us to imagine citizens as reasonable deliberators. Third, the inclusion principle posits citizens as motivated to reach universal agreement. At least in some instances, it thus avoids the problem of indeterminacy that can result when reasonable citizens disagree about the legitimacy of a particular instance of coercion. These three features make the inclusion principle a useful tool for developing an account of democratic rights.[22]

Individual Point of View

The inclusion principle asks whether persons, thinking as citizens, can reasonably accept or reject a given act of coercion. To apply the test effectively, we must recognize that persons are situated in particular contexts and social positions and that their distinct interests are implicated differently by each coercive law or institution. Because of these differences, many policy disputes over coercion will be fueled by clashing points of view. In criminal punishment, relevant points of view include those of criminals on trial in addition to those of victims and potential victims. Pertinent to justifications of property are the interests of both the person who finds himself excluded from wealth and the property owner who has an interest in not having her property taken or taxed.

Aggregative accounts of equality resolve these tensions by asking persons to abstract into a generalized perspective in which their interests are interchangeable with those of other persons. The democratic inclusion principle, on the other hand, seeks to justify coercion while respecting the distinct interests that arise within these particular points of view. The best way to give meaning to

---

and his idea of "a point of view." See Scanlon, *What We Owe to Each Other*. Unlike Scanlon, however, my view, like Rawls's principle of liberal legitimacy, is a distinctly political theory with an emphasis on democracy's core values. Like Rawls, I put the values of free and equal citizenship at the center of my theory and demonstrate a commitment to a "criterion of reciprocity." Although Rawls does not develop this idea, there is a suggestion in *Political Liberalism* that the "criterion of reciprocity" is an extension of Scanlon's theory of reasonableness; see in particular *Political Liberalism*, xliv, n. 14. Also like Rawls, I invoke a conception of public reason; see *Political Liberalism*, Lecture 6, 212–54.

[22] David Estlund, "The Democracy/Contractualism Analogy," *Philosophy and Public Affairs* 31, no. 4 (October 2003): 387–412. The inclusion principle should be understood as a procedure-independent standard for evaluating rights, and should clearly not be regarded as a device or democratic procedure. As Estlund argues, the ideal of justifiability to all would itself likely be a flawed procedure because giving each citizen veto power would amount to a conservative stalemate, leaving the status quo in place (397–99). This understanding is consistent, however, with the recognition that the contractualist framework is appropriate to theorizing rights. This view is compatible with a variety of democratic procedures. For instance, majoritarianism might be a legitimate democratic procedure, though it is rightly limited by protection of democratic rights.

this principle is to assess coercion's impact on different individuals from the perspective of those individuals' particular social contexts. We thus can distinguish between the general point of view embraced by aggregative accounts of equality and the particular points of view embraced by democratic contractualism. I acknowledge the importance of this component of the inclusion principle in subsequent chapters; for example, I discuss punishment from the perspective of criminals in chapter 5 and taxation from the perspective of property owners in chapter 6.

Persons as Reasonable Citizens Embracing the Core Values

In the lexicon provided earlier in this chapter, I distinguished between "persons," who hold a variety of reasonable and unreasonable views, and the ideal of the "citizen," who reasons according to the core values. The inclusion principle's standard of reasonableness rules out a variety of interpretations of the core values as inconsistent with democratic reasoning. Among those unreasonable views, for instance, might be the view of criminals who reject any punishment or restriction on their freedoms. They might claim that no limit on their freedoms to travel or to kill wantonly is acceptable. However, the inclusion principle distinguishes between what persons actually reject and those instances of coercion that they, as citizens, reasonably can reject. The assertion of a "right to murder" would be paradigmatic of an unreasonable interpretation of the core values. Murder entails a failure, in the most basic sense, to respect citizens' status as free and equal; therefore, no reasonable citizen could assert a right to commit such a crime.

This point highlights why the test is not predictive of what persons *will* do and think but is a normative claim about how they *should* act and think. If persons seek to find democratically legitimate limits to coercion, they should advance only those interests that are reasonably consistent with the core values. Ideally, all persons will participate in this type of justificatory deliberation in a democracy and will think of themselves as citizens, but it is especially important for officials who exercise the coercive power of the state to turn to this independent standard of legitimacy. Legislatures and judges, who directly determine coercive measures, claim to act with legitimate authority. The inclusion principle suggests that part of this task involves an element of empathy. They should evaluate the substance of policy by imagining the arguments that might be made by persons subject to coercion who think of themselves as citizens. This process of "putting oneself in the shoes" of those subject to coercion is an important means of ensuring that addressees of law are treated in a democratic manner.

Motivation to Reach Universal Agreement

The requirement that interpretations of the core values be reasonable further limits the value theory's conception of legitimate coercion. Nevertheless, the requirement of reasonableness does not produce enough determinacy to generate an account of rights. Certain citizens still could reasonably accept a large number of arguments that others would reject. With no motivation to resolve their differences, these disagreements might result in considerable indeterminacy. Such indeterminacy would respond inadequately to the task of legitimizing coercion, a task to which the account of democratic citizenship is meant to respond.

Because of the need to reconcile competing interests and to avoid indeterminacy, the inclusion principle conceives of citizens as motivated to seek universal agreement. Positing such a motivation models the ideal of reciprocity—that citizens should take seriously each other's status as free and equal. Without such a motivation, citizens would be content merely to disagree with each other about whether many instances of coercion were justifiable. In self-government, we share not only an obligation to participate in lawmaking, but also a common fate in its effect. The democratic ideal requires that citizens seek to balance their own interests with the interests of others through a process of mutual justification, in which citizens are committed not only to recognizing each other's status but also to reaching conclusions about where the boundaries of coercion lie.[23]

Of course, some persons qua persons might reject the project of seeking democratic rights justifiable to all. My account of citizenship, however, is an ideal for thinking about politics (that is, thinking as person qua citizen), not a description of actual motivation.[24]

Substantive Rights

The inclusion principle is useful for discerning the content of the substantive democratic rights required by the core values. Some instances of coercion will be so essential to the preservation of all citizens' status as free and equal that

---

[23] In positing such a motivation, I follow many other theories that seek to give content to the value of reciprocity, from Scanlon's moral theory to theories of deliberation.

[24] Indeed, the very capacities of citizens are normative attributes that suggest a way of treating citizens in a democracy. This moral notion of capacity can be contrasted with a naturalized account of democratic capacities such as that of Josiah Ober, "The Democratic Animal: Nature, History, and Politics" (Stanford University Wesson Lectures, 2004). Indeed, if Ober's account is correct, I take it only to reinforce my normative conception, although I rely on no such naturalized view.

they rightly are regarded as reasonably acceptable to all. For instance, laws prohibiting assault obviously are reasonably acceptable because they limit individuals' freedom in order to preserve the most basic interests of potential victims. Such a law might be rejected by some violent members of society, but any reasonable citizen motivated to come to agreement with her fellow citizens would recognize that it is fundamental to ensuring the status of all citizens as free and equal. In contrast, I argue in the following chapters that other laws or social institutions coerce citizens without respecting the core values. While the principle of democracy's public reason reveals why some laws generally do not respect these values, the inclusion principle helps to highlight coercion that reasonably is rejected by particular citizens impacted by that coercion even when they are motivated to recognize the interests of their fellow citizens and to seek universal agreement. The inclusion principle suggests further limits on democratic coercion and lays additional groundwork for theorizing a set of democratic rights that delineate these limits.[25]

V. Conclusion

I argued in the last chapter that rights against coercion associated with the rule of law were paradigmatic rights of addressees. Bills of attainder, for instance, are obvious candidates for reasonable rejection because they clearly undermine citizens' entitlement to equality, autonomy, and reciprocity. While these are easy cases that violate the inclusion principle, I suggest that this principle is also useful in discerning the content of rights in more controversial areas. I will argue in the chapters to come that rights often associated with the liberal tradition can be rearticulated in terms of democratic justification. In chapter 4, I argue that negative rights to privacy, or what is sometimes called "decisional autonomy," are aspects of an important democratic right against the state. This right protects citizens from laws against sodomy and other incursions into sexual decision making. But democratic contractualism does not require protections for all aspects of life traditionally regarded as private. I argue that the inclusion principle and the principle of democracy's public reason help to distinguish the boundaries between the right to privacy and reasonable state

---

[25] While the inclusion principle suggests a set of democratic rights, there will be a variety of areas of democratic debate within the boundaries established by democratic rights. For instance, many budgetary debates about the allocation of resources are not about basic rights or constitutional essentials. In such cases the inclusion principle will likely be neither useful nor appropriate. Legitimacy in such matters, as opposed to those that are relevant to basic rights, might depend entirely on whether a legitimate procedure is followed.

coercion. For instance, not all incursions into family life rightly are regarded as violations of a democratic right to privacy. Democratic contractualism ensures protections for individual citizens, and at times this will mean that a role for the state in protecting women from domination within the home is reasonably acceptable to all.

In addition to helping to discern when rights of privacy limit legitimate coercion, the inclusion principle also suggests limits on punishment, even for those who have violated legitimate laws. In particular, I will argue in chapter 5 that it is useful in delineating democratic rights through its recognition of the point of view of criminals qua citizens. While citizenship is often associated with individuals in their capacity as makers of the law doing their civic duty, democratic rights for addressees offer guarantees for even those who flout their most basic duties. Criminals qua citizens could reasonably reject punishments that strip them of all their rights. Thus, I argue that even the worst citizens are entitled to some limits on punishment, and—to the extent that it is possible while recognizing the entitlement of democratic societies to punish—the preservation of their democratic rights.

While privacy and criminal justice rights are "negative" rights against state coercion, I argue in chapter 6 that democratic contractualism also requires "positive" rights to welfare guarantees for all citizens if private property is to be justified. The coercion at issue in justifications of private property is the right of property owners to exclude their fellow citizens through exclusive ownership. Citizens who have their economic interests neglected in a regime of private property still could, given a motivation to reach universal agreement, reasonably reject the right to exclude. I argue that in order to justify the legitimacy of exclusive ownership to the poorest citizens, the state must provide them with basic welfare guarantees. These democratic rights to privacy, to restrictions on punishment, and to welfare are necessary conditions of democratic legitimacy justified by appeal to the principle of democracy's public reason and the inclusion principle.

In sum, the framework of democratic contractualism offers two principles for discerning democratic limits on coercion and the democratic rights required by the core values. The principle of democratic public reason holds that citizens should evaluate coercive policies in terms of the core values that define their shared status as citizens. The inclusion principle holds that coercion should also be evaluated based on its impact on individual citizens with distinct points of view. Having drawn on the insights from the previous chapter to develop democratic contractualism's justificatory framework, we can now extend this framework to more controversial terrain, beginning with privacy.

CHAPTER 4

PUBLIC JUSTIFICATION AND THE RIGHT TO PRIVACY

> RS: And if you make the case that if you can do whatever you
> want to do, as long as it's in the privacy of your own home, this
> "right to privacy," then why be surprised that people are doing
> things that are deviant within their own home? . . . Whether
> it's polygamy, whether it's adultery, whether it's sodomy,
> all of those things, are antithetical to a healthy, stable,
> traditional family . . . The definition of marriage has not
> ever to my knowledge included homosexuality. That's not
> to pick on homosexuality. It's not, you know, man on child,
> man on dog, or whatever the case may be . . .
> AP: I'm sorry, I didn't think I was going to talk about "man on
> dog" with a United States senator, it's sort of freaking me out.
> —*Interview with U.S. Senator Rick Santorum (R-PA),*
> *April 7, 2003, Associated Press*

I. Introduction

In this chapter I propose and defend an account of the right to privacy from
the perspective of democratic contractualism, the value theory's framework for
justifying coercion. I am particularly concerned with the issue of "decisional autonomy," the individual's right to a sphere of intimate decision making free
from state coercion and public scrutiny.[1] Given that democratic contractualism
advances an ideal of political justification, both of state coercion and of the
rights of democratic citizens, this ambition might appear paradoxical. Courts
interpreting the Constitution and political theorists who have offered defenses
of privacy doctrine have defended individuals' rights to make personal decisions
about issues ranging from life and death to sexual activity. They argue that

---

[1] This issue can be distinguished from "informational privacy." For an elaboration of this type of
privacy, see Samuel D. Warren and Louis D. Brandeis's discussion of the right to control which personal information is published in the press in Warren and Brandeis, "The Right to Privacy," *Harvard Law Review* 4, no. 5 (December 1890): 193–220.

because these decisions concern the most intimate areas of life, they are distinct both from the idea of public justification among citizens and also from politics generally. Not surprisingly, then, most modern defenses of privacy have stressed the dignity of individual persons as distinct from and more fundamental than citizenship in the state and the polity. They have not sought to establish a public justification for privacy but rather to protect persons' inherent human dignity from the constraints of democratic authority.

The reluctance to defend privacy in public-regarding terms, however, conflates the right of citizens to privacy guarantees with the task of justifying that right. While I defend the view that citizens should not be subject to the requirements of public justification in a variety of personal matters, I argue that the boundaries of the privacy right—boundaries enforced by the state through coercion—should be delineated through public justification with reference to the core values of democracy. When privacy is justified in this manner, status quo understandings of the boundary between public and private must be redefined.

The right to privacy plays a prominent role in contemporary constitutional law and in the limits it imposes on legislation. The Supreme Court has grounded the right to privacy, or what is sometimes called "decisional autonomy," in the constitutional doctrine of "substantive due process." It has relied on this doctrine to overturn legislation that restricts personal decisions about life, death, marriage, sexual activity, abortion, and the use of contraception. Traditional liberal appeals to the prepolitical rights of individuals are often present in the Court's reasoning.[2] In contrast to this way of reasoning, democratic contractualism offers an attractive conceptual starting point for theorizing privacy because it avoids the problem of constraint that accompanies these other defenses.[3]

---

[2] In *Meyer v. Nebraska*, 262 U.S. 390 (1923), which struck down a state law that forbade schools to teach German to students not yet in ninth grade, substantive due process was defended on the grounds that it is "the right of the individual . . . to engage in any of the common occupations of life, to acquire useful knowledge, to marry, establish a home and bring up children, to worship God according to the dictates of his own conscience, and generally to enjoy those privileges long recognized at common law as essential to the orderly pursuit of happiness by free men." Also consider Brennan's claim in *Eisenstadt v. Baird*, 405 U.S. 438 (1972): "If the right of privacy means anything, it is the right of the individual, married or single, to be free from unwarranted governmental intrusion into matters so fundamentally affecting a person as the decision whether to bear or beget a child." Justice Douglas's opinion in *Griswold v. Connecticut*, 381 U.S. 479 (1965), voices the same belief in prepolitical individual rights: "We deal with a right of privacy older than the Bill of Rights—older than our political parties."

[3] My approach in this section shares a similar ambition to a work in progress by Joshua Cohen, "Democracy and Privacy." For a Habermasian approach to the relationship between democracy and

I begin in section II by distinguishing democratic contractualism's account of a right to privacy from views that theorize privacy as an a priori guarantee, or that see it merely as instrumental to political participation. My argument is that privacy is intrinsically valuable but its boundaries must be publicly justifiable. This means that democratic privacy is presumed by contractualism but also that this presumption can be overcome in the face of good democratic reasons. I argue in section III that "morals legislation" limiting citizens' right to make their own decisions in sexual matters is not supported by democratic reasons and therefore fails to overcome the presumption of privacy. Given the hostility of antisodomy laws to the core values, the principle of democracy's public reason clarifies the need for a right to sexual privacy akin to that defended by the Supreme Court in *Lawrence v. Texas*. A democratic right to privacy, however, does not cordon off a domestic sphere immune from public justification. In section IV, I argue, in part by appeal to feminist theorists such as Susan Okin, that the core value of equality suggests instances in which the state should intervene in intrafamily matters. I distinguish this understanding of democratic equality from perfectionist accounts of equality invoked by some feminist theorists.

II. SITUATING DEMOCRATIC PRIVACY: A CRITIQUE OF LIBERAL AND REPUBLICAN ACCOUNTS

When the right to privacy is defended by an appeal to democratic contractualism, it can be formulated in a manner that avoids problems present in both traditional liberal and republican conceptions of privacy, the two dominant approaches in the literature of political theory. In particular, it draws on a feminist critique of some liberal views.[4] When privacy is assumed a priori or defined with reference to current cultural boundaries between the public and the private, feminist critics have argued that it serves to protect, or at minimum to ignore, intrafamily injustices. In response to this criticism, I propose that the boundaries of privacy should not be drawn prior to normative argument, but rather by appeal to a justifiable normative standard. Because the value theory

---

privacy, see Jean Cohen, *Regulating Intimacy: A New Legal Paradigm* (Princeton: Princeton University Press, 2002).

[4] For an example of this critique see: Susan Moller Okin, *Justice, Gender, and the Family* (New York: Basic, 1989), and "Political Liberalism, Justice, and Gender," *Ethics* 105, no. 1 (October 1994): 23–43; and John Exdell, "Feminism, Fundamentalism, and Liberal Legitimacy," *Canadian Journal of Philosophy* 24, no. 3 (September 1994): 441–64. A good example of this critique from a nonliberal perspective is Wendy Brown, *States of Injury: Power and Freedom in Late Modernity* (Princeton: Princeton University Press, 1995).

articulates the right to privacy only with reference to democratic justification, it does not assume that the traditionally private realm of the family is somehow "off limits" to coercive laws and institutions. Instead, it is designed to balance concerns about the equal interests of vulnerable members of the family with concerns about the general value of privacy.

In contrast to liberal theorists who have been criticized for making privacy too central to their theories, some republican theorists regard privacy as being at best an instrumental value of democratic theory. In Constant's terms, many of their accounts value the "ancient liberty" of political participation over the "modern liberty" to be free from state coercion.[5] These republican accounts criticize dominant conceptions of liberalism that overvalue the private sphere and devalue political participation. There are strong and weak versions of this republican account of privacy. The strong version is exemplified in some of Rousseau's work, which seems to suggest that the ancient liberties can only be revived if the individual constantly thinks of herself as a public being, "transparent" to her fellow citizens in all aspects of life. The less extreme version values privacy rights only because they are instrumental to robust public life. Along these lines, Frank Michelman suggests that privacy is useful because it produces diversity to the benefit of public discourse and, ultimately, democracy.[6] Michelman's work is helpful in theorizing a democratic account of privacy because of its recognition of privacy's instrumental value in contributing to democratic participation. It contains, however, the same limitation as the preconditional theories of rights examined in chapter 1; on Michelman's view, privacy would cease to be a legitimate right if it failed to be instrumentally valuable for participation. Democratic contractualism avoids this limitation by suggesting why privacy can be defended both as a substantive right and as an intrinsically valuable aspect of the democratic ideal.

In sum, democratic contractualism rejects both liberal accounts of privacy as prior to, or independent of, public justification and republican accounts of privacy as solely instrumental to participation. Instead, its account defends privacy rights, like democratic rights to speech and conscience, by appeal to the ideal of democratic citizenship.

The starting point for thinking about democratic privacy rights is the notion of freedom implicit in the requirement that coercion be justifiable to citizens.[7] Coercion is not justified unless it appeals successfully to citizens' status as rulers, following democracy's public reason and the inclusion principle. Thus,

---

[5] Benjamin Constant, "The Liberty of the Ancients," 307–28.

[6] Michelman, "Law's Republic": 1534–36.

[7] For a related argument, see Philip Pettit, *Republicanism: A Theory of Freedom and Government* (Oxford: Clarendon, 1997).

democratic contractualism presumes citizens to be free in the absence of good democratic reasons for coercion. This presumption of freedom is implicit in the argument of chapter 2 that individual citizens as addressees of law are entitled to reasons explaining why they are coerced. The example of Larry Legislator in that chapter helped to illustrate why a lack of freedom from state control, despite the retention of procedural rights of participation, violates the basic entitlements of addressees of law. The examples of ex post facto laws and bills of attainder demonstrated why citizens' freedom cannot be limited by arbitrary dictates of the state. Drawing on these examples, democratic contractualism sets a standard of justification that must be met in limiting or overcoming the presumption of freedom.

The presumption of freedom also might be regarded as a presumption of privacy, or as it sometimes is called, "the right to be let alone."[8] By itself, however, this presumption does not give rise to a generalized right of privacy.[9] For instance, citizens do not have a right to be free from state prohibitions against physical assault, since state coercion in such instances clearly is justifiable. To demonstrate a right to privacy, it is necessary to show that arguments for coercion are incompatible with the core values as articulated in the democratic contractualist framework. In other words, privacy rights are justifiable when they protect against coercion that is not supported by democracy's public reason or the inclusion principle.

A presumption of a right to privacy is defensible in part because privacy is necessary for individuals to develop the capacity to reason autonomously as citizens. In deciding how to vote, citizens are entitled to freedom from coercion and to a "private space" in which to make up their own minds through the exercise of political judgment. The privacy of the voting booth serves to enhance this sense that we are free to make our own decisions without external coercion. This rationale also extends beyond procedural protections in the paradigmatic case of voting to the general role privacy rights play in citizens' capacity to think of themselves as rulers. Citizens do not think about politics at a particular moment or in a particular space that can be limited politically. Rather, our private and public thoughts intermingle.[10] We think metaphorically about politics through our private experiences, and at times the opinions we have developed in the public realm influence our private thoughts. Since our capacity for political thought is intertwined throughout life with our capacity for thought in general, a society concerned to respect either of these capacities should value citizens' ability to be free from coercion.

[8] Warren and Brandeis, "The Right to Privacy," 195.

[9] It might thus be called a prima facie freedom or right.

[10] I thank George Kateb for this formulation.

Following Rawls, I want to suggest that the presumption of privacy respects citizens' capacity for a "conception of the good."[11] Such a capacity entails the ability to see one's interests as distinct from the interests of others and is implied by the democratic idea that each citizen is entitled to justification that addresses him or her as an individual. It is also implicit in the meaning of democratic autonomy, which suggests that citizens should view themselves as independent rulers entitled to have their interests respected. Rawls argues that basic liberties best respect and allow citizens to develop this capacity. He writes, "For this conception of the good to be possible we must be allowed . . . to fall into error and to make mistakes within the limits established by the basic liberties."[12] Although Rawls makes this statement to defend freedom of conscience, I believe it serves as one reason to support a general presumption against state intervention. The ability to make mistakes and to explore a conception of the good is not limited to contemplation. It includes the way one lives—and the way one experiments with living—in accordance with a particular conception of the good. Therefore, there is reason to support not just freedom of conscience but a general presumption against state intervention in the absence of justifications consistent with democratic contractualism.

Related to the core democratic value of autonomy is the capacity of citizens to exercise independent judgment. Although one can be made aware of the interests of others through discussion and can exercise reciprocity in public, the capacity for judgment is fundamentally private. In order to judge, one must have some critical distance from public discussion and a conceptual space within which to make up one's mind. Here, too, freedom of conscience cannot suffice. Rather, to regard oneself as free to explore a variety of conceptions of the good allows one to make independent decisions.

While a presumption of privacy respects the capacities for a sense of the good and for judgment, nothing in my claim relies on the suggestion that privacy is an empirically necessary condition for these capacities to develop. Indeed, persons might develop these capacities in completely undemocratic regimes with no freedom at all. Slave narratives, for instance, provide evidence of persons' ability to develop such capacities despite their utter lack of freedom. Nonetheless, a presumption of privacy respects citizens' capacities for a sense of the good and for judgment even if they could be developed in regimes that offer no such respect.[13]

[11] John Rawls, *Political Liberalism*, 19.

[12] Ibid., 314.

[13] In his later work, Rawls uses the notion of a capacity for justice as a way to understand the ability to recognize the interests of others in contrast to his use of the capacity for a sense of the good to explain citizens' ability to recognize their own interests as distinct from others'; see Rawls, *Political Liberalism*, 19.

The arguments for a presumption of privacy can also be bolstered by an independent principle that stems from the very idea of self-rule. If citizens are granted the right to make decisions for others by virtue of their participation in the political process, it should follow that they have the right to make decisions for themselves in the most important matters of personal life. For instance, the decision to marry, which the Supreme Court protected in *Loving v. Virginia* with reference to the right to privacy, is among the most important decisions in life. If the state prevents one from making this choice as one sees fit, it trivializes political rights such as the right to vote.[14] This argument can be reinforced by the inclusion principle. Imagine the point of view of an individual who is denied the fundamental right to decide with whom he will share his life despite his reasonable objection to such a prohibition. It would be reasonable for this individual to view the right to make broad decisions for others through voting as hollow.[15] To allow citizens rights to rule others but not to rule themselves is morally inconsistent. The example of Larry Legislator again illustrates this general principle. It seems intuitively true that Larry's total lack of personal freedom due to government coercion amounts to a lack of *democratic* freedom. We can explain this intuition in part by recognizing that political freedom of the type Larry enjoys normatively presupposes some personal freedom of the type he is denied. Like those who are denied the right to marry, any political freedom Larry enjoys would be rendered hollow by his lack of personal freedom.

So far in this chapter I have emphasized why democratic contractualism suggests a presumption of freedom from coercion. We are now in a position to evaluate how to draw the boundary between public coercion and privacy rights that limit that coercion. In the next section, I begin by examining laws that fail

---

[14] This reasoning not only applies to the ability of individuals to make these decisions free from state intervention, but also to the freedom from legal coercion that would force them to explain these decisions to others. For instance, the reason for striking down spousal consent in abortion laws, which the Court did in *Planned Parenthood of Southeastern Pennsylvania v. Casey*, 505 U.S. 833 (1992), follows a similar logic. In that case, the Supreme Court considered whether the right to an abortion could constitutionally be made contingent on a woman securing permission from her husband. There are good democratic reasons for rejecting such a restriction—reasons similar to those for rejecting restrictions on decisional autonomy. In order for these decisions about marriage or abortion to be truly independent for individuals, they must be made according to individual judgments, without a requirement to explain them to others. Freedom from transparency means not only freedom in decision making, but also freedom to rely on one's own reasons without the need for explanation.

[15] This point suggests that there are reasons against intervention into areas also deemed fundamental rights by the Court. The decision of whether and when to have children is equally fundamental to one's life plan. Individuals forced to carry a baby to term or forced to decide between their ability to have sex and their decision not to have children would likely be unable to think of themselves as truly independent individuals with the ability for independent authorization.

to overcome the democratic presumption of freedom. I argue that restrictions on sexual intimacy do not pass the standard of democracy's public reason and thus violate the democratic right to privacy.

III. Relevance and the Boundaries of Privacy

The Supreme Court's doctrine is a good starting point for articulating what protections the right to privacy should ensure according to democratic contractualism. Indeed, while it often is dismissed as oxymoronic because of the contrast between procedure and substance, the name of the Court's constitutional doctrine for protecting privacy, "substantive due process," evokes the value theory's ambition to offer a democratic theory of both substantive and procedural rights.

In chapter 2, I examined democratic arguments for rights associated with the rule of law and free speech. Unlike these rights, however, the Court's privacy doctrine is not commonly accepted as democratic. Indeed, the primary challenge to judicial enforcement of privacy rights is that privacy is undemocratic because it is enforced in a countermajoritarian manner (that is, in opposition to laws passed by a legislative majority).[16] In chapter 7, I examine how to resolve conflicts between democratic procedure and substantive rights like the right to privacy. In this chapter, however, I first must ask a more fundamental question: Can the value theory of democracy justify a substantive right to privacy?

Before attempting to answer this question, it is necessary to clarify further the constitutional doctrine of privacy. The Supreme Court has grounded the right to privacy in substantive due process by appealing to choices that individuals should be able to make free from government coercion. As such, privacy is approached as a negative right to be free from state intervention, also known as "decisional autonomy." In a series of cases beginning with *Griswold v. Connecticut*, the Supreme Court has applied the privacy doctrine to the right of citizens to make their own choices in a variety of areas.[17] *Griswold* articulated a right of families to use contraception in the manner in which they choose; *Eisenstadt v. Baird* extended the right to use contraception to all individuals.[18] This doctrine also has served to protect individuals' rights in such areas as interracial marriage, euthanasia, and abortion. Recently, in *Lawrence v. Texas*, the Court extended decisional autonomy to intimacy within gay couples.

---

[16] See Bickel's discussion of the "countermajoritarian difficulty" in *The Least Dangerous Branch*, 16.
[17] 381 U.S. 479 (1965).
[18] 405 U.S. 438 (1972).

Writing for the majority in *Lawrence*, Justice Kennedy reasoned, "The issue is whether the majority may use the power of the State to enforce these views [against sodomy] on the whole society through operation of the criminal law. 'Our obligation is to define the liberty of all, not to mandate our own moral code.'"[19] On Kennedy's account, justifications for "morals legislation" are insufficient to trump the right of individuals to make their own decisions free from state interference. Reversing a previous decision of the Court, he concluded that the Constitution prohibits state interference with consensual sexual relationships and extended the right to privacy to protect both gay and straight citizens in this area.

In one sense, Kennedy's distinction in his opinion between liberty and a "moral code" is flawed. The contention that liberty should be respected is itself a moral claim. Moreover, given Kennedy's recognition that there are appropriate limits on liberty, there is no morally neutral way to draw the boundary between protected privacy and justifiable coercion. Kennedy's distinction is accurate in another sense, however, for one need not invoke a "moral code," or a comprehensive conception of morality, to draw this boundary.

I argued in chapter 1 that comprehensive conceptions cannot form a legitimate basis for democracy. Instead, I proposed the value theory of democracy, which is grounded in the core democratic values of equality of interests, political autonomy, and reciprocity. The value theory respects the sovereign status of citizens because it does not impose a moral view that is required of them as democratic citizens. The core values identify a type of morality that is relevant specifically to determining legitimate state coercion and its limits. According to the value theory's framework of democratic contractualism, the boundary between the "liberty of all" and legitimate coercion lies in an appeal to citizens' common status as recognized through the core values. I highlighted in the previous section of this chapter why democratic contractualism calls for a presumption of freedom from coercion. In the absence of a good justification for coercion, as understood through democracy's public reason and the inclusion principle, the state cannot justifiably restrict the decisional autonomy of its citizens. The principle of democracy's public reason asks whether a coercive policy treats citizens in general as free and equal. The inclusion principle ensures that the coercive policy also respects the interests of individual citizens.

We are now in a position to bring the principle of democracy's public reason to bear on the issue of sexual privacy raised in *Lawrence v. Texas:* are the argu-

---

[19] 539 U.S. 558 (2003). Kennedy is quoting from *Planned Parenthood of Southeastern Pennsylvania v. Casey*, 505 U.S. 833, (1992), 850.

ments for sodomy laws consistent with the core values? My view is that these arguments are inconsistent with the core values and thus can be ruled out at the level of democracy's public reason, even without appeal to the inclusion principle. Indeed, many of the arguments are not only inconsistent with, but openly hostile to, democratic values. Thus, Kennedy is correct to extend privacy protections as he did in *Lawrence*, not because the legislation at issue is "moral," but because it appeals to a conception of morality that conflicts with the core values of democracy.

Senator Santorum's comments quoted in the epigraph of this chapter are paradigmatic of attempts to invade private life on grounds irrelevant to and inconsistent with democracy's public reason. Santorum attacks what he calls a "right to privacy lifestyle" and discusses why he finds certain forms of sexual life to be deviant. But Santorum's own sexual morality is irrelevant to drawing the boundaries of coercion according to citizens' status as free and equal. Santorum's comments might be appropriate to a religious discussion group or to an ethics of sexuality class, but not as grounds for legitimizing coercion. The right of privacy is not about a lifestyle; it is about the conditions necessary to treat citizens as free and equal.

Drawing on my discussion in chapter 2, we can reject three types of reasons for restricting decisional autonomy at the level of democracy's public reason. All of these, like Santorum's arguments, are inconsistent with the core values and therefore are insufficient to overcome the presumption of personal freedom against state coercion. In the first category are reasons openly hostile to democratic values; as such, they easily can be dismissed. In the second category are reasons that appeal to a particular comprehensive doctrine, such as natural law or perfectionism, as the basis for drawing the limits of coercion. I argue that when these comprehensive doctrines are inconsistent with the core values, free and equal citizens reasonably may reject them. In the third category, which I will examine in the next section, are reasons that appeal directly to the core values, but to a perfectionist conception of them.

Reasons for restricting decisional autonomy that are most obviously irrelevant to democracy are those openly hostile to the values of political equality and autonomy. Arguments for laws banning so-called miscegenation are one example of such reasoning. Here it is helpful to explore the case of *Loving v. Virginia*, which examined the constitutionality of a Virginia law prohibiting interracial marriage.[20] Laws like Virginia's were motivated by racist ideology thinly veiled by language that claimed to support a "separate" equality. These laws were

[20] 388 U.S. 1 (1967).

attacks on the status of African Americans as free and equal citizens, and the reasons supporting them directly challenged democratic values. Because of this incompatibility with the core values, such laws can be rejected at the level of democracy's public reason.

The second category of reasons for restricting decisional autonomy—those appealing to a comprehensive conception—is exemplified in the currently popular conservative positions in favor of sodomy laws like those struck down in *Lawrence*. Some prominent arguments in the academic literature that defends these positions appeal to natural law theories that claim to define a reasonable type of sexuality appropriate to all citizens.[21] These new natural law arguments voice a respect for gay citizens as equals in democratic life but reject their decisional autonomy to have homosexual relationships. Following the common Christian injunction to "love the sinner but hate the sin," some claim to respect gay citizens but not homosexual acts.

However, these natural law arguments are irrelevant to drawing the boundaries of state coercion because they are based on a particular conception of the good life that is not acceptable to all reasonable citizens.[22] New natural law theorists claims that law should be designed to promote a plurality of "basic human goods," such as life, procreation, and aesthetic appreciation, that are intrinsic parts of human flourishing and give people noninstrumental reasons to desire things.[23] Further, they contend that only the basic human goods of procreation and marriage are reasons for people to engage in "reasonable sex." While sex often furthers both of these basic goods, new natural law theorists justify sex even between infertile heterosexual couples because it "realize[s] the intrinsic good of marriage itself as a two-in-one-flesh communion of persons."[24] They restrict this justification to genital intercourse, however, because they argue that only this specific act truly embodies the biological unity that forms a critical part of the marital relationship. New natural law theorists thus argue that nongenital sex acts, whether homosexual or heterosexual, cannot be justified by reference to the basic human good of marriage. Rather, people who engage in such acts violate their integrity by using their bodies as instruments in the pursuit of

---

[21] For a defense of this argument, see John Finnis, "Law, Morality, and 'Sexual Orientation,'" in *Same Sex: Debating the Ethics, Science, and Culture of Homosexuality*, ed. John Corvino (Lanham, Md.: Rowman and Littlefield, 1997), 31–43. See also Robert P. George, *In Defense of Natural Law* (Oxford: Clarendon, 1999). For a critique, see Stephen Macedo, "Homosexuality and the Conservative Mind," *Georgetown Law Journal* 84 (December 1995): 261.

[22] Such arguments are often labeled "perfectionist."

[23] George, *In Defense of Natural Law*, 103.

[24] Ibid., 282.

their desires instead of pursuing the basic human goods that ostensibly define their human nature. Based on this reasoning, some new natural law theorists argue that sodomy should be banned.[25]

Such natural law arguments against sodomy are unacceptable because of their incompatibility with the core values, at the levels of both democracy's public reason and the inclusion principle. The core values are defined by their compatibility with a variety of reasonable conceptions of the good. But the new natural law theorists argue from a particular conception of the good about which there is clearly reasonable disagreement, one that requires that sex be justified either by the goods of procreation or marriage. It follows that the appeals to procreation and heterosexual marriage as part of a general conception of the good life are inconsistent with respecting citizens' common status as free and equal. Thus, natural law arguments are based on reasons that are inappropriate for citizens to appeal to at the level of democracy's public reason.

The appeals to procreation and marriage also rightly are rejected at the level of the inclusion principle. In the case of procreation, some citizens reasonably choose not to have children at all, or to live lives that involve sexual intimacy without the aim of procreation. Citizens who wish to have sex but do not wish to have children reasonably could reject the explicit aim of promoting procreation as a reason for sodomy laws. In the case of marriage, some citizens espouse reasonable conceptions of the good life that involve intimate relationships outside of the formal institution of marriage. Such citizens reasonably could reject the appeal to marriage to justify sodomy laws. Thus, both straight and gay individuals could reject sodomy laws on the basis of their promotion of goods that are irrelevant to justifying coercion.

A similar argument could be made against attempts to reframe sodomy laws in line with utilitarian or aggregate justifications. Some conservative thinkers claim that social stability would be promoted if the government identified the good of procreation within the context of marriage as the sole reason to have sex. Although I find this statement empirically dubious, it is also incompatible with the core values. Aggregative theories do not value individual citizens as

---

[25] Though Finnis argues that the law should discourage homosexual conduct, he opposes such a ban. See John Finnis, "Is Natural Law Theory Compatible with Limited Government?" in *Natural Law, Liberalism, and Morality: Contemporary Essays,* ed. Robert P. George (Oxford: Clarendon, 1996), 17. George, however, leaves open a possibility that such legislation could be legitimate. He argues that the positive law should be derived from the natural law in George, *In Defense of Natural Law,* 107–9, and rejects the decisional conception of the right to privacy underlying the protection of homosexual conduct in idem, *Making Men Moral: Civil Liberties and Public Morality* (Oxford: Clarendon, 1993), 210–17.

rulers as the inclusion principle demands; rather, they appeal to the good of the social whole.[26]

This discussion suggests that is not necessary to show that a reason is false in order to dismiss it as irrelevant to democratic reasoning about policy. One need only show that the view is inappropriate to democratic justification of state coercion, or that it fails to succeed as a democratic justification. The same is true of certain kinds of arguments against new natural law theorists, such as that made by Stephen Macedo. Macedo challenges the contention of new natural law theorists that only sex among consenting heterosexual couples should be permissible because it best reflects "biological complementarity." These new natural law theorists insist that male and female bodies are the only ones that naturally fit together because they are designed for procreation. Macedo cites the case of infertile couples to argue that this contention is flawed, and I have much sympathy for his argument.[27] But in a public forum where the lines of political coercion are being drawn, Macedo's critique is unnecessary because the arguments of Santorum and the new natural law theorists should be deemed irrelevant at the level of democracy's public reason. They need not be disproved.

I regard arguments that defend the virtues of homosexual relationships as the flip side of arguments that defend the immorality of homosexuality.[28] Both of these views appeal to conceptions of the good life, or personal virtues, by staking claims on when coercion is justified. This strategy is irrelevant to the task of drawing the boundaries of privacy, however. While I am sympathetic to those

---

[26] Ruling out the procreation argument not only suggests why arguments for sodomy laws are indefensible at the level of democracy's public reason, but also why laws banning contraception, such as those struck down in *Griswold* and *Eisenstadt,* are also indefensible at the level of public reason. The arguments for prohibiting contraception similarly appeal to the good of procreation. If this criterion is inadmissible, laws that are justified on this basis are also illegitimate. Thus, although the view of new natural law theorists is protected through freedom of conscience, it should not be imposed through state coercion as a binding principle for all.

[27] Stephen Macedo, "Homosexuality and the Conservative Mind," 261.

[28] Andrew Koppelman, "Homosexual Conduct: A Reply to the New Natural Lawyers," in Corvino, *Same Sex: Debating the Ethics, Science, and Culture of Homosexuality,* 44–57. Koppelman disputes the new natural law theorists' claim that sex can never be justified solely by the instrumental reason of producing pleasure, but he maintains nonetheless that homosexual sex often serves higher ends. He admits, "It makes moral and prudential sense to distinguish more valuable from less valuable expressions of sexuality and to discourage the latter" (54). He argues, however, that some homosexual sex serves as a meaningful and crucial part of intimate relationships just as much as heterosexual sex, so one can encourage sex justified by noninstrumental reasons and discourage sex pursued for instrumental reasons without regard for whether it is heterosexual or homosexual.

who appeal to virtue theory in defense of gay rights, their views do not get to the heart of the democratic justifications for the right to privacy.

In defense of their approach, virtue theorists argue that failing to discuss the goodness of gay relationships risks reinforcing status quo prejudices by focusing defensively on rights rather than positively on virtues. By their logic, those who defend gay rights on privacy grounds risk expanding the American military's "Don't ask, don't tell" policy into a general political principle.[29] This move is a mistake, virtue theorists argue, because it diverts attention from the fact that good gay relationships exhibit many of the merits of other good relationships. By ruling out discussion of similarities, privacy theorists seek legal toleration while abandoning the very strategy that ultimately can win full acceptance of gays. Virtue theorists' arguments thus can be seen as an indictment of my approach to privacy. My appeal to the core values of democracy, one could argue, neglects the most forceful argument in defense of gay rights.

However, by appealing to the core values of democracy as the basis of privacy, I need not deny the legitimacy of invoking the virtues of gay relationships to change social attitudes. The issue I am concerned with is how best to delineate the boundaries of legal coercion. I argue that democratic values are the most relevant criteria in this task, but these are not the only values relevant to convincing citizens that they have reasons personally to respect gay relationships.

Jean Cohen's *Regulating Intimacy* is instructive in elaborating the distinction between the irrelevance of personal virtue discussions in delineating the boundaries of coercion and the potential benefits of such discussions in public argument. Cohen distinguishes between a duty of privacy and the legal right to privacy.[30] She argues that one could recognize that individuals have no duty to keep quiet about the virtues of gay relationships, or to disclose their own sexual orientation, yet still hold that there should be a right of decisional autonomy with regard to gay relationships. It is consistent to be both a strong promoter of the virtues of gay relationships and to rely on the privacy doctrine as a way of reasoning about politics. One's position on a right to privacy does not limit one's ability to speak out about the virtues of gay relationships, nor does it suggest a normative position about the legitimacy of remaining in the closet.

In this section we have examined perfectionist arguments for limitations on the privacy rights delineated by the Supreme Court. These are fairly easy cases

---

[29] One defender of these arguments has suggested that privacy theorists support an "epistemology of the closet." My argument draws from Jean Cohen's reply in chap. 2 of *Regulating Intimacy: A New Legal Paradigm* (Princeton: Princeton University Press, 2002), 77–124, to Eve Kosofsky Sedgwick, *Epistemology of the Closet* (Berkeley: University of California Press, 1990).

[30] Cohen, *Regulating Intimacy*, chap. 2.

from the standpoint of democratic contractualism because they appeal to values either irrelevant or hostile to the core values of democracy. In the next section, I examine a class of cases that appeal directly to the three core values to justify limits on freedom. Specifically, I distinguish those justifications that satisfy the demands of democracy's public reason and the inclusion principle from perfectionist appeals to the values of autonomy and equality. While perfectionist appeals to these values might seem to be democratic on the surface, a closer look reveals that they are not.

IV. Privacy, Equality, and Democratically Justifiable Coercion

If democratic contractualism is to prove to be a sound framework for identifying legitimate forms of coercion, then there must be limits on the scope of negative liberty that it protects; that is, it must account for why some instances of coercion are reasonably acceptable. If it cannot do so, the theory would suggest that no state action is permissible, and even that the state itself is illegitimate. In this section, I begin by explaining why appeals to the core values at times justify coercion and trump the presumption of privacy. I then distinguish between democratic reasons for coercion and perfectionist arguments that advocate limits on privacy, especially with regard to equality. I suggest that these perfectionist arguments are insufficient to trump the presumption of privacy.

There are many instances in which democratic contractualism can justify state coercion, but by way of example I want to focus specifically on arguments for state intervention into intrafamily issues based on the value of equality. Democratic contractualism does not presuppose an a priori protection of the family. Nor does it propose that all interventions that would promote equality within the family are justifiable. Instead, the framework suggests that interventions on the grounds of equality should be limited to institutional equality in a family. This means that interventions cannot dictate the content or completely control the dynamics of these personal relationships. In clarifying the role of democratic contractualism in intrafamily relationships, I also contrast the democratic meaning of equality of interests with a perfectionist meaning of equality.

The easiest cases for justifying state action concern criminal laws prohibiting physical violence by one citizen against another, such as assault, rape, and murder. In many liberal theories, such crimes are paradigmatic rights violations. For instance, natural law theories rule them out a priori. According to the value theory of democracy, there are no such a priori rights violations. Rather, the account of rights rests on the democratic account of justification. But on this account, physical violence clearly is ruled out at the levels of both democracy's public reason and the inclusion principle. At the level of public reason, legislatures pass laws to ensure that citizens are able to live lives such that they are free to pursue their own conceptions of the good as equals. This gives rise to rights of citizens against interference both by the state and by fellow citizens. While limits on the state are needed to prevent state interventions into these pursuits, state action also is needed to prevent persons from intervening in each other's projects. These limitations are necessary to protect individual rights to autonomy and equality.

At the level of the inclusion principle, laws that prohibit assault and other violent crimes are reasonably acceptable to all. Admittedly a criminal might object that these limits prohibit her from pursuing her own conception of the good, a conception that includes a tendency to commit violent acts. But such a pursuit would not be a reasonable interpretation of the core values or advance any reasonable interest arising from a particular point of view. Any reasonable citizen thinking in terms of the inclusion principle would recognize that violent action is inconsistent with the desire to reach universal agreement because it rules out the security that is a precondition for citizens to pursue their projects as individually autonomous persons. Laws against violent actions therefore are easy for the value theory to accept because they limit acts that clearly conflict with a reasonable interpretation of the core values.[31]

Feminist critics often have pointed to liberalism's inadequate attention to intrafamily injustice. They argue that because liberalism posits a strong divide between the public and private realms, it cannot adequately address the most graphic injustices within the home. But the value theory of democracy does not establish the right to privacy by appeal to a distinction between private and public life that exists independently of public justification. Rather, the legitimacy of coercion, and thus the distinction between the public and private realms, is justifiable by appeal to democratic contractualism. Thus, there is no reason to presuppose that intrafamily relationships are any more or less public or private than any other relationships. On this point the value theory breaks from many arguments in the history of liberal theory—such as Locke's claim that husbands have authority over their wives in the "private" sphere—that are inconsistent with the ideal of treating individual citizens in accordance with the core values.[32] Regardless of their marital situation, individuals within a family

---

[31] Of course, laws relating to self-defense and other justified violence are different from laws limiting battery or other violent crime. My point is not about the legitimacy of these defenses of violence but about generalized laws prohibiting violence in the first place.

[32] Locke is clear that husbands do not have political authority over their wives, but he suggests that this view is consistent with private authority: "If therefore these words give any Power to Adam, it can be only a Conjugal Power, not Political, the Power that every Husband hath to order

remain the sovereign source of authority from the standpoint of the state. Thus, their rights as individuals must be protected.

So far I have attempted to delineate the easy cases of unjustified state intervention (to bar consensual homosexual and heterosexual sex) and justified intervention (to protect against assault and domestic violence). But a harder set of cases involves instances in which methods more subtle than violence undermine women's equality. Within the space often taken to be protected by liberal rights against coercion can lie an interpersonal dynamic of inequality of husbands over wives and boyfriends over girlfriends. This dynamic is captured by the feminist slogan that "the personal is political."[33] Of course, men in heterosexual relationships do not have a monopoly on treating their domestic partners as unequal. Most of the feminist arguments articulated in this section also can be applied to gay relationships or those in which women undermine the equal status of their male partners.

Before we can establish that some feminist appeals to equality are congruent with democratic contractualism, we must clarify the type of equality at issue. Some appeals to autonomy are perfectionist because they suggest that the state should promote this value in all aspects of citizens' lives. These, I will argue, are not properly understood as democratic appeals to that value. Similarly, appeals to equality demonstrably must be democratic, not perfectionist, interpretations of the core value of equality of interests.

Consider an example inspired by Pat Mainardi's article, "The Politics of Housework."[34] Roger and Glenda both vote for policies that treat men and women as equals and are egalitarians in public debate. But at home, Glenda assumes a traditional female role by taking care of the children and doing all the housework. Hence, the couple's public egalitarianism and their private inegalitarian relationship are incongruous. To what extent should democratic contractualism be concerned with justifying state intervention into this domestic relationship on the grounds of promoting equality of interests?

One feminist argument is that this private inequality is no less politically relevant than any other form of inequality. The family often is the basis of education and personality formation. Therefore, it is at least as relevant to one's status as a citizen as more traditional public relations. Using a phrase coined by

---

the things of private Concernment in his Family . . . but not a Political Power of Life and Death over her, much less over any body else" (Locke, *Two Treatises of Government*, 174).

[33] Carol Hanisch, "The Personal is Political," in *The Radical Therapist*, ed. Jerome Agel (New York: Ballantine, 1971), 152–57.

[34] Pat Mainardi, "The Politics of Housework," in *Sisterhood is Powerful: An Anthology of Writings from the Women's Liberation Movement*, ed. Robin Morgan (New York: Vintage, 1970), 501–10.

Nancy Rosenblum, we might understand this argument to imply that democratic contractualism requires a "logic of congruence."[35] Under the logic of congruence, equality must go "all the way down" into relationships both in civil society and within the family for democratic equality to be obtained. Thus, a congruent interpretation of the value of equality requires that it be instantiated in all aspects of persons' decisions and relationships. To emphasize the belief that equality is relevant to persons' decisions in all aspects of life, I call the congruent understanding of this core value "perfectionist equality." The problem with this understanding is that while it seems to appeal to the democratic value of equality, it ignores the distinction between ensuring democratic treatment for citizens and promoting equality in all aspects of persons' lives. In clarifying why the perfectionist understanding of equality is not democratic, I will be in a position to suggest when feminist appeals to equality are appropriate in limiting decisional autonomy and when they are not.

From the perspective of democratic contractualism, the question of whether the state justifiably can intervene in Glenda and Roger's relationship requires determining whether an appeal to the value of equality rightly overrides the default against state coercion. Here it is fundamental to clarify the democratic meaning of equality rather than invoking an overly generalized understanding of the value. The question in regard to Glenda and Roger is not whether they are equal in a perfectionist sense, but rather whether they are equal in the sense relevant to their status as rulers, that is, consistent with the meaning of democratic contractualism's interpretation of the value of equality.

To develop the distinction between perfectionism and democratic contractualism, it is helpful to postpone our discussion of Glenda and Roger to draw on some suggestive examples. In these examples, I will extend my consideration of "perfectionist equality" to "perfectionist autonomy," which similarly holds that the core value of autonomy should be applied throughout citizens' lives. Imagine, for instance, a person thirty years of age who defers to his parents' opinion of what he should do in all cases. When it comes to political matters, he always asks how he should vote and follows their advice in each instance. In matters of personal decision making, such as whether to get married, he also follows their advice regardless of whether it conflicts with his own preferences. Evaluated in psychological terms, this person is not autonomous. Therapists might recommend, for instance, that he be psychologically separated from his parents and learn to make his own decisions before he can be regarded as autonomous.

However, the question of whether this person is autonomous in the demo-

[35] Nancy L. Rosenblum, *Membership and Morals: The Personal Uses of Pluralism in America* (Princeton: Princeton University Press, 1998), 36.

cratic sense is independent from this sort of psychological evaluation. For instance, if the thirty-year-old retains a right to vote and other fundamental liberties, we likely still would consider him politically free even if his choices in voting were unduly influenced by his parents. If the state were to intervene on behalf of his political autonomy by barring him from seeing his parents prior to voting, this would be a paradigmatic violation of his democratic right to freedom of conscience. That this would be undemocratic illustrates why the state cannot promote the core values in all instances, but must be content to respect citizens' right to privacy even when their psychological autonomy seems threatened.

Consider the inverse of this example. Nelson Mandela was said to possess immense integrity and inner strength despite facing extreme hardship and a lack of any privacy rights while in prison on Robben Island. In this case it seems reasonable to claim that Mandela was psychologically autonomous despite his confinement. It would, however, betray our most basic intuitions to claim that he was treated as autonomous in the democratic sense. These examples suggest why we should distinguish sharply between democratic and perfectionist interpretations of the core values. This distinction entails that the core values be understood to respect citizens' status by ensuring them democratic treatment as citizens, not by guaranteeing that they will be fully autonomous and equal in their self-conception and in all of their life choices. While concerns about psychological autonomy and equality might be central if we interpreted these values as perfectionist, the democratic sense of these values entails that we are concerned with conditions of equality and autonomy.

To return to the problem of Roger and Glenda, the nonperfectionist democratic meaning of the core values as applied to the conditions of coercive institutions and laws by no means entails an indifference to inequalities within the family. Rather, it calls for a set of structural conditions in the family that make equal treatment of women possible. For example, according to Susan Okin, the state should ensure that relationships are structured in a way that gives individuals within them the option to leave. This involves both formal exit options through liberalized divorce laws and material options, such as guaranteeing financial resources to individuals within relationships.[36] I take Okin's contribution to this debate to be her recognition that a lack of freedom within the home—including the lack of an ability to leave a relationship—in many cases will cripple one's sense of self so severely that it is impossible to view oneself as an equal and autonomous citizen. While conceptions of privacy that protect the family might appear to grant freedom, they in fact can leave women who are

---

[36] Okin proposes a mandatory sharing of paychecks between husbands and wives in *Justice, Gender, and the Family*, 180. The proposals for a basic income discussed in chapter 6 might achieve the same effect.

subject to domination and abuse in conditions in which they lack freedom. On the grounds of democratic contractualism, exit laws that guarantee women's ability to leave relationships are justified from the point of view of women whose equality and autonomy otherwise would be threatened.

However, if institutional conditions, such as a right to exit, are met, there is a residual question of whether unequal relationships such as Glenda and Roger's still require state intervention. The resolution of this question resembles the case for intervention into the relationship between the thirty-year-old and his parents. The question here concerns the deeply psychological characteristics of a relationship. Arguably, Glenda is dominated psychologically by her husband despite conditions of political equality, so a perfectionist who sought full equality might argue for intervention. It is not clear, however, that this type of inequality is democratically relevant or that it justifies further state intervention. From the standpoint of democratic contractualism, Glenda has the option to leave the relationship, both legally and materially, even if she remains psychologically unequal with her husband. As in the case of the thirty-year-old, this relationship rightly is regarded as psychologically, but not democratically, unequal.

The right of decisional autonomy grants citizens the ability to make their own decisions even when this allows them to enter into relationships that seem inconsistent with psychological autonomy and equality. For instance, while Roger and Glenda's relationship undermines Glenda's equality in a meaningful sense, state intervention prohibiting them from forming such an unequal relationship itself would undermine their status as rulers. In contrast, state support of equal treatment for women by creating exit options and by preventing domestic violence is consistent with democratic contractualism's guarantee that all persons be treated as citizens. Here, the state is ensuring rights to conditions that respect citizens' equal interests; it is not attempting to promote equality in a psychological sense.

The flaws of the logic of congruence are apparent in Catharine MacKinnon's arguments about sexuality and privacy. MacKinnon argues that democracy fundamentally is about equality, so equality should trump autonomy whenever they conflict. This has led her to contend that First Amendment speech guarantees should not protect pornography.[37] According to MacKinnon, the harms of pornography are twofold. First, it encourages men to view sex as a form of dominance and thus impairs their ability to see women as equals.[38] Second, it teaches women that they should sexualize domination and thus contributes to

[37] See Catharine A. MacKinnon, *Only Words* (Cambridge, Mass.: Harvard University Press, 1993), 85.

[38] MacKinnon also, more controversially, argues that pornography leads to rape, but I do not consider this empirical claim; see *Only Words,* 16.

their own failure to see themselves as equal citizens. MacKinnon's main point is that pornography is not rightly regarded as free speech because it is not an idea but rather a form of behavioral conditioning that promotes a deeply inegalitarian understanding of sexuality.

MacKinnon's logic, which invokes equality in a perfectionist sense, seems to suggest that there should be no distinction between the right to own pornography and the right to engage in sex that also might lead to inequality. Her argument, after all, is that pornography is a behavior rather than speech; therefore, there would seem to be no principled difference between regulating sex on screen and sex in the bedroom. This point suggests that sexuality itself needs to be politicized and should not be protected under the conceptual framework of privacy.[39] If it were to turn out, for instance, that some sexual practices reinforce the idea that women are unequal in a psychological sense, MacKinnon's logic could be used to argue that these practices should be discouraged or even criminalized. This reasoning parallels the new natural law theorists' case for moral sexuality in the private sphere. Like the natural law account, MacKinnon's view is hostile to the core values. Her argument for equality should not overcome the presumption of privacy because it appeals to perfectionist rather than democratic equality.

The distinction between conditions of psychological and political inequality is not always easy to draw. Certainly a widespread instance of inequality in the deep perfectionist sense could point to institutional problems. A hard case illustrating this point concerns the question of whether democratic contractualism requires that the right to marry extend to polygamous relationships. Some cases involving the right to marry are easy from the perspective of democratic contractualism. For instance, prohibitions on interracial marriage clearly fail at the level of democracy's public reason. As discussed earlier, the Supreme Court in *Loving v. Virginia* nullified such a law on the grounds that it was patently hostile to the right to equal protection as well as to substantive due process rights to make basic life choices. In contrast, however, one might argue that polygamous marriages threaten to undermine women's equality.

The right way to frame this question from the perspective of democratic contractualism is to ask whether such arguments appeal to the democratic value of equality of interests or to an account of psychological equality.[40] In the nineteenth century, suffragists sought to extend the vote to women in Utah. The

---

[39] See "Privacy v. Equality: Beyond *Roe v. Wade* (1983)," in MacKinnon, *Feminism Unmodified: Discourses on Life and Law* (Cambridge, Mass.: Harvard University Press, 1987), 93–102.

[40] Rosenblum, "Democratic Sex: *Reynolds v. U.S.*, Sexual Relations, and Community," in *Sex, Preference, and Family: Essays on Law and Nature,* ed. David M. Estlund and Martha C. Nussbaum (New York: Oxford University Press, 1997), 63–85.

suffragists believed that participation in the political process is a fundamental right for all citizens conceived of as free and equal. In addition to expanding participation, they also hoped that the extension of this right would lead to the abolition of the institution of polygamy, an institution that they believed dominated women and prevented their equality. In their view, polygamous relationships were yet another way in which a fundamentally patriarchal Mormon society succeeded in undermining women's identity as equals. Empowered with the right to vote, suffragists believed, Mormon women would seek to abolish polygamy. Surprisingly, however, the women of Utah actually voted to reinforce its role and prominence in the life of Utah's citizens.[41] Given free choice in voting, women sought to affirm the institution of polygamous marriage that Mormon men always had claimed the women supported. Faced with the realization that women voted to undermine what the suffragists believed to be a fundamental democratic outcome, the suffragists decided it would be wise to revoke women's right to vote until the institution of polygamy could be abolished.

The position of the suffragists in this case was patently undemocratic. Taking away suffrage for any reason, most of all as a means of silencing citizens' substantive political views, clearly violates democratic values. However, this case raises another question for democratic theory that is not as easily resolved: Are there democratic grounds for prohibiting the practice of polygamy based on equality, given women's political and individualized consent to enter polygamous relationships? The suffragists' argument against polygamy sometimes is couched as a concern that women not be in relationships in which they are dominated by men. One could bolster this argument by claiming that the conditions and institutions of polygamy structurally promote women's inequality. For instance, because of the young age at which girls usually enter into these relationships, they often lack the education or monetary independence to have genuine exit options. Also, given the history of non-egalitarianism in polygamous marriages, the institution of polygamy might seem to lack the basic conditions of equality and thus be undemocratic. These structural supports for unequal treatment would differentiate women in polygamous marriages from those in Glenda's situation whose psychological domination by their husbands provides insufficient democratic reasons for state intervention in their private lives.

These arguments, however, concern empirically contingent circumstances and would not prohibit a right to polygamous marriages on principle. Indeed, one can imagine polygamous relationships that have the structural conditions of equality that I have suggested are democratically relevant. For instance, a woman might have the maturity and the independent financial security to enter

[41] Ibid., 76.

freely into and remain in a polygamous marriage, fully aware of her exit options. Those in such a relationship reasonably could reject the prohibition on polygamous marriage on the grounds that it did not consider their individual interests and circumstances. Thus, although there are structural grounds for prohibiting polygamy at the generalized level of democracy's public reason, some individuals may have good democratic reasons to object to such a prohibition at the level of the inclusion principle. Hypothetically, the spouses in a relationship in which all parties were equally well educated and financially independent could reasonably object to restrictions on polygamy on the grounds that they would undermine their decisional autonomy for no good democratic reason.[42]

The best argument for prohibitions on polygamy is that they protect conditions of women's equality, but such an argument at best is a blunt edge that risks violating the rights to marry of many who wish to enter polygamous relationships. The more democratic way to ensure that conditions of equality are not undermined by polygamous marriages is to follow Susan Okin's lead and guarantee the right to enter such relationships as long as the conditions that would support women's equality and their ability to make their own decisions is not undermined. Exit options for all spouses, for instance, should be ensured. Moreover, there is good reason to prevent children from entering such marriages given their special vulnerability to domination. The task, in short, is to ensure conditions that would protect women from the traditional subservience associated with polygamy; given such conditions, there is no reason why the right to marry should not extend to these relationships as well.

It is important to clarify that these arguments about privacy apply to adults, and there is an important contrast between the proper role of the state in protecting the privacy rights of adults and its duties to protect children. Not only do children not have the same privacy rights as adults but, as some commentators have emphasized, there is a role for the state in promoting children's self-conception as autonomous equals through education.[43] Such an education

---

[42] As it happened, polygamy eventually was abolished by federal statute, thus overriding the Mormon women's decision at the state level and their individual decisions to participate in polygamous marriages. In *Reynolds v. United States*, 98 U.S. 145 (1878), the Court considered whether the Mormon practice of polygamy was entitled to a religious exemption from this statute based on the First Amendment's protection of religious freedom. It reasoned that because there was a legitimate state interest in abolishing despotic relationships that threatened democracy and the law in question regulated actions instead of opinions or beliefs, the law should stand despite the claim of religious exemption.

[43] Stephen Macedo, *Diversity and Distrust: Civic Education in a Multicultural Democracy* (Cambridge, Mass.: Harvard University Press, 2000), especially "Civic Purposes and Public Schools," 231–53. For a discussion of this issue, see also Callan, *Creating Citizens: Political Education and Liberal Democracy.*

arguably is a precondition for ensuring that citizens will respect the core values as adults. Of course, this conception of civic education clearly is coercive, and it is because we are speaking of children that there is not a problem with forcing them to go to school and encouraging them to internalize these values. Were we to speak in the same way about adults, we would cross the line from a respect for decisional autonomy to an illegitimate promotion of the psychological senses of the values. While no parent should claim a right of decisional autonomy to prohibit her own children's access to education, parents themselves should not be forced to attend educational sessions on the value of democracy. Such a conception essentially would be cultural reeducation, without regard for democratic freedom.

V. CONCLUSION

In this chapter I have sought to resolve whether the right to privacy is necessary for democratic legitimacy according to the value theory of democracy. Radical republican and feminist critics of liberalism suggest that privacy is incompatible with robust conceptions of democracy. However, unlike liberal theories that claim a priori legitimacy for private space, I have sought to justify the boundaries of privacy on the grounds of democratic contractualism. These boundaries must be democratically justifiable, even though choices within the boundaries (the sphere of decisional autonomy) may not be.

A paradigmatic democratically justifiable privacy right is sexual privacy for gay and straight couples. The major reasons for legislation limiting these rights are perfectionist in nature. Perfectionist arguments, however, appeal to conceptions of the good in a way that is incompatible with the core values of democracy.

Democratic contractualism proposes limits on state power, but it does not suggest that all state action is illegitimate. Some coercive measures—such as laws prohibiting violence, including violence in the home—reasonably are accepted by citizens and thus are consistent with democratic contractualism. Laws meant to protect equality are more complicated to evaluate. I have argued that the value theory of democracy justifies laws preventing institutional inequality but not psychological domination. For instance, polygamy is objectionable to the extent that it carries institutional inequalities. There would, however, be no principled argument against polygamy on the basis of democratic contractualism if those institutionalized inequalities did not apply.

This chapter has delineated the broad contours distinguishing decisions protected by the right to privacy from those subject to legitimate coercion. Now it is necessary to consider how legitimate coercion can be institutionalized and enforced. Though there are many cases where democratic contractualism justifies coercion, such coercion cannot be enforced through any method of punishment. Rather, I argue that some punishments necessarily conflict with the core values no matter what the crime. Thus, the question of legitimate punishment raises another set of substantive rights issues. Whereas privacy rights limit the type of laws that legitimately can coerce citizens, democratic rights against certain forms of punishment limit the methods by which laws legitimately can be enforced.

CHAPTER 5

THE RIGHTS OF THE PUNISHED

I. INTRODUCTION

In the previous chapter, I argued that a right to privacy, or decisional autonomy, is a necessary aspect of an ideal democracy. I also argued that in some instances decisional autonomy must be limited. This is the case, for instance, when the state seeks to protect its citizens from violent crime. Yet the claim that state coercion can be justified raises a distinct question: what forms of state coercion are legitimate? In this chapter, I examine the question of *how* the state should coerce through the lens of democratic contractualism. I argue that although some forms of criminal punishment are legitimate means of coercion, the substantive rights of convicted criminals guarantee certain limits on punishment.

In an ideal democracy, the state enforces prohibitions against violence through the criminal law, not merely on an ad hoc basis. I argued in chapter 2 that the rule of law is necessary for any legitimate democracy, and the guarantee to procedural due process rights, foremost to a fair trial, is accepted widely as a crucial component of this institution. My aim in this chapter, however, is to move beyond the procedural aspects of due process in a democracy into substantive questions about democratically acceptable forms of punishment. According to the value theory of democracy, substantive rights of self-government constrain not just lawmaking but also legitimate punishment.

In providing a specifically democratic account of punishment, I face a significant obstacle. Democratic contractualism requires that punishment, like all forms of coercion, be justifiable to individuals qua citizens. Yet when it comes to criminal punishment, this task is complicated by the fact that actual criminals punished by the state often do not accept the core values of democracy or indeed the ideal of democratic justification. Even if they claim to endorse the core values of equality, autonomy, and reciprocity, their very actions seem to renounce these values. Those who commit the worst crimes do not respect fellow citizens as free and equal; through their crimes, they violate their victims' sovereign status. Therefore, the persons to whom this coercion must be addressed seem the very opposite of reasonable citizens.

I aim for democratic contractualism to be a comprehensive framework for legitimate coercion. Therefore, its success rests in part on its ability to offer a theory of punishment, one of the most central institutions of state force. It cannot acknowledge a limitation when dealing with criminals who have flouted their democratic duty. As I suggested in chapter 3, the ideal of democracy entitles all persons subject to coercion to be viewed *as if* they accepted the core values of democracy. Since criminals face a paradigmatic instance of state coercion, it follows that they, too, should be treated as citizens. In part, this means formulating legitimate punishments in a manner consistent with the core values. Such a process would entail extending democracy's public reason and the inclusion principle to issues of punishment. In other words, we should ask which punishment a criminal qua citizen reasonably could accept.

Thus, the issue of punishment for democratic contractualism is not whether criminals, given their empirical disposition (or lack thereof) toward reasonableness, would actually accept a punishment or not. Rather, the issue is whether a particular criminal who has committed a particular act could *reasonably* accept a given punishment. In other words, contractualist justification is concerned with punishment addressed to the criminal qua citizen, and whether those who have committed crimes could reasonably accept such punishments. The goal is not to legitimize only those punishments that criminals would actually accept, but rather to assess which punishments a criminal might reasonably accept were she motivated to find universal agreement about how to balance her interests with the interests of others. Given such a motivation, I am also concerned to identify those punishments that citizens could reasonably reject. My aim is thus to use contractualist justification to rule out certain punishments as inconsistent with legitimate state coercion. It is important to note that on at least some issues of punishment—for instance, regarding crimes for which there are incremental differences between possible punishments—there will be reasonable disagreements about which punishments are legitimate. I do not take up these harder cases; instead, I focus first on showing that contractualism can generate at least minimal standards for punishment.[1]

The democratic contractualist approach to punishment is usefully contrasted with two other prominent theories of punishment. In section II, below, I argue that it rightly rejects the Hobbesian view that criminals are enemies of the state not entitled to justifications of punishment. In section III, I acknowledge that retributive theories avoid the flaw of the Hobbesian approach because they offer an account of justifiability to persons. I argue, however, that these theories

---

[1] For a discussion of reasonable disagreements, see Amy Gutmann and Dennis Thompson, *Democracy and Disagreement* (Cambridge, Mass.: Harvard University Press, 1996).

still are flawed because they focus on criminals' moral desert in isolation from a general political theory of what citizens are owed. Democratic contractualism, in contrast, theorizes punishment in the context of a political theory of justifiability to criminals qua citizens. I argue that this account of justification requires rights of criminals against punishments that undermine their status as citizens. While some forms of confinement are consistent with this status, other punishments, notably the death penalty, are not.

II. THE NEED FOR JUSTIFICATION TO CRIMINALS QUA CITIZENS: THE PROBLEM WITH PUNISHMENT AS WAR

The first objection to the requirement of justifying punishment to criminals qua citizens is rooted in the work of Thomas Hobbes. On one reading of Hobbes, the state is justified in the first place because it preserves the lives of its subjects better than they could preserve their own lives in the state of nature. The desire for security, Hobbes thinks, would compel rational actors to give up the liberty of nature for the security guaranteed by his account of the Leviathan state.

This theory, however, presents a complication. In order to provide security successfully, Hobbes thinks the state must retain the institution of capital punishment. Capital punishment, however, is a denial of self-preservation, and thus it dissolves the social contract between the criminal and the state.[2] Hobbes therefore recognizes that at the moment the state seeks to execute an individual, it no longer exists in a contractual relationship with that individual. Such a person would gain nothing from the state and therefore would lack any moral obligation to obey a death sentence.[3] For Hobbes, the state's relationship to violent criminals is characterized not by the metaphor of contract, but by that of a war between an "enemy" and the state.[4] Hobbes claims that the state can jus-

---

[2] "There be some Rights, which no man can be understood by any words, or other signes, to have abandoned, or transferred. As first a man cannot lay down the right of resisting them, that assault him by force, to take away his life; because he cannot be understood to ayme thereby, at any Good to himselfe" (Thomas Hobbes, *The Leviathan* [Amherst, N.Y.: Prometheus, 1988], 68).

[3] "'Tis one thing to say, *Kill me, or my fellow, if you please;* another thing to say, *I will kill my selfe, or my fellow*" (Hobbes, *Leviathan*, 114).

[4] Among others who commit capital crimes, the traitor "suffers as an enemy" when he or she is executed. Moreover, such persons are to be regarded as outside the law, so their treatment is not considered "punishment"; see Hobbes, *Leviathan*, 166. It is hard to see references to enemies without thinking of the Bush administration's position that those prisoners accused of terrorism held at Guantanamo Bay are "enemy combatants" not subject to limits of law. For an argument against this categorization, see David Cole, *Enemy Aliens: Double Standards and Constitutional Freedoms in the War on Terrorism* (New York: New Press, 2003), especially "The Bill of Rights as Human Rights,"

tify execution to society as a whole on security grounds, but he recognizes it has no justification for capital punishment that can be addressed to, or that is acceptable for, the condemned.

Although Hobbes clearly does not endorse the notion of justifying punishment to criminals qua citizens, he does suggest that even though it is a state of war, the state exists in a type of rights-based relationship with individual criminals—the same relationship that exists among persons in the state of nature; namely, the condemned retain rights to self-defense that conflict with the state's right to defend itself. This account sharply contrasts with democratic contractualism and the inclusion principle, which posit that criminals remain citizens within the contractualist framework of justification. Thus, democratic contractualism offers a theory of punishment in which even those guilty of the worst crimes are not exiled from the contractualist framework. Rather, democratic contractualism aims to include the points of view and accommodate the reasonable interests of all criminals as a requirement of democratic legitimacy.

Any reasonable citizen would recognize that convicted murderers must forfeit some rights of citizens in a scheme of democratic contractualist justification. On my view, however, it is too extreme to claim that they must forfeit all of their rights associated with democratic legitimacy. For example, it is plausible to maintain that murderers should give up the right to travel about freely because a society should be able to protect citizens by restraining those who are unwilling to respect their fellow citizens' rights. This recognition does not entail that such persons should lose their status as citizens. The goal of restraint is compatible with the idea that some punishments are unreasonable because they are entirely inconsistent with the requirements of contractualist justification to citizens. In contrast to Hobbes's idea that many crimes require an alienation of citizenship, I contend that a good democratic theory of punishment will uphold the state's right to punish those who violate the core values, yet still justify punishment in a way consistent with those values. Thus, the democratic contractualist approach to punishment can be clarified by contrast to the Hobbesian "contractarian" approach. Whereas Hobbes labels criminals "enemies" outside the social contract, contractualist justification views even the worst offenders as citizens and requires that the coercion they face be reasonably acceptable to them.

A potential response to the democratic contractualist approach to punishment is that regardless of its position on obligation, it still overextends its account of justification. One could argue that citizens are entitled to procedural

---

211–27. Although part of his argument rests on an account of inherent dignity, mine rests on a specifically moral conception of citizenship, a position he does not address.

guarantees that ensure that only the guilty are punished, but that they "forfeit" a right to contractualist justification once their guilt has been determined. On this line of argumentation, those who have flouted the most basic requirements of the social contract do not deserve to be treated according to it. Furthermore, one could contend that nothing in this view entails that such criminals have *no* rights. Rather, one might reconstruct the Hobbesian view to explain the practice of extending rights to the guilty (for instance, in the Eighth Amendment to the U.S. Constitution) on the basis of natural law or other metaphysical accounts of human dignity.[5] In sum, this objection follows Hobbes in arguing that criminals retain natural rights while not retaining all contractual rights, but it breaks from Hobbes in defending a broader set of natural rights than those he identifies in the state of war.

Although this reconstructed approach is perhaps more compelling than a pure Hobbestian account of punishment, I believe that the contractualist theory should resist this view; in fact, it would fail in its most basic ambition if it were to concede this point. Democratic contractualism aspires to be a theory of legitimate coercion. Never is the state more coercive than when it punishes. Therefore, if punishment is a paradigmatic example of coercion, and contractualism hopes to justify coercion, it must explain how punishment can be justified within the contractualist framework. If it cannot, this speaks ill of contractualism's core ambition. Indeed, the need for a theory to extend to those who do not comply with its dictates is not peculiar to contractualism. Most moral and political theories aim both to give an account of ideal action and to offer principled responses to those who fail to live up to this ideal. Such is the requirement of any theory that is not purely utopian and that aims to take "men as they are and laws as they might be."[6] For instance, Kant's categorical imperative need not be abandoned when persons fail to treat each other as ends. Rather, it suggests how to act in the face of such flouting of the categorical imperative. If democratic contractualism is to provide an account of political legitimacy, therefore, we should inquire into its account of treatment for those citizens who flout its most basic requirements.

[5] George Kateb, *The Inner Ocean: Individualism and Democratic Culture* (Ithaca, N.Y.: Cornell University Press, 1992), 4–5, 201; idem, "What Do Citizens Owe Their Constitutional Democracy?" (Delivered at the Center for Human Values Twentieth Anniversary Celebration. Unpublished [2000].) For a criticism of the idea of inherent dignity, see Hugo Adam Bedau, "Abolishing the Death Penalty Even for the Worst Murderers," in *The Killing State: Capital Punishment in Law, Politics, and Culture,* ed. Austin Sarat (New York: Oxford University Press, 1999).

[6] Jean-Jacques Rousseau, "On the Social Contract," in *Basic Political Writings: Discourse on the Sciences and the Arts, Discourse on the Origin of Inequality, Discourse on Political Economy, On the Social Contract,* trans. and ed. by Donald A. Cress (Indianapolis, Ind.: Hackett, 1987), 141.

In chapter 2, I argued that the requirement to justify coercion to the coerced was implicit in the democratic commitment to treat citizens as addressees of law. I demonstrated why the rule of law calls for democratic rights against ex post facto laws and bills of attainder, even for the worst criminals. The Hobbesian refusal to justify punishment to all individuals, such that they are obligated to abide by them, abandons this aspect of the democratic ideal.

In exploring why political justification should entail justification to the individual, it is important to refer to the lexicon of chapter 3. Democratic legitimacy depends on justification to a people. In turn, this "people" comprises individual citizens. According to democratic contractualism, the ideal of the citizen serves to justify coercion by regarding all persons subject to state force as free and equal. In contrast to legal citizenship, the moral ideal of democratic citizenship requires that all persons subject to coercion have rights guarantees that limit the type of punishment the state can impose upon them.[7]

III. State Punishment as an Issue of Political Morality:
Punishing Criminals qua Persons versus Criminals qua Citizens

In the previous section, I rejected Hobbes's notion that criminals are "enemies" of the state, arguing that justifications of state punishment should take seriously the interests of criminals qua citizens. This section examines another account of punishment, retributivism, that sees criminals as moral agents entitled to justifications but still fails to recognize their status as citizens. Traditional retributive accounts of punishment suggest two ways in which to regard criminals as moral persons. First, they require that punishment only be given to those who are morally guilty of crimes. Second, they require that the amount of punishment be proportional to the crime committed.[8] Unlike Hobbes's war-like account of punishment, retributive accounts do not abandon the need for justifications of punishment but instead couch all criminal justice questions within the framework of moral justification. I will argue that while a moral

[7] As I suggested in chapter 3, the moral ideal of citizenship in matters of state punishment should be extended to all persons subject to coercion regardless of their legal status. For the reasons I stated in that chapter, however, this need not mean that all persons are entitled to voting rights associated with legal citizenship in every democratic country.

[8] Joel Feinberg, "The Classic Debate," in *Philosophy of Law*, 5th ed., ed. Joel Feinberg and Hyman Gross (Belmont, Calif.: Thomson Wadsworth, 1995), 614; Herbert Morris, "Persons and Punishment," *The Monist* 52, no. 4 (October 1968): 475–501. For an attempt to formulate retributivist responses to death penalty cases, see Jeffrey H. Reiman, "Justice, Civilization, and the Death Penalty: Answering van den Haag," *Philosophy and Public Affairs* 14, no. 2 (Spring 1985): 115–48.

stance on when and how criminals should be punished is important to any account of criminal justice, a narrower focus on the unique political questions raised by state punishment—a focus provided by democratic contractualism—should replace the retributivist focus on broad questions of moral desert.

Traditional retributive accounts of punishment differ from democratic contractualism most significantly in terms of the context within which they frame the problem of punishment. Retributive accounts focus on the moral worth of either the criminal or the criminal's particular action, in isolation from the criminal's relationship with the state. In this sense, they justify punishment for persons, not punishment for citizens. The apolitical nature of these accounts is demonstrated by the priority they give to the question of what the criminal qua person deserves rather than the question of what punishment the state rightfully can impose.

In order to highlight the problem with an apolitical account of punishment, consider the following example: suppose a child molester and murderer is sentenced to death. Assume that the punishment is justified. While on Death Row, the child molester is killed by a fellow inmate who is outraged by his crime. In some sense, the child molester received what he "deserves," since we have stipulated that the appropriate punishment is death.[9] However, there is something troubling about this "vigilante" approach to justice. One obvious concern is that the fellow inmate might choose a less humane form of punishment than the state. If, however, we alter the example so that the criminal is electrocuted by his cellmate, just as he would have been by the state, we still are left with a problem. The trouble is that punishments that the state legitimately might carry out are not necessarily justified when they are inflicted by private persons. The retributive account, centered entirely on what criminals qua persons deserve, cannot acknowledge a moral distinction between state punishment and private punishment carried out in the same manner.[10] Since retributivism focuses exclusively on guilt, it evaluates the child molester example simply by concluding that he is guilty, deserves death, and has received what he deserves, just as he would have at the hands of the state.

Retributivists' apolitical accounts of punishment also are problematic because their focus on criminals' moral worth as persons ambitiously is grounded in a comprehensive moral code instead of a narrower conception of politically

---

[9] This stipulation aside, my view, developed at the end of this section, is that there is no good democratic justification of capital punishment.

[10] Some retributivist arguments, such as Locke's, suggest a pragmatic reason for the state, rather than individuals, to punish. This argument refers to the coordination problems (including the inability of the weak to punish the strong) that come from allowing private individuals a right of punishment; see Locke, *Two Treatises of Government,* 351.

legitimate actions. As such, they risk privileging one particular viewpoint over other reasonable viewpoints held by citizens of a polity. This reliance on comprehensive conceptions, as I suggested in earlier chapters, undermines citizens' status as free and equal.

The virtue of the democratic contractualist account over the traditional retributive view is that it can explain why state punishment is justifiable within a political theory that recognizes persons' status as citizens. Because this account is framed by the value theory of democracy, it also is subject to the limits imposed by the value theory. Although democratic contractualism grants the state certain powers that are not justifiable to private persons, such as the seizure of property or the imprisonment of citizens, the legitimate democratic state's need to respect the status of its citizens limits its actions. To highlight further the differences between the democratic contractualist emphasis on legitimate state treatment of citizens and the retributivist emphasis on moral desert, it is helpful to consider examples that illustrate why the punishment that criminals deserve as persons is distinct from the punishment that is justifiable to them as citizens.

A contemporary example illustrates an instance in which moral desert and state legitimacy conflict: the theoretical punishment of terrorist Osama bin Laden. In a televised debate between the candidates for the 2004 Democratic Party presidential nomination, Senator John Kerry challenged his opponent, then Vermont Governor Howard Dean, over his comment that he would give bin Laden a fair trial for his crimes if he were captured alive. Kerry responded with moral outrage, asking, "What in the world were you thinking?" Dean's reply was paradigmatic of the distinction between moral desert and legitimate state conduct:

[A]s an American, I want to see Osama bin Laden get what he deserves, which is the death penalty.

But . . . a candidate for president of the United States is obligated to stand for the rule of law. . . . if I was the president and the troops had Osama in their sights—we would shoot to kill. But the fact is, if we captured him alive, we have to stand for the rule of law.

I have no doubt that if we capture Osama bin Laden, he will end up with the death penalty. But as president of the United States, I'm obligated to stand for the rule of law.[11]

---

[11] "Transcript: Democratic Presidential Debate in Iowa," *Washington Post* on the Web, available at <http://www.washingtonpost.com/ac2/wp-dyn/A54363>−2004Jan4?language=printer>.

A private person well might believe that a mass murderer such as bin Laden deserves brutal, spontaneous, even bizarre retribution, perhaps at the hands of the victims of his attacks.[12] As Dean suggested, however, legitimate state conduct implies a commitment to the rule of law, in particular the institution of a fair trial. Of course, the point here should not be limited to a claim about fair procedures. If the state were to administer a ghastly death to bin Laden, even with due process, it would not behave legitimately, although it might satisfy most people's sense of what bin Laden deserves. Whatever the moral qualities of a particular individual, a state acts legitimately when it treats individuals as rights-bearing citizens.

The distinction between a punishment that a criminal deserves and a punishment that the state legitimately is authorized to carry out can be developed by examining the principle of *lex talionis* (lit., law of retaliation). A literal interpretation of the principle "an eye for an eye and a tooth for a tooth" demands not only that punishments be deserved but also that they match the crime. Those who are assaulted, for instance, might think it appropriate to assault their attackers in retribution for their crimes. Again, the principle does not obviously seem wrong as a response from a victim. However, a state that physically assaults criminals in exactly the same manner as they assaulted their victims rightly is regarded as morally suspect according to democratic ideals. Such a state clearly would engage in cruel and unusual punishment because of its deliberate infliction of pain. This example suggests that a democratic state's approach to punishment should be substantively distinct from private approaches to punishment.

Without more precise guidelines, however, it is difficult to determine which punishments should be prohibited in a democracy and which are acceptable. The principle of democracy's public reason can help to evaluate the legitimacy of particular state punishments. This principle first rules out any punishment based on the Hobbesian concept of the criminal qua enemy who has no rights. Hobbes's concept directly contrasts with the ideal of treating those subject to coercion as citizens because it rejects the idea that criminals are entitled to treatment that is justifiable to them in any way, much less the right to be treated in accordance with the core values. The principle of democracy's public reason also rules out the overly ambitious concern of retributivists to give a person what he deserves. Morally speaking, criminals might deserve a range of punishments from humiliation to pain. I have argued, however, that this question

[12] Some might believe that bin Laden merits the Hobbesian "enemy" label, especially since he is not a U.S. citizen. For the purposes of the argument here, however, I follow contractualists such as Rawls in referring to a moral ideal of citizenship that suggests a way of treating all persons subject to state control. Another project would take up a defense of this use in relation to noncitizens.

should be bracketed in favor of a more specific question about which punishments a democratic state rightfully can impose.

Democracy's public reason only goes so far in providing guidelines for state punishment. It excludes some theories of punishment as irrelevant to the core values because they fail to account for the status of citizens as rulers. But we must consider the more specific inclusion principle to distinguish between punishments that are legitimate in the democratic state because they are reasonably acceptable to citizens and those that are illegitimate because they reasonably are rejected by citizens.

IV. DEMOCRATIC RIGHTS AGAINST PUNISHMENT

Although democratic contractualism is compatible with many forms of punishment, some rights of criminals never should be abridged. In determining the contours of these rights, we should ask what forms of punishment a rightly convicted criminal qua citizen reasonably could accept or reject. The inclusion principle cannot resolve every hard case, but it can rule out several types of punishment and identify some basic rights that even the worst criminals should retain.

What punishment can a violent criminal, thinking of himself as a citizen, reasonably accept? I have suggested that restraint is legitimate if it respects criminals' continued status as citizens to the greatest extent possible. Punishments that deliberately inflict pain for no plausible democratic reason reasonably are rejected. Such punishments do not serve to confine, nor are they consistent with the reasons why persons rightly are imprisoned in the first place. A democracy legitimately can prohibit violent crime. However, guards' wanton infliction of pain on prisoners merely repeats this same offense at the hand of the state.

While wanton violence is an easy case of illegitimate coercion, a harder case could arise in which a guard has reason to act violently, but not a reason that is justifiable to prisoners qua citizens. For instance, suppose a guard believes that extremely violent responses to prisoners' minor misbehavior will help to pre-empt more violent misbehavior or attacks. Such an approach, it might be argued, is justified on the grounds that guards should protect themselves at all costs. Although this is arguably a "plausible" reason for the guard's violent action, such an approach should be rejected as inconsistent with the legitimate punishment when forming state policy for how to treat prisoners. It is not enough that public policy be based on "plausible" reasons; rather, democratic contractualism specifically demands reasons that uphold the values of free and equal citizenship. It follows that policy should respect the reasonable interests of all citizens, not just the interests of specific individuals or groups. In this case, policy should reflect the interests of both guards and prisoners, not merely those of the former. Although a policy that allowed guards to defend themselves from violent prisoner attacks certainly would respect the interests of all, a policy allowing guards to commit extremely violent acts in response to minor infractions would ignore the possibility that prisoners might comply with prison rules and refrain from violence against guards as a result of other means. This policy clearly would serve the interests of the guards at the expense of those of the prisoners. Thus, it should be dismissed as inconsistent with democratic contractualist justification.

When carried out properly, imprisonment balances the need for incapacitation of criminals with a respect for their status as citizens and the maintenance of some rights. If we want to know which rights criminals should retain, we should begin with the most paradigmatic rights held by those outside prisons and ask whether they reasonably can be retained by criminals qua citizens. Free speech, for instance, is a paradigmatic democratic right that is necessary for the state to respect citizens' entitlements to hear arguments about which there is reasonable disagreement and to listen to those they disagree with, and generally to respect the freedom of conscience inherent in the status of free and equal citizenship. But should such a paradigmatic democratic right be extended to prisoners in a legitimate society?

Prisons primarily are responsible for preventing criminals from harming their guards, society, and one another; thus, prison guards should prevent speech that could serve to coordinate an escape attempt or to provoke violent riots. Such an argument, however, does not explain why prisoners should not retain some free speech rights. For instance, prisoners could retain a right to communicate with those outside prison walls without necessarily posing a security threat. Such communication both gives prisoners some continued status as citizens in the wider community and affirms the "listening" rights of nonprisoners articulated in chapter 2. Given that this aspect of free speech still must be balanced with security, there is reason to think that prisoners' right to communicate with those beyond the prison walls should be retained. Another means of honoring prisoners' free speech rights would be to offer them a forum for civic dialogue, particularly about their own imprisonment, to compensate for the abridgement of their rights in other settings.[13] In general,

---

[13] By allowing prisoners to reflect on their punishment, such forums would treat prisoners as reasonable moral agents capable of seriously assessing the legitimacy of their punishments. For justifications of punishment that stress the importance of moral reasoning by the criminals themselves, see Jean Hampton, "The Moral Education Theory of Punishment," *Philosophy and Public Affairs* 13, no. 3 (Summer 1984): 208–38, and R. A. Duff, "Penal Communications: Recent Work in the Philosophy of Punishment," *Crime and Justice* 20 (1996): 1–97. Interestingly, Hampton

prison policy should provide for restrictions on prisoners' rights that infringe as little as possible on the legitimate exchange of ideas, especially in their communication with the outside world.[14]

Another case to consider through the lens of democratic contractualism concerns criminals' right to vote. Several states deny felons the right to vote even after they are released. The idea here seems to be that citizens should forfeit this basic right of citizenship because they have violated the rights of others. This interpretation of reciprocity, however, mistakenly extends the idea that citizens surrender some of their rights when they violate their duties as citizens to conclude that they give up all of their rights and their status as citizens. Requiring life-long disenfranchisement even for those who have completed their punishment would create a group of second-class citizens who do not enjoy democratic treatment.[15] According to democratic contractualism, therefore, those who have served their time reasonably could reject attempts to deny them the franchise even after they are released.

A much harder case concerns whether citizens should be allowed to vote while in prison. There clearly are good reasons to disenfranchise imprisoned felons, particularly in local elections, to prevent them from exerting political influence to secure a pardon or other potentially improper changes in the law. A reasonable criminal would recognize that a balance therefore must be struck that protects prisoners' continued status as citizens while denying them the power to undermine the effectiveness of legitimate criminal laws. One possibility, for example, might deprive prisoners of the right to elect the local sheriff while preserving their voting rights in national elections, in which their votes would not threaten prison security.

Society's interest in security justifies punishments that restrict criminals' freedom of action, but legitimate punishment also must preserve criminals' moral status as citizens. Most obviously, this means limiting cruel and unusual punishments and preserving democratic rights to the greatest extent possible.

---

draws a specific connection between her moral education theory of punishment and democracy; see Hampton, "Moral Education Theory of Punishment," 220.

[14] Similar reasoning could justify the idea that prisoners should retain rights to free exercise of religion. Joshua Cohen, for instance, has argued that given reasonable religious disagreements, no state can claim the right to coerce citizens concerning their religious beliefs; see Cohen, "Procedure and Substance in Deliberative Democracy," 103. Such coercion would betray the ideal that coercion originates in a respect for citizens' common status. Restrictions on religion within the prison walls can be reasonably rejected because they fail to respect this status.

[15] One possible consequence of such disenfranchisement is that, without this basic right of citizenship, former prisoners might feel no reciprocal obligation to respect the basic requirements of law.

V. CAPITAL PUNISHMENT

Although some of the limitations required by a democratic contractualist account of punishment are relatively easy to identify, there of course are harder cases. On my view, democratic justification to criminals implies a substantive limit on any form of punishment that undermines their status as free and equal citizens. In this section, I argue that the practice of capital punishment is inconsistent with respect for the status of criminals qua citizens. Democracy requires a right not to be executed, even for the worst offenders. Criminals qua citizens reasonably can reject capital punishment.

In contemporary political theory, those condemned to death often are extended certain rights against state coercion. But the arguments in this tradition often have focused on highlighting the "inherent dignity" retained even by the worst offenders, dignity that is violated when the state kills.[16] For these thinkers, my argument seems backwards: I attempt to argue against capital punishment from a political conception of the citizen when the problem with the practice is that it robs *persons* of their humanity. Certainly, the worst thing about being executed by the state is not that one has lost one's political status as free and equal; it is that one is dead.[17] From the point of view of democratic contractualism, however, justifying punishment is not about the moral desert of persons. It is, rather, about how to punish in a way consistent with the ideals of free and equal citizenship.[18] Capital punishment is inconsistent entirely with this ideal. There are two main arguments for this point.

The first argument stems from the nature of the state as a fallible agent. Ideally, a democratic state never would punish the innocent. But institutions are not ideal. They comprise individuals and mechanisms that sometimes simply do not work. As recent DNA evidence has illuminated, the state is prone to err even when it sanctions the most severe punishment, death.[19] The most obvious

---

[16] Kateb, *Inner Ocean,* 4–5, 201; Kateb (2000) "What do Citizens Owe Their Constitutional Democracy?" For a criticism of the idea of inherent dignity, see Bedau, "Abolishing the Death Penalty Even for the Worst Murderers."

[17] For discussion on this point, I thank Gilbert Harman.

[18] For a detailed examination of the relationship between my argument and the older tradition of opposing capital punishment, see my "Dignity, Citizenship, and Capital Punishment: The Right of Life Reformulated."

[19] For instance, the ACLU claims that from 1976 to April 2005, 119 prisoners convicted of capital crimes were found innocent and released from death row. American Civil Liberties Union, "National Death Penalty Fact Sheet" (2005), available at <http://www.aclu.org/capital/facts/10593res20050216.html> (accessed June 23, 2006).

condition necessary for justifying punishments to criminals qua citizens is that they must be guilty to be punished. Therefore, the actual innocence of individuals, despite the Rehnquist Court's recent rulings, should be grounds for an appeal.[20] The state's fallibility necessitates that democratic procedures always allow the innocent to prove that they have been punished wrongly, and this is possible only if they are alive.[21]

It is easy to see how this guarantee can be made consistent with life imprisonment. Prisoners can try to prove their innocence through appeal, and many have done so successfully. Yet this right of appeal is denied to persons after they are executed. While the family of an executed prisoner might prove his or her innocence post mortem when the state makes a mistake, the state cannot make amends to the wronged party directly. In contrast, imprisonment does not eliminate the possibility of some rectification to an unfairly convicted individual. If such an individual can prove his innocence, it is possible to recognize the illegitimacy of his punishment.

According to this argument against capital punishment, a procedural right to appeal presupposes an appellant who is alive. Therefore, the procedural right demands a more fundamental right: the right to life. Many opponents of capital punishment object to this line of reasoning because it suggests that a more fundamental right depends on a less fundamental procedural right. But nothing in the nature of democratic justification necessitates that we always appeal to the inherent value of life, or indeed to any metaphysical argument when seeking to limit state punishment. The issue here is not divine or even moral justice in general, but the specific dynamic between citizen and state within a legitimate democracy. While death may be a just punishment for certain offenses in the pure theory of moral desert, this does not legitimize a penal institution that puts individuals to death without certainty that they actually have committed a crime. The fallibility of the criminal justice system suggests that what criminals deserve and what constitutes legitimate state conduct are distinct questions. Because state institutions do not perfectly administer justice, they should embody reasonable balances between the interests of society and

[20] In *Herrera v. Collins*, 506 U.S. 390 (1993), the Court found (roughly) that the possibility of actual innocence does not constitute grounds for an appeal if procedural rules have been followed.

[21] In *United States v. Quinones*, 205 F. Supp. 2d 256 (S.D.N.Y. 2002), District Court Judge Jed S. Rakoff invoked a version of the fallibility argument when he suggested that the danger of executing innocent people made the death penalty unconstitutional. In Rakoff's words: "Given what DNA testing has exposed about the unreliability of the primary techniques developed by our system for the ascertainment of guilt, it is quite something else to arbitrarily eliminate, through execution, any possibility of exoneration after a certain point in time. The result can only be the fully foreseeable execution of numerous innocent persons." The decision was reversed on appeal.

those of the accused. Since capital punishment deprives individuals of the ability to prove their innocence in a judicial system that frequently makes mistakes, it reasonably is rejected by convicted criminals.

Some have argued that courts will get better and better at proving guilt with the improvement of DNA evidence and other criminal justice techniques, such that the possibility of wrongful convictions no longer will be cause for concern. Although this level of sophistication is unlikely in the near future—especially given the corruption and inequalities of representation in many criminal justice systems—it is worth asking whether, even given an infallible state, capital punishment would ever be justifiable in a democracy. I contend that the answer is no.

Consider a second distinct argument that appeals directly to democratic citizenship as an ideal of justification. Rousseau famously argues that because persons would agree to the death penalty when considering what the general will requires of them as citizens, a person convicted of a capital crime would have to acknowledge that she should consent to her own death. As a theory of what actual criminals will, this view is implausible. In my discussion of Rousseau in chapter 3, I called this view the "problem of false attribution." The implausibility of Rousseau's view is not its only problem, however; the very notion that citizens ever could have an obligation to destroy their own existence is problematic. In short, while the person-citizen distinction is useful, citizenship presupposes a person who can be treated in accordance with the core values.[22]

Fundamental to democratic contractualism and central to my rejection of the Hobbesian notion of punishment is the right of each person to have coercion justified to him or her as a citizen. This right is so fundamental that it should be considered inalienable. If citizenship is inalienable, however, one cannot alienate one's own right to life either, because citizenship presupposes personhood.

This argument from citizenship against capital punishment also has roots in constitutional law. Writing for the majority in *Trop v. Dulles*, Chief Justice Warren held that to strip persons of their legal citizenship as punishment is unconstitutional because it constitutes cruel and unusual punishment, insofar as it denies them any political identity.[23] Several years later, in an opinion in *Furman v. Georgia*, Justice Brennan drew on this reasoning to suggest that if citizenship could not be stripped as a punishment, then the death penalty never could be

[22] The classic counterexample arguably is found in Plato's "Crito," where Socrates argues that he is obligated to consent to his own death sentence. See Plato, Five Dialogues, 2d ed., trans. G.M.A. Grube, rev. John M. Cooper (Indianapolis, Ind.: Hackett, 2002), 45–57.

[23] 356 U.S. 86 (1958).

justified.[24] In short, he reasoned that it is impossible to execute persons without thereby stripping them of their citizenship.

As a moral ideal, citizenship should frame all acts of coercion. Drawing on the Warren-Brennan reasoning, my theory suggests that the need always to justify coercion to persons qua citizens presupposes their existence and therefore protects them from execution by the state. The state's fallibility is one justification for this protection; because the state never can be sure that the person it would execute is guilty, it must leave some room for correction. A deeper justification, however, stems from the value of never terminating the relationship between citizens and the democratic state, a relationship that itself is the foundation of the state's authority.

In this regard, Rousseau's account of capital punishment actually might work against his conclusion in support of the death penalty. Although he agrees that citizenship never should be revoked, his support of capital punishment leads him to adopt a counterintuitive position. On the one hand, the condemned citizen recognizes that he must will his own death because the death penalty is justifiable. In Rousseau's words: "Whoever wills the end also wills the means."[25] On the other hand, Rousseau argues that one's status as a citizen, and in turn as an essential part of the general will, is inalienable. Thus, he claims that one dies not as a citizen but as an "enemy" at war with the state. He reasons, "Thus one of the two must perish; and when the guilty party is put to death, it is less as a citizen than as an enemy."[26] Rousseau argues that because citizenship is an inalienable part of the general will, the citizen cannot be banned from the social contract. Given this justification of the death penalty, however, the actual person who has committed a crime should die. The result is the strange conclusion that citizenship cannot be alienated and that one cannot be killed as a citizen, but nonetheless can be killed as a person. On my account, citizenship is a moral ideal distinct from personhood, but it still presupposes the existence of a flesh-and-blood person. Justification to citizens is not justification to inanimate objects; at a minimum, citizens must be living persons. By contrast, Rousseau's account borders on versions of idealism, in which an individual can continue to exist as a citizen without being a person.

One objection to my argument against capital punishment is that the state does place citizens in life-threatening situations when, for instance, it conscripts soldiers and sends them to war. Here, however, the state neither acts directly to kill the soldiers nor demands that they take their own lives. The

[24] 408 U.S. 238 (1972).
[25] Rousseau, "On The Social Contract," 159.
[26] Ibid.

difference is one of intention. The aim of sending citizens to participate in a just war is to defend their nation. The unintended and regrettable result of this defense is that they often die in the process. However, ideal democracies continue to respect soldiers' status as citizens by pursuing strategies that risk as few lives as possible. By contrast, the clear intention and goal of capital punishment is to end the life of the condemned. Furthermore, soldiers in just wars who risk their lives to defend their country rightly are regarded as heroes, whereas prisoners condemned to die, Socrates notwithstanding, are anything but venerated.

A related question concerns whether my account of democratic limitation on capital punishment also should limit citizens who want to take their own lives.[27] Here, there is an important difference between the state granting a right to suicide and requiring a prisoner to submit to capital punishment. If the state were to grant a right to suicide, it would not by any means force citizens to exercise this right. When the state metes out capital punishment, however, it gives no such choice to persons. Thus, there is a distinction between granting permission to kill oneself, which demands no action from citizens and arguably enhances their autonomy, and a requirement that is enforced through the coercive institution of capital punishment.

VI. Conclusion

Democratic justification requires specific limitations on state punishment. One limitation requires rejecting the Hobbesian idea that criminals who have committed certain offenses no longer deserve to have acts of coercion justified to them. This is an unacceptable departure from democratic justification. In contrast, I have suggested a way of understanding justifications of punishment as addressed to criminals qua citizens. Here, there is an important contrast between a general moral account of punishment, such as those offered by retributivists, and a specifically democratic account of state punishment. Some punishments that are justifiable on retributivist grounds are inconsistent with criminals' status as free and equal citizens because they take as criteria for punishment what is morally deserved by criminals rather than how the state rightly treats them.

In contrast to Hobbesian and retributivist approaches to punishment, democratic contractualism offers an account of punishment as an essential part of a

[27] This question was raised by Austin Sarat in his response to my paper during our panel on capital punishment at a conference on "Law and Humanities," Austin, Texas, Association for the Study of Law, Culture, and the Humanities, 2001.

more general theory of political legitimacy. In turn, this theory requires substantive rights that restrict how citizens can be punished. While certain punishments are justifiable in a democracy, they always should be formulated to allow citizens some degree of democratic freedom through rights such as free speech, the right to vote and the right to live.

CHAPTER 6

PRIVATE PROPERTY AND THE RIGHT TO WELFARE

Regardless of the light in which [the rich] tried to place their
usurpations, they knew full well that they were established on
nothing but a precarious and abusive right, and that having
been acquired merely by force, force might take them away
from them without their having any reason to complain. Even
those enriched exclusively by industry could hardly base their
property on better claims. They could very well say: "I am the
one who built that wall; I have earned this land with my
labor." In response to them it could be said: "Who gave you
the boundary lines? By what right do you claim to exact
payment at our expense for labor we did not impose upon
you? Are you unaware that a multitude of your brothers
perish or suffer from need of what you have in excess, and
that you needed explicit and unanimous consent from the
human race for you to help yourself to anything from
the common subsistence that went beyond your own?
—*Rousseau, "Discourse on the Origin of Inequality"*

I. INTRODUCTION

The past two chapters examined democratic contractualism's approach to laws
that limit decisional autonomy and to state punishment, both important instances of state coercion. I suggested that democratic contractualism requires
"negative" rights, rights against the state, that protect citizens against certain
restrictions on decisional autonomy and against particular punishments. In this
chapter, I argue that democratic contractualism also requires rights to welfare.
Specifically, I propose that all citizens in an ideal democracy are entitled to a
basic set of welfare guarantees. In contrast to *negative* rights against the state,
these welfare rights are *positive* rights of individuals to be given some particular good by the state.

The democratic contractualist defense of welfare rights conflicts with some
liberal theories, specifically libertarian theories that describe the right to private

property as incompatible with the right to welfare. These theories defend a "minimal state" exclusively dedicated to protecting the fundamental right to private property. Unlike some defenders of positive rights, I do not reject entirely the libertarian contention that the state has a role in protecting the negative rights of property owners. I argue, however, that the state's guarantee of welfare rights is a necessary condition for legitimizing private ownership. On the democratic contractualist account, positive rights limit the right to property by justifying taxation to fund welfare provision. In my view, democratic theory can embrace the institution of private property, an institution that historically has accompanied democracy, provided that it does so in a manner that honors the three core values of democracy. This necessitates a guarantee of welfare rights.

My argument proceeds in three stages. First, I maintain that "private" property, at least in its modern form, depends upon state coercion for its existence. Second, I argue that because of this reliance on state coercion, private property should be subject to justification that appeals to democracy's public reason and the inclusion principle. Following this account, the institution of private ownership is only justifiable if the coercion necessary to its existence reasonably can be accepted from the point of view of all citizens, including the least well-off. Third, I suggest that *if* private ownership is to be made acceptable to all, the state must guarantee welfare rights to all citizens.[1] My inquiry, however, concerns only a necessary condition for private property's legitimacy. I leave the much larger project of examining the sufficient conditions for its legitimacy for another place.

II. The Right to Private Property and State Coercion

In chapter 3, I proposed that democratic contractualism is a particularly appropriate framework for applying the value theory of democracy to justifications of state coercion. Criminal law and punishment, the subject of chapters 4 and 5, were obvious candidates for this examination. The relationship between private property and state coercion is less obvious, however; at first glance, therefore, it may be unclear why democratic justification is required to demonstrate its legitimacy.

---

[1] The idea of welfare as a conditional requirement for private ownership differs from many accounts of welfare rights that aim to defend them with reference directly to their role in meeting basic needs. See Michael Walzer, *Spheres of Justice: A Defense of Pluralism and Equality* (New York: Basic, 1983), 78.

The very use of the word "private" to describe property not held by the state suggests that ownership exists independently of politics and the state. This common understanding is reinforced by the fact that private law, including the law of real property, concerns conflicts between private parties, seemingly without state involvement. Moreover, libertarians often argue that, far from depending on the state for its existence, private property is threatened most by state power. The authors of the United States Constitution perceived such a threat, as they sought to limit the state's ability to seize private property. If this popular understanding of property as *private* were correct, there would be no need to justify private ownership along the lines of democratic contractualism.[2]

Contrary to its popular understanding, however, private ownership *does* involve state coercion and thus should be subject to democratic justification. There is an analogy here between the often tacit coercion present in what is commonly thought to be the private sphere of the family and that which is tacit in private property. I argued in chapter 4 that the boundaries of privacy should be subject to democratic justification, and the same holds true for the contours of private property.

If so many individuals regard private property as distinct from the state, why is it subject to public justification? Here, the distinction between property as "a thing" to be possessed and the *right* to private property upon which modern ownership rests is fundamental. One common understanding of private property, although one not often held by property theorists, is that ownership is about possession and therefore does not involve the state. Although one sometimes possesses property, possession is a very weak account of what it means to have a *right* to private property.[3] Many forms of ownership do not involve tangible resources that can be possessed. For example, if one owns stock in a company, one does not fully possess any particular object. Likewise, it would be odd to claim that the value of a labor contract is possessed like a thing. These modern forms of ownership suggest that the right to private property cannot rightly be understood as possession of objects.

Many modern property theorists suggest that private property can be understood better as a bundle of rights. Property owners can take advantage of their property's fungibility (trade it for another resource of similar value), use the re-

---

[2] While such justification might be necessary if the state tried to take property, an obvious form of coercion, it would not at core be required to justify private ownership itself. Such ownership would exist independently of the state.

[3] Thomas C. Grey, "The Disintegration of Property," in *NOMOS XXII: Property,* ed. J. Roland Pennock and John W. Chapman (New York: New York University Press, 1980), 69–85. Grey refers to the "possession" view as a "layman's" view of ownership. For a similar view, see Leif Wenar, "Original Acquisition of Private Property," *Mind* 107, no. 428 (October 1998): 799–819.

source to produce more resources (as with farm land or rental property), or choose not to use it at all. I call these rights "vertical" rights of ownership because they fundamentally concern the owner's relationship to the resource that is owned. In contrast to these vertical rights, a series of "horizontal" rights also are necessary to the right to property. Horizontal rights concern the relationship between the owner and other citizens instead of the relationship between the owner and the thing owned.

The most fundamental horizontal right is the right to exclude. This right entails that ownership depends, in large part, on one's ability exclusively to control resources. To have exclusive control, however, one must be able to prevent nonowners from intervening in one's decisions regarding those resources, such as by taking them. The power of coercion clearly is necessary to enforce the right to exclude; the issue that remains is whether the libertarians' contention that the state need not enforce this right is correct.

The argument for understanding property as a bundle of rights rather than as possession is sufficient to dispense with the understanding of private property as solely about the relationship between the owner and the thing she possesses, such that the state is irrelevant to the right to private property. This understanding fails to acknowledge the variety of rights involved in the right to private property, and it cannot account for complex modern forms of ownership, such as stocks, in which no thing is possessed.

A more sophisticated understanding of property, however, might accept that property is a bundle of rights and recognize that private ownership fundamentally requires a right to exclude, even while maintaining that these rights need not be guaranteed by the state. For instance, some libertarians might suggest that owners in the state of nature could enforce the right to exclude, either independently or by banding together. If libertarian thinkers successfully could prove that the protection of private property does not require the state, they would go a long way toward showing that public justification is irrelevant to private property. An owner who toils on and successfully protects his or her property would not need to provide any reasons to non-owners for their exclusion. While the state might have a justificatory relationship with its citizens, private individuals would have no such relationship with each other with regard to private property. If owners owe any justification to non-owners, libertarians might argue that they merely must demonstrate that through their labor they cultivated property, and through their strength they exercise their right to exclude others.

One way to refute the libertarian contention that private property is a natural phenomenon existing independently of the state is to contest directly the idea that private property can exist without the state. In *The Cost of Rights,*

Stephen Holmes and Cass Sunstein argue that the institution of private property could not exist without the active support of the state.[4] They note that private property relies on the contribution of taxes by citizens to pay for a state police force to protect property rights, and for courts and a legal system to help regulate these rights. Holmes and Sunstein's rejection of the idea that property could ever exist in a state of nature can be seen as a challenge to the libertarian contention that private property should be excluded from public justification. Since private property requires institutional enforcement, it cannot conceivably exist except in the context of state coercion. In light of this view, one could argue that the justification of private property must be publicly defensible.

This debate over private property's existence in the state of nature is among the most fundamental in political theory. Because contemporary ownership in the modern state *does* rely on state protection and enforcement, however, property as it currently exists is not subject to the same debate. Therefore, it is not necessary to prove Holmes and Sunstein's position and to disprove the libertarian thesis of natural ownership in order to make my point that private property requires public justification. Modern property arrangements implicate the state because there is a legally enforced duty to respect the right to exclude.[5] Property owners today undeniably depend on state law enforcement agencies to protect their property by enforcing laws against theft, trespass, and other property-related crimes, and they rely on the state judicial and criminal justice systems to punish violators and ensure that the law is implemented accurately. Moreover, even when the state does not actively coerce, individuals are deterred from violating the right to exclude by the threat of force. Regardless of whether, or how, the right to exclude might be enforced in the state of nature, private property in the contemporary state is distinctive because of the way the right to exclude is enforced.

Another alternative for libertarians is to defend a wholesale end to the state's role as the enforcer of private property. They might, for instance, defend exclu-

---

[4] Stephen Holmes and Cass R. Sunstein, *The Cost of Rights: Why Liberty Depends on Taxes* (New York: Norton, 1999). Similarly arguing that government and taxes are necessary for the market to function, Liam Murphy and Thomas Nagel conclude, "It is therefore logically impossible that people should have any kind of entitlement to all their pretax income" (Murphy and Nagel, *The Myth of Ownership: Taxes and Justice* [Oxford: Oxford University Press, 2002], 32). Their argument reinforces my contention that private property must be legitimated with reference to a more general political justification.

[5] Samuel Freeman suggests that libertarianism is best understood as a feudal view that offers no justification for the state. But even if property might be enforced without the state, many modern libertarians claim that the state does have a role in protecting private property. Thus, they still must give an account of state ownership; see Samuel Freeman, "Illiberal Libertarians: Why Libertarianism Is Not a Liberal View," *Philosophy and Public Affairs* 30 (2001): 105–51.

sively private enforcement of property. As Samuel Freeman suggests, however, the claim that property enforcement is not an aspect of the state's legitimacy more closely resembles feudalism than any recognizable liberal view.[6] The refutation of such a view is outside the scope of this chapter, as this claim does not defend anything resembling the right to private property as it currently exists. I do not aim to abandon the contemporary institution of private ownership, but to inquire into the legitimizing conditions for the state's role in protecting it. What, then, are the necessary conditions for making private ownership consistent with the core values of democracy?

III. Democratic Contractualism and the Right to Private Property

At the level of democracy's public reason, we can rule out arguments about the legitimacy of private property that are incompatible with the three core values. Some such arguments evaluate the legitimacy of private property on the basis of a "true" comprehensive moral theory. For instance, Locke grounds his defense of private property in natural law. Similarly, Marxian arguments, which reject the legitimacy of private property altogether, appeal to a "true" theory of history. Democracy's public reason rules out both of these theories because they appeal to comprehensive conceptions of truth, not values that stem from a shared conception of political morality based on the ideal of democratic citizenship. Theories of truth do not provide acceptable justifications or refutations of private property given the value theory of democracy that I developed in chapter 1.

Having dispensed with theories of truth as the basis for our justification, we now can ask in what sense the three core values are compatible with the institution of private property. The clearest defense of private ownership through the core values can be drawn from the argument I made for privacy in chapter 4. There, I argued that democratic contractualism's respect for autonomy requires a respect for citizens' ability to develop and pursue their own conceptions of the good. Control over resources and the fungibility inherent in private ownership give individuals the power to pursue and enact their life plans. Nothing in the structure of private ownership forces individuals to use private property in any particular way, or, indeed, to use it at all. Instead, private ownership simply expands the realm of possible decisions, thus honoring citizens' decision-making ability.

Clarifying the distinction between state ownership and private ownership can help to illuminate why private ownership enhances the value of individual

[6] Ibid.

119

autonomy. In a system of state ownership, decisions about the use of resources are centralized and therefore taken away from individuals. In contrast, private ownership allows individual citizens to make a plethora of such decisions. The decision-making power afforded by private property increases the level of autonomy for individual citizens. Thus, if privacy rights are necessary to respect individuals' autonomy, the institution of private property potentially enhances the worth of this core value.

This initial discussion of the relationship between the core value of autonomy and private ownership so far has taken place at the generalized level of democracy's public reason. If, however, private property is to be legitimized as part of an ideal democracy, we also should determine its compatibility with the inclusion principle. We can do this by asking the following question: can all citizens reasonably accept the right of owners to exclude nonowners? I have argued that the right to exclude is the coercive aspect of the institution of private property. This right is not coercive in the sense that owners routinely assault nonowners for trespassing. Instead, the coercive apparatus of the state reveals itself in a powerful, albeit tacit, form at the moment an individual attempts to trespass on land or take another's property. A guard need not be present at the boundaries of each person's property for the threat of state sanction to be real. Property crime in contemporary states is a common reason for state punishment and imprisonment, yet the legitimacy of ownership is not widely challenged in contemporary society. The question raised by the inclusion principle is whether the boundaries of property that are so widely accepted by *persons* actually can be justifiable to *citizens* from a variety of points of view.

From what points of view, then, is the duty to respect the coercive boundaries of private ownership reasonably acceptable? Economic interests are among the most fundamental considerations in addressing this question. Therefore, in analyzing the legitimacy of excluding a particular citizen from a particular property, we must consider the amount of property that she already owns, or her economic status.

From a strictly economic perspective, those who have the greatest reason to accept the boundaries of private property are those who own a good deal of it. Even the wealthiest citizens are limited by the right to exclude, as they are subject to exclusion from other citizens' property. There is, however, reason for them to accept this exclusion because they retain the right to exclude others in exchange for respecting the rights of other owners to exclude them. The inclusion principle thus is satisfied here because there are reciprocal reasons for this form of coercion available to property owners. In addition to the core value of reciprocity, this form of coercion also respects the value of autonomy because owners are provided conditions that assure their control over their own resources to further their life projects.

However, the real challenge, for the theorist who seeks public justification for exclusion is to justify exclusion to those with the least interest in respecting the boundaries of private property—namely, the least well-off, whose interests are served least by private ownership. Rousseau's work is helpful in approaching this problem. Although I criticized aspects of Rousseau's theory in chapter 3, his concept of self-governance shares with mine the ideal of including all citizens in an account of democratic legitimacy. This led him, in particular, to recognize the conundrum of justifying private ownership to those with little or no private property. In the epigraph with which I began this chapter, Rousseau acknowledges that the problem of exclusion poses a difficulty in legitimizing private property. He imagines a potential trespasser asking an owner about the legitimacy of the "boundaries" that exclude him from the owner's property. The institution of private property does not serve this potential trespasser's interests as a free and equal citizen, so the owner cannot merely assert his ownership of the property to justify the coercion implicit in his exclusion of the potential trespasser. How, then, can the owner justify this coercion?

This question of how to justify exclusion to the least well-off members of society is my subject in the next part of this chapter. I begin by asking whether the right to exclude could be justified to a person with minimal or no ownership. Ultimately, I argue that no satisfactory justification could be given to anyone who falls below the threshold established by a set of welfare rights. But before I articulate this argument, it is worth considering positions that accept the burden of providing justification to the excluded but deny my contention that legitimate states must ensure welfare rights. In the rest of this chapter, I shall use the term "minimal owner" to refer to a person whose level of ownership falls below a certain basic level of welfare, and shall refer to a person with a greater level of ownership simply as a "property owner." At times I also will express this distinction by contrasting "owners" with "the excluded."

One way to demonstrate that exclusion is justified to the minimal owner is to show that her exclusion from private property somehow serves her reasonable interests. One strategy prominent in the literature considering justifications of private property is to demonstrate that the act of excluding the minimal owner actually benefits her more substantially in the long run, despite its apparent detriment to her immediate interests. For instance, some defenders of libertarian views of private property appeal to the aggregate benefit that private ownership brings to society as a whole.

These thinkers invoke a familiar skepticism regarding the productivity of common ownership. According to their view, it is only when land and wealth

121

are privately owned that they can be productive for the entire society. Private individuals who claim exclusive ownership over land and wealth can be confident that they will reap all of the benefits of their property increasing in value, so they have an incentive to use it as productively as possible. In contrast, individuals in a system where land and wealth are owned communally know that the benefits resulting from effort on their part to increase the value of the community's property will be spread among all members of society. The return on the individual's effort is much less in this system of common ownership, so she has less incentive to use her property productively. An implication of this argument is that since the benefits to society increase as more property is held privately, the government should not force individuals to reduce their level of ownership by imposing taxes.

Libertarians who embrace such reasoning contend that property ownership is not a zero-sum game in which society must divide up a given amount of wealth. Rather, private ownership increases the overall amount of wealth that exists in a society, and this aggregate increase in turn benefits all. To quote a common saying, "a rising tide raises all boats."[7]

The problem with this justification as stated, however, is that it establishes a benefit to society as a whole without addressing the reasonable basic interests of all citizens, including their basic material needs. Specifically, it risks ignoring the interests of those citizens who are minimal owners. Even if the overall benefits to society are greater under a system of private ownership than under a system with no private ownership, minimal owners reasonably could reject such a scheme because their reasonable interests are sacrificed for the interests of others in society. These minimal owners have no reason that appeals to them for accepting the right to exclude; such a justification thus fails the test of the inclusion principle. Consider the following exchange:

> PROPERTY OWNER: I accept the challenge of showing that those who are excluded from private ownership actually have their interests served. Society as a whole has more goods than it would if I left my gates open, as nobody would use my property productively if it were owned communally. Because I make my property useful, others have their interests served.
>
> MINIMAL OWNER: But to whom is the property useful?
>
> PO: To society, which has more goods than it would if my gates were forced open. Property is not, as you have implied, a fixed amount of

---

[7] For an extension of this reasoning to an argument against the welfare state, see David Schmidtz's argument in Robert E. Goodin and David Schmidtz, *Social Welfare and Individual Responsibility* (Cambridge: Cambridge University Press, 1998).

goods to be divided up, but rather is a positive-sum game that serves the interests of all. For instance, my trading partners have more now than they would otherwise, the school I give to has more resources, and the soup kitchen I give to can provide to those in need.

MO: I'll take you on your word as a matter of economics. But you slip quickly from "the aggregate wealth is increased" to "everybody has his interests served." You need to address your argument to me, standing at your gates. To ask me to be happy for others when I myself do not have my most basic interests served is to ask too much. I cannot sacrifice my most basic interests as a citizen for the good of the whole.

PO: Okay, I see your point. You want me to show you how my property ownership not only serves others but also helps to meet your reasonable interests. I accept the challenge. You could go to the soup kitchen or get your name on the list of the housing charity I support. You should be grateful for society's charity.

MO: Your desire for gratitude is the mistake here. I deserve to have my reasonable basic interests met in exchange for respecting your right to exclude me from your property, because meeting my reasonable basic interests is the basis for justifying the right to exclude. My reasonable basic interests are understood best as rights, and meeting them is not charity.

In contrast to libertarian theories that attempt to defend private property as a right distinct from political justification, the property owner's argument here appeals to the interests of the minimal owner and is set in terms of public reason. The problem with the property owner's argument, however, is that it relies on an aggregate conception of interests.[8] Aggregate conceptions of interests easily can ignore entirely the interests of particular individuals, and thus are incompatible with the inclusion principle. Thus, the minimal owner reasonably could reject the legitimacy of state enforcement of the right to exclude, since her reasonable basic interests are not met.

Despite the failure of the utilitarian approach, the normative requirement of justification of property rights to excluded individuals can be met given certain guarantees for all citizens. Reciprocal reasons for the right to exclude could be given to all citizens if, for example, property owners were taxed at a level sufficient to guarantee that the reasonable basic interests of all citizens were met. In other words, if the state could guarantee that no one was in the position of the

[8]John Stuart Mill and Jeremy Bentham, *Utilitarianism and Other Essays*, ed. Alan Ryan (New York: Penguin, 1987). See also J.J.C. Smart and Bernard Williams, *Utilitarianism: For and Against* (Cambridge: Cambridge University Press, 1973).

minimal owner and that all citizens had their reasonable basic interests met, all individuals would have reason to respect the right to exclude. For instance, those in the middle class, who have fungible resources and whose reasonable basic interests are met, have reason to accept the right of their wealthier neighbors to exclude them from their property. The system that excludes a particular member of the middle class from the use of others' property also protects his right to exclude and respects his status as free and equal by ensuring that his reasonable basic interests are met and that he has resources to pursue his particular conception of the good. Though this member of the middle class might not be able successfully to realize particularly extravagant conceptions of the good, he does have some resources beyond those necessary for subsistence that he can use towards whichever conception of the good he chooses to pursue. Thus, my suggestion is that all citizens would have a reason to respect the right to exclude if they were granted some level of welfare rights that ensured them a basic level of ownership, defined by their reasonable basic interests. In contrast, those who fall below this level of ownership would lack a strong contractualist reason to respect the right to exclude.[9] It follows that the state that seeks to legitimize its role in protecting the right to exclude should guarantee that no one falls below this basic level of ownership.

Before I explain the nature of these rights and why they justify private ownership, it is worth considering one more objection to my view. A critic could contend that I have set the burden of justification too high. Why cannot the legitimizing condition for the right to exclude simply be that the minimal owner suffers no loss as a result of her lack of ownership? For instance, those who seek to show that property ownership causes no detriment to minimal owners might argue that the absolute economic status of a minimal owner will not change after an owner has acquired property.[10]

As I have framed it, however, the question of political justification concerns why coercion itself is acceptable, not whether persons are worse-off after coercion than they were before. A good justification of coercion will seek to legitimize it by appeal to the interests of those who it most adversely affects and in

---

[9] For Holmes and Sunstein, one justification for basic welfare stems from the need to keep poor citizens from rebelling. Such a conception would set the level of welfare in a manner dependent on citizens' willingness to resist the law. But on my view the burden for the property owner is not to keep the minimal owner from storming the gates. Rather, it is a moral challenge to justify the institution of private property to the minimal owner as free and equal citizen.

[10] Alternatively they could argue that there is a benefit compared to the state of nature. Both Locke and Hobbes argue in this way. See John Locke, *Two Treatises of Government,* ed. Peter Laslett. (Cambridge: Cambridge University Press, 1988), and Thomas Hobbes, *Leviathan* (London: Penguin, 1985).

particular by asking whether they reasonably can reject such coercion. In the case of property, the excluded are the persons to whom such justification should be addressed. Therefore, the relevant question does not involve a comparison of pre- and postcoercion status, but rather asks whether the society can justify coercion by explaining how it is consistent with meeting people's reasonable basic interests. I have suggested that one can justify property rights by showing that they meet the needs of all citizens, not just of some subset of society. In societies that fail to guarantee all individuals' reasonable basic interests, there is reason for citizens reasonably to reject the right to exclude. Thus, the legitimacy of the institution of private property in such societies is called into question.

I began this chapter with Rousseau's challenge to the property owner to justify his ownership to all. I have argued that this challenge can be met if state enforcement of private property rights is justified to the excluded by appeal to the fact that their reasonable basic interests are met. Material rights to welfare compensate for exclusion. Although my argument is incompatible with some libertarian conceptions of the right to property, it is grounded firmly in the liberal tradition.[11] Consider the following argument made by John Locke, the paradigmatic defender of liberal property rights, regarding owners' obligation to ensure minimal owners' right to subsistence:

> We know God hath not left one Man so to the Mercy of another, that he may starve him if he please: God the Lord and Father of all, has given no one of his Children such a Property, in his peculiar Portion of the things of this World, but that he has given his needy Brother a Right to the Surplusage of his Goods; so that it cannot justly be denied him, when his pressing Wants call for it. And therefore no Man could ever have a just Power over the Life of another, by Right of property in Land or Possessions; since 'twould always be a Sin in any Man of Estate, to let his Brother perish for want of affording him Relief out of his Plenty. As *Justice* gives every Man a Title to the product of his honest Industry, and the fair Acquisitions of his Ancestors descended to him; so *Charity* gives every Man a Title to so much out of another's Plenty, as will keep him from extream want, where he has no means to subsist otherwise.[12]

[11] Samuel Freeman, "Illiberal Libertarians: Why Libertarianism Is Not a Liberal View," *Philosophy and Public Affairs* 30, no. 2 (April 2001): 105–51.

[12] Locke, *Two Treatises of Government*, 170. Locke did not seek to ensure this right through taxation, yet he arguably saw a role for the state in the guarantee of welfare rights. Specifically, he suggested that the state should fine parishes that failed to secure basic welfare for the poor. See John Locke, "An Essay on the Poor Law," in *Political Essays*, ed. Mark Goldie (Cambridge: Cambridge University Press, 1997), 198. It should also be noted that one of Locke's conditions for the legitimate appropriation of land was that there be "enough, and as good left" for other individuals

This passage is striking for two reasons. First, Locke acknowledges that the institution of private property partly is justified by its ability to provide for the welfare of minimal owners. Second, and more fundamentally, Locke regards basic welfare claims as "rights" on the "title" of property owners. Even for Locke, then, property rights are justifiable in part because they provide for the basic needs of the least well-off. I do not, however, merely want to endorse Locke's understanding of the relationship between welfare and property. For instance, Locke is unclear about how welfare rights should be enforced. Although he claims that there should be penalties on owners who do not meet the basic needs of minimal owners, he never outlines a system of state provision. In contrast, I argue that the state should enforce welfare rights because they are necessary to legitimate the right of property, which itself depends on state enforcement.

IV. Democratic Proposals for Welfare Rights

We have established that welfare rights compensate for the right to exclude. But how should the resources to satisfy these rights be distributed? I suggest three proposals as reasonable approaches to implementing welfare rights. All three proposals are crafted with the aim of inclusion required by democratic contractualism and appeal to the reasonable interests of both the property owner and the person excluded from ownership.

The Right to a Job

One possible form of the welfare-right entitlement appeals to the core value of reciprocity: the right to work for a just wage. Here, the state does not confer economic benefits directly, but rather guarantees each individual the potential to accrue resources. Owners generally acquire their property through labor, and they reasonably could object to the government distributing resources to individuals who exerted no effort to merit compensation. Thus, a right of the excluded should parallel property owners' opportunity to acquire resources, without necessarily paralleling the result of the owners' labor. It follows that the excluded should have a right to work and thus to acquire property.

Although the right to a job is one of opportunity, it still requires the state to guarantee a positive right. In an agrarian economy with an abundance of farmland and agricultural training for citizens from a young age, citizens would have

---

(Locke, *Two Treatises of Government*, 291). Thus, Locke held that a person's acquisition of land was legitimate only if it did not prevent others from meeting their basic needs.

endless opportunities to acquire resources. In the Lockean account of the state of nature, therefore, citizens' opportunity to work does not rely on state-provided rights. No such commons exist in modern economies, however; workers must compete for income in the labor market instead of simply finding a plot of land. Given inevitable economic fluctuation, the free market often does not provide enough jobs for all citizens to labor. The state, however, must ensure that all citizens are provided basic opportunities to work because it enforces the right of private property, which depends on coercion that must be justified by appeal to citizens' status as free and equal. If the market cannot provide sufficient jobs, therefore, the state should guarantee that they exist.

The public-policy proposals for guaranteeing the opportunity to work range from those that embrace New Deal–style, state-sponsored work programs to modern proposals for "fair workfare."[13] These latter proposals require the state to provide payment adequate to meet basic needs in return for work, but also suggest the possibility of public-private partnerships in providing jobs. Amy Gutmann and Dennis Thompson argue in *Democracy and Disagreement* that income must be linked to a citizen's willingness to participate in society.[14] They contend that the government is obliged to provide work opportunities for the unemployed, but they also maintain that the state has no responsibility to support those able-bodied persons who still do not work because they have not fulfilled their part of the mutual obligation between the citizenry and the state.[15] Gutmann and Thompson reason, "If they choose to spend their life surfing at Malibu, they cannot reasonably expect their fellow citizens to support them."[16] Reciprocity implies as much.

These proposals for the right to work best reflect the value of reciprocity. As discussed earlier, for minimal owners to make a unilateral claim on others' property would be unreasonable because they would be demanding the product of

---

[13] Judith Shklar, *American Citizenship: The Quest for Inclusion* (Cambridge, Mass.: Harvard University Press, 1991).

[14] Amy Gutmann and Dennis Thompson, *Democracy and Disagreement* (Cambridge, Mass.: Harvard University Press, 1996).

[15] Cf. L.T. Hobhouse, *Liberalism* (New York: Oxford University Press, 1964), 86.

[16] Gutmann and Thompson, *Democracy and Disagreement* 280. The distinction between work and contribution also is relevant to the current debate over workfare. In the United States, Aid to Families with Dependent Children (AFDC) was replaced in 1996 with a new welfare program, Temporary Assistance for Needy Families (TANF). While AFDC provided welfare recipients with unconditional state aid, TANF makes aid conditional on the fulfillment of work requirements. For a detailed analysis of the distinction between AFDC and TANF, see Vee Burke, "IB93034: Welfare Reform: An Issue Overview," Congressional Research Service, March 15, 2001, available at <http://www.ncseonline.org/NLE/CRSreports/Economics/econ-107.cfm?&CFID=11461009& CFTOKEN=78975792>.

the owners' labor without exerting the effort that was necessary for its production. Thus, the minimal owners would seek to acquire property on different terms than those by which the owners originally acquired it. Such redistribution would not be defensible to all reasonable citizens, violating the value of reciprocity in a way that would seem to be based on nothing more than resentment or envy. In contrast, a demand for a right to work would ask only that all citizens share the same opportunity to acquire resources, which would allow them to make autonomous decisions about the good life. Given its parallel opportunities for property owners and those without property, therefore, the right to work is a reasonable demand acceptable to all.

A Right to In-Kind Resources to Meet Basic Needs

While the right to a job appeals to the core value of reciprocity, the idea that welfare should be distributed in a manner that ensures that the basic needs of all are met appeals to all of the three core values of autonomy, equality, and reciprocity. Before a person can live an autonomous life or regard herself as an equal citizen, her needs for shelter, food, and health care must be met. Rights fulfilling the values of autonomy and equality are worthless for the starving and homeless. Moreover, reciprocal reasoning certainly cannot justify a system in which certain individuals own property while the most basic needs of others are unmet. One prevalent way of thinking about how to meet basic needs is through the in-kind distribution of resources, such as food stamps, health insurance, and housing vouchers. Though these in-kind resources are not fungible, they give citizens the ability to meet their basic needs.

In a society whose institutions are justified by a contractual account of legitimacy, such as one that embraces the right to a job, the state would have to provide for the basic needs of those who are unable to work, whether due to injury, age, or impairments. These citizens continue to be members of democratic societies and still are subject to the duties of citizens, including those created by the right to exclude. While the right to a job and the opportunity to acquire resources that comes with it might justify exclusion to able-bodied citizens, they do not for those who cannot work; opportunities to work are meaningless for those who have no ability actually to do so. Though the reasons for exclusion based on the idea that everyone can work might be reasonably acceptable from the point of view of able-bodied citizens, therefore, they reasonably are rejected by those who cannot work. In contrast, provisions to meet basic needs through in-kind resources potentially could serve to justify the right to exclude to citizens who cannot work. Although such citizens cannot make use of the opportunities of the right to work, they can be compensated for their exclusion if the state ensures them the preconditions of autonomy. Thus, any reasonable account of "fair workfare" should ensure that the basic needs of those who cannot work are met. In this sense, the right to work and the right to in-kind benefits to meet basic needs are compatible methods of ensuring welfare rights.

A harder question concerns whether those who choose not to work despite the opportunity to do so also should be guaranteed in-kind resources to meet basic needs. I suggested the argument for rejecting the extension of this right in the previous section: property owners could eschew the right of all citizens to receive in-kind resources because this would give welfare recipients the results of labor without the parallel obligation of work. Though this is an understandable claim, I want to outline an opposing response.

Two points support why the distribution of in-kind benefits to all persons, including those who choose not to work despite the opportunity to do so, is compatable with democratic contractualism. First, citizens' right to be respected as free and equal derives directly from their status as members of democratic polities, and should not be contingent upon their participation in the workforce. Indeed, it should not depend on any particular duty of citizens. Even if individuals flout their duty to work, then, they still are entitled to have their basic needs met because any other policy would result in an underclass of citizens whose very poverty would violate their status as equals. Such a circumstance would be unacceptable in a society in which coercion is justified by appeal to all citizens' status as free and equal.

The second reason to extend in-kind welfare benefits to all is that this method can better accommodate particular individuals' reasons not to work. Among these reasons might be individuals' decision to contribute to society in ways besides working. Those activities that the market deems work are not the only ways that individuals can contribute to society. Some might choose to contribute by taking care of children or through other forms of unpaid domestic work.[17] Others might pursue art or writing despite the lack of monetary compensation.

Basic income

A proposal for implementing welfare rights through a guaranteed minimum income for all appeals more directly to the core value of autonomy than do proposals for in-kind benefits. If the previous section's argument that all citizens

---

[17] Hobhouse argues that a mother who simply cares for her children often is "doing better service to the community and [is] more worthy of pecuniary remuneration" than if she were to take a job and leave her children "to the chances of the street"; see Hobhouse, *Liberalism*, 94.

are entitled to have their basic needs met is correct, then the manner in which these needs are met should itself reflect this core value. Specifically, advocates of a basic income, or a basic stake, offer an alternative to in-kind distribution that allows citizens fungibility in how to use the resources allocated to them. Defenders of a basic income contend that in-kind resources unduly limit citizens' autonomy in deciding how to use resources to meet their life plans. For instance, while some citizens might choose to allocate a large portion of their resources to health care, others might desire to increase the standard of their housing beyond the level preferred by their fellow citizens. In contrast to in-kind distributions, basic income allows citizens autonomy in determining how best to meet their basic needs.

Additionally, the argument for basic income more directly parallels the appeal to the value of autonomy that originally justified private ownership in terms of the core values. I suggested that private ownership could be justified to property owners on the grounds that it empowered them to choose for themselves how best to use resources to pursue their particular life plans. The institution of private property thus enhances autonomy for owners in a way that centralized ownership might not. Basic income schemes can, however, also be justified with reference to autonomy because they give more citizens control of economic resources. Basic income schemes thus offer the same type of reason for exclusion from others' property as that available to property stakeholders in contemporary society. Recipients of basic income should accept owners' right to exclude them because the system of ownership as a whole respects their status as free and equal by producing wealth that is directly distributed to them in the form of basic income. In this way, basic income schemes enable the institution of private property to satisfy the value of reciprocity.

Among the proposals for distributing resources in a manner that enhances autonomy, those of Philippe Van Parijs and Carole Pateman propose an unconditional minimum basic income for all citizens.[18] Bruce Ackerman and Anne Alstott's "stakeholding" proposal suggests giving every citizen an $80,000 lump payment on her eighteenth birthday.[19] Both proposals aim to ensure basic

[18] Philippe Van Parijs, "Why Surfers Should be Fed: The Liberal Case for an Unconditional Basic Income," *Philosophy and Public Affairs* 20, no. 2 (Spring 1991): 101–31, and Carole Pateman, "Freedom and Democratization: Why Basic Income is to be Preferred to Basic Capital," in *The Ethics of Stakeholding*, ed. Keith Dowding, Jurgen De Wispelaere, and Stuart White (London: Palgrave Macmillan, 2004).

[19] Bruce Ackerman and Anne Alstott, *The Stakeholder Society* (New Haven, Conn.: Yale University Press, 1999), 4.

welfare while empowering citizens to make autonomous decisions about how best to meet their life goals.

Issues of Deliberation

In deliberations about these three proposals, several concerns arise in addition to the basic question of whether able-bodied workers should receive such benefits. One issue concerns whether income should be structured to ensure that it is not wasted at one point. The lump-sum payment, in particular, carries this risk. In contrast, an annual basic income would ensure that citizens continually had the means to meet their needs. Resolving this issue inevitably involves a tradeoff because the proposals that carry the greatest risk of waste also allow citizens the most autonomy in determining their spending across time. Citizens reasonably will disagree about where to strike the balance between these two concerns, so contractualism cannot be said to require any one particular arrangement.

Another question concerns the amount that must be provided in a basic income. On a fundamental level, citizens will differ about what counts as a basic need. Moreover, while some citizens will argue that the payment should be enough only to provide for basic needs, others will contend that it should go beyond that to allow recipients to pursue life plans beyond the most rudimentary. Again, citizens reasonably will disagree about these questions, so there is no scheme of basic income that unequivocally is the best at meeting the core values.

Given that citizens will differ about the amount that must be provided in a basic income (or the amount of benefits that must be provided in an in-kind distribution of resources), one might be tempted to conclude that the most generous approach should be implemented because it would include all of the benefits that less generous approaches would provide. This reasoning, however, overlooks another important tradeoff inherent in any policy that funds welfare programs through taxation. The increased autonomy that welfare benefits provide the least well-off comes at the price of less autonomy for property owners, whose ability to determine how to allocate their resources to pursue their life plans is hampered by taxation.

Finally, one further issue concerns how to guarantee welfare rights without bringing a stigma upon recipients. The idea that welfare is a basic right, not charity, entails that policy should be designed not to ostracize or penalize recipients. In distributions of in-kind resources, for instance, policymakers would do well to choose methods that allow recipients to remain anony-mous.[20]

My ambition in this section has not been to offer a specific policy proposal for implementing the right to welfare. Rather, I have outlined three views of how to implement this right that all are reasonable applications of the con-tractualist test and the values of public justification. Regimes that implement one version of these policies therefore could be said to offer reasonable at-tempts to guarantee welfare rights. Moreover, it is plausible to think that de-bates about implementing welfare rights would produce some hybrid view com-bining a right to work, a right to in-kind distribution of resources, and a right to income.

The three proposals I have presented all are reasonable interpretations of the right to welfare. Because all three are reasonable, I suggest in the next chapter that a democracy grounded in the value theory of democracy would not allow courts to dictate one particular proposal over any of the others; instead, the choice of a proposal and the development of a subsequent policy would occur within majoritarian institutions. The debates within these institutions should appeal to the core values in advancing policy that meets the basic welfare guar-antee.

V. OBJECTIONS

My claim that a right to welfare is a necessary condition to justify private prop-erty is open to the objection that it is overly statist. One could argue that citi-zens' needs should be met through voluntary gifts to charity in the context of free markets, not through state protection. I call this the "objection from free markets."

The objection from free markets fundamentally is about the best method for securing basic rights and, as such, does not really challenge my view. I ac-knowledge that private ownership protected by the state could lead, in many in-stances, to the guarantee of welfare rights for some citizens. Those who are em-ployed by property owners and have salaries to cover basic needs might not need help from the state. Indeed, I have acknowledged that private ownership, in contrast to a system of common ownership, likely would increase the num-

---

[20] Examples include distributing basic income through checks that are mailed to the recipients' homes, as opposed to requiring visits to a central office, and distributing food stamps through debit cards.

ber of people covered in this way. But when I considered the utilitarian claim that benefits need be secured only in the aggregate, I stressed that it is not enough even for *most* citizens to have these rights secure. Rather, these rights must be extended to *all* citizens. I do not rule out the possibility that this can be achieved best through the free market. Indeed, private contributions that secured welfare rights for all would achieve the core values better than state provision of welfare rights. In nonideal circumstances where this is not achieved, however, the state has an obligation to rectify the failure of the market. In this sense, the state's role can be understood as providing a safety net to secure basic welfare rights without requiring that in each instance the state provide welfare rights directly.

This formulation of the state as a guarantor of last resort is similar to its role in securing negative rights. For instance, property owners' right to exclude often is upheld by other individuals of their own volition, especially in stable states. In this case, the state does not secure property rights through continual threats. Rather, private persons simply acknowledge their obligation as citizens to respect the property of their fellows, such as by not trespassing. When there is a breakdown in respect for these duties, however, the state plays a role in sanctioning violators. Similarly, when private persons insure that welfare rights are provided to all through charitable contributions or the market, the state need not intervene to ensure those rights. When welfare rights are not provided for in this way, however, the state has a role in taxing and distributing resources to ensure that all citizens' welfare rights are met.

Another form of the "statist" objection appeals to concerns about the relationship between a right to welfare and autonomy. This position maintains that a state role in creating a safety net increases state power in a way that undermines the independence or autonomy of citizens. According to this objection, it would be self-defeating to make the state the guarantor of welfare rights because autonomy means independence from the state. Another way to put the point is to claim that there is a fundamental inconsistency between the enforcement of the rights to private property and to welfare. Although private property enhances autonomy, a right to welfare undermines it. I offer two responses to this view.

First, minimal owners depend on either the market or the charity of private individuals for the resources to meet their basic needs. The question, then, is not whether state-guaranteed welfare rights make citizens dependent, but whether they create greater conditions of dependence than otherwise would exist. I believe that a right to welfare could be structured in a manner that makes citizens less dependent on the government than they otherwise would be on charity or the marketplace.[21] While charity workers can stipulate conditions for those who receive benefits—religious observance, for instance—a right to welfare is ensured on the basis of one's citizenship and without requirements that infringe unreasonably on individual life choices. Compared to many charities, therefore, welfare rights give citizens more autonomy than they otherwise would have.

The right to welfare also protects citizens from a dangerous form of dependence on the market. If one is at the complete mercy of an employer for subsistence, one might have to accept degrading work assignments or deal with humiliation and harassment without complaint. In contrast, the right to welfare allows citizens to choose to work, but protects them from the economic need to accept work that is debasing, and therefore undermines their status as free and equal.

Second, regarding the claim that welfare rights increase state power, Holmes and Sunstein point out in *The Cost of Rights* that it is not obviously true that securing positive rights requires more state action than protecting negative rights. Indeed, given the number of people in prison for property-related crimes, the state perhaps is most active when enforcing the right to exclude. A large and active police force is necessary even when property rights are conceived of solely as the right to be free from intervention by the state or from other citizens. After all, the police in such a regime will need to protect the wealthy from the minimal owners. While the right to welfare might require a state agency to ensure a basic income for all, distribute in-kind resources, or guarantee the availability of work, this likely would be a bureaucracy more benign than the police. Moreover, even if one takes the perspective of those who fear any increase in state power as a loss for individual autonomy, on balance the creation of agencies to support a right to welfare could reduce the size of the state. For instance, if such agencies led to a reduction in the crime rate, as some have suggested they might, the level of state action could decrease, not increase.[22]

[21] See Michael B. Katz, *The Price of Citizenship: Redefining the American Welfare State* (New York: Metropolitan, 2001), esp. p. 348–54.

[22] That a state guarantee of the right to welfare will lead to a reduction in the crime rate arguably is implicit in Holmes and Sunstein's contention that a state guarantee of basic subsistence is necessary to provide incentives for the poor to engage in social cooperation and to obey the law; see Holmes and Sunstein, "Rightsholders as Stakeholders," in *The Cost of Rights*, 189–203. Without such voluntary self-restraint by the poor, a far larger and more powerful state would be necessary to protect property rights. For a discussion of several explanations for the relationship between a right to welfare and decreased crime, see Philippe Van Parijs, "Competing Justifications of Basic Income," in *Arguing for Basic Income: Ethical Foundations for a Radical Reform*, ed. Van Parijs (London: Verso, 1992), 35–36n45.

A third version of the free market objection argues that if citizens were provided with adequate education and health care, the market could secure basic income for all. According to this view, the empirical reason why individuals lack income in society is that they lack basic education and health care. These are the necessary conditions for playing a role in the market. Here, I offer the same response that I did to the original objection from free markets: if the free market economy can meet the basic needs of all without state intervention, then so much the better. But if it fails to do so, the state has an obligation to function as a safety net.[23]

VI. CONCLUSION

The concepts of property and welfare often are considered distinct in political theory. I have argued that although they indeed are conceptually distinct, their justifications are related. Private property is not just about a relationship between an owner and the thing that she owns. Its meaning also stems largely from the right it confers owners to exclude others from their property. Because of the coercive nature of property rights, in particular the right to exclude, these rights must be justifiable to the persons who are excluded from ownership. The best way to justify this exclusion to minimal owners is to demonstrate how it is part of a regime that also ensures that their reasonable basic interests are met. A right to welfare, therefore, is one necessary condition in the larger project of providing a democratic justification for private property. I have argued that any one of three types of welfare rights—or a combination thereof—could meet these interests.

We are now in a position to understand how Rousseau's property owner in the epigraph to this chapter can reply to the minimal owner who stands at his gates. In an earlier passage, Rousseau's hero declares: "You are lost if you forget that the fruits of the earth belong to all and the earth to no one!"[24] In response, the property owner could argue: "It is by allowing private ownership that the 'fruits of the earth' can best be cultivated and guaranteed for all."

[23] It should be noted that this objection is inconsistent with much contemporary economic thought. Many economists recognize that any given economy has some "natural rate of unemployment" that would exist even if all workers had full access to education and health care. For a discussion of this topic, see Olivier Blanchard and Lawrence F. Katz, "What We Know and Do Not Know About the Natural Rate of Unemployment," *Journal of Economic Perspectives* 11, no. 1 (Winter 1997): 51–72.

[24] Rousseau, "Discourse on the Origin of Inequality," 60.

CHAPTER 7

JUDICIAL REVIEW: BALANCING DEMOCRATIC RIGHTS AND PROCEDURES

I. INTRODUCTION

In this book I have proposed the value theory of democracy as an alternative to procedural and epistemic theories. One of the virtues of the value theory is that it resolves the problem of constraint by defending substantive rights through an appeal to citizens as addressees of law. In the previous three chapters, I made the case for a democratic account of rights to privacy and against certain forms of criminal punishment. I also argued for a democratic right to welfare as a necessary condition for legitimizing property rights. The value theory suggests that ideal democracies will protect these rights and that regimes that fail to do so rightly are criticized for falling short of the democratic ideal.

Because my emphasis in this book has been on the substantive rights protected in an ideal democracy, I have departed from many works of democratic theory by not formulating an ideal procedure. Nevertheless, the core values that ground my theory do provide useful parameters for formulating such a procedure. Ideally the procedure by which all policy is made in a democracy directly would reflect the core values. It would respect all individuals' autonomy by guaranteeing a right to participate in political discussion and to have a role in decision making. It also would respect equality of interests by granting equal voting power to all citizens. Finally, it would instantiate reciprocity through institutions that encourage reasoned debate among all citizens.

Even if we can imagine an ideal democratic procedure that reflects the core values, however, such a procedure sometimes might fail to protect the basic democratic rights I have defended: the right to privacy, the rights of criminals, and the right to welfare.[1] What is to be done in such nonideal circumstances?

---

[1] I do not claim to have formulated such a procedure in this book, but rather have focused on the distinct question of whether procedure-independent rights are an essential aspect of democratic legitimacy. My aim in this chapter is to consider, given the values that I have argued must underlie such a procedure, how to understand the conflict between a democratic procedure (whatever that might be) and democratic outcomes. See chapter 1 for a discussion of theories that attempt to

This question shifts our discussion from what is required in an ideal democracy to what the most democratic response is to nonideal circumstances. What constitutes the best democratic response given a tension between substantive democratic rights and democratic procedures? Inevitably, circumstances in which a democratic procedure produces outcomes that undermine or fail to respect basic democratic rights will result in a failure to live up to the democratic ideal, what I call a "loss to democracy." There is a loss to democracy if the decision is allowed to stand because democratic rights have been violated, and there also is a loss if the decision is overturned because this would undermine the ideal that citizens make policy through participation in democratic procedures. Thus far my thesis has been that ideal democracies recognize both procedural and substantive ideals. Now I want to explore what should be done when these ideals conflict.

The very idea that democracy comprises two ideals that sometimes can be in tension distinguishes the value theory of democracy from three rival conceptions. First, it conflicts with traditional liberal conceptions that do not perceive a tension *within* democracy but instead focus on a tension *between* democracy and a theory that constrains it. I suggested in chapter 1 that subsuming this tension within an account of democracy has the advantage of resolving the problem of constraint.

Theories that view democratic procedure as the primary value in political decision making also are at odds with the value theory's recognition of the tension between procedure and substance. I have called this type of theory "pure proceduralist." Such theories are "pure" because they suggest that any outcomes of democratic procedures (procedures that accord with the minimal conditions I outlined above) are democratically legitimate entirely by virtue of having been produced by such procedures.

Finally, "pure outcomes" theories also refuse to acknowledge a tension between substance and procedure. According to such theories, democratic procedure is merely instrumental to producing democratic outcomes. By "democratic outcomes," I mean outcomes that protect the substantive rights required by the democratic ideal, such as those I have argued for in the past three chapters. Following this line of argumentation, there is no loss to democracy when democratic procedures are overturned to ensure democratic outcomes.

Unlike both pure procedural and pure outcomes theories, the value theory responds to conflicts between democratic procedures and outcomes, acknowledging the intrinsic value of both. I argue against pure outcomes and pure pro-

---

define an ideal procedure. My arguments about rights are potentially compatible with a variety of possibly ideal procedures, although not with claims about the sufficiency of democratic procedures for democratic legitimacy.

cedural theories on the grounds that both of these views neglect crucial implications of the core values. By contrast, the value theory distinguishes itself by recognizing that there will be a loss for democracy whenever democratic procedures produce nondemocratic outcomes. The issue for those confronted with such a tension who wish to be true to the core values is how to act most democratically by minimizing the loss to democracy.

My response to this dilemma is that while there always is a loss to the democratic ideal when democratic procedures are overturned, at times the loss to democracy is greater if these procedures are not overturned. Judicial review in defense of basic democratic rights is justifiable in some of these instances, given the failure of majorities to respect these rights. On my account, a Supreme Court or Constitutional Court rightly intervenes to overturn legislation that threatens rights to privacy, which I defended in chapter 4, or rights of convicted criminals, which I defended in chapter 5. However, the combined weight of the intrinsic value of democratic procedures and pragmatic considerations about how democratic outcomes best can be achieved suggests that judicial review is not an appropriate way to implement the welfare rights I defended in chapter 6, although it might be appropriate for courts to acknowledge their existence.[2]

I began this book by discussing the recent Supreme Court decision in *Lawrence v. Texas,* in which the Court struck down legislation that outlawed gay sex on the grounds that this legislation violated the right to privacy. Later, I developed a partial response to the concern that the Court acts undemocratically when it strikes down legislation that threatens basic rights such as privacy. I also suggested that substantive rights like privacy are necessary aspects of an ideal democracy. In this chapter, I take the argument one step further by defending judicial review as a democratic response to procedural failures to protect certain democratic rights. The Court's doctrine of substantive due process thus is defensible on the grounds that there are substantive rights essential to the ideal of self-government.

Justice Tension's Dilemma

In order to highlight the advantages of a theory of democracy that embraces the tension between substance and procedure, it is helpful to consider a hypothet-

---

[2]The idea of nonjustifiable welfare rights is prominent in international law. The International Covenant on Economic, Social and Cultural Rights, for instance, proposes a robust set of welfare rights as aspirations but does not provide for their judicial enforcement. U.N. General Assembly, "International Covenant on Economic, Social and Cultural Rights," adopted by General Assembly resolution 2200A (XXI) of December 16, 1966; text available at <http://www.unhchr.ch/html/menu3/b/a_cescr.htm>.

ical example. This example will introduce some of the key issues to be explored in the rest of this chapter. Justice Tension is a democratic theorist who finds herself on the Supreme Court of a country that has both judicial review and a national plebiscite system. In such a plebiscite, procedural rights of participation (including deliberative rights) are guaranteed for all adults in the entire polity, and the procedure dictates that a majority of eligible voters can make politically binding decisions on matters of public importance. Justice Tension is confronted with the question of whether she should strike down a plebiscite.[3] Her concern solely is to determine whether striking down the plebiscite would be the right decision from the standpoint of democracy.

Justice Tension finds herself on the bench with two other justices named Justice Process and Justice Results. Both think that they can answer this question a priori. Justice Process offers the following argument: "The people have already spoken. If we are going to make a democratic decision, it demands letting people determine for themselves what is right. The best way to do this is to maximize the number of opinions taken into account and then to let the outcome stand. Any intervention on our part is a loss to democracy."

Justice Tension's other colleague, Justice Results, counters: "Democracy fundamentally is about certain core values underlying self-government. We should ask whether the plebiscite's outcome undermines these values. If it does, we should strike it down—not on our own behalf, but in the name of democracy."

My view is that both Justice Process's statement (an example of pure proceduralism) and Justice Results's statement (an example of pure democratic outcomes theory) suffer from the same flaw. Before they look at any particular case and the specific democratic right at issue, both Justices know what their primary concerns will be. For Justice Process the question of whether the plebiscite is democratic depends entirely on whether the majoritarian procedure was followed. For Justice Results the issue entirely is whether the outcome supports core democratic values; the procedure used to determine the outcome is irrelevant.

Although her fellow justices would advise otherwise, I think Justice Tension should consider carefully the details of the case and the democratic right at issue, from the perspectives of both procedure and outcome, before making up her mind. If the outcome is ratified by the national plebiscite system, there is reason to think it has some democratic weight. I argue in section II, below, that the very fact that actual persons have made a decision has weight democratically because one aspect of political autonomy demands deference to actual persons' decisions. If such a decision affirms the core values of democracy and the

---

[3] Again, this hypothetical is meant to illustrate the tension between democratic procedures and democratic outcomes. I turn from an application of this hypothetical to the American case of judicial review in a later section.

status of all citizens as free and equal, then all the better for democracy. But, as I will discuss in section III, a dilemma arises if the outcome of this decision undermines the core values. When a democratic procedure fundamentally threatens citizens' democratic status, there is a loss to democracy. This is a problem for Justice Tension because the result is a tension internal to democracy between substantive and procedural implications of the core values. Here the advice of both Justice Process and Justice Results is unhelpful. Justice Tension is left with a choice that requires her to determine which decision least harms democracy by balancing the intrinsic weights of democratic procedures and democratic rights that both reflect the core values and are central to the ideal of self-government. Although taking this approach makes her job more difficult than that of her colleagues, it allows her to be more transparent about the inevitable value conflicts that occur within a democracy.

For the purposes of this discussion, I stipulate that Justice Process correctly claims that his country's majoritarian plebiscite is a paradigmatic democratic procedure. I do not attempt to argue, however, that such plebiscites are the only truly democratic procedures, or that representative democracy is not an instance of self-government. Debates about the best democratic procedure long have had a central place in democratic theory, and my aim is not to resolve them. Rather, I want to begin with the more limited claim that majoritarian procedures in which citizens deliberate about how best to implement the core values are one example of a democratic procedure. I take this to be the case because majoritarianism as a means of decision making is widely regarded as an essential aspect of democratic legitimacy. This procedure is stipulated as paradigmatically democratic to serve the main focus of this chapter, namely, to highlight the tension between procedural and outcomes-based views of democracy.[4]

II. The Limits of a Pure Outcomes-Based Theory

Since I contend that some substantive outcomes must be protected in a legitimate democratic polity, it might seem at first glance that my position is the same as Justice Results's. After all, one might think that any theory embracing the notion that democracy requires substantive constraints must see procedure as merely instrumental to certain outcomes. (In the cases of both Justice Re-

---

[4] I suggested previously that contractualism itself, while a good account of justifying democratic rights, should not be taken literally as a democratic procedure because it would both be conservative in its defense of the status quo and unworkable given its allowance for individual veto power. See Estlund, "The Democracy/Contractualism Analogy," 397–99.

sults and the value theory, the desired outcomes are those that protect the core values.) If this were the case, Justice Results would be right to claim that Justice Tension's first concern should be to promote good outcomes consistent with both the core values and the democratic rights they demand. The value of any particular procedure would depend entirely on whether it promoted these particular outcomes. To the extent that majoritarian procedures violate the core values, they could be written off as undemocratic. By elaborating on why Justice Results's view ignores the importance of democratic procedures, however, I hope to distinguish my own account from hers.

One theoretical defense of Justice Results's view is developed by Ronald Dworkin. He argues that since the meaning of democracy depends fundamentally on the idea that citizens have equal status, the sole question in assessing a policy's democratic legitimacy is whether it protects or undermines this status. In instances in which judicial review overrides either the decision of the legislature or a plebiscite, there is, in his words, "no moral cost" to democracy. No citizen is "worse off" from the standpoint of democracy.[5]

Dworkin would wholeheartedly endorse Justice Results's solution to the legal dilemma. Justice Tension should have no qualms about overriding a majority decision when a majority enacts an undemocratic outcome. This could take place if most voters are indifferent to the idea of a democratic outcome that reflects equal status. An override also might be necessary if voters attempt to enact policy that respects equal status but fail to do so. Since institutional structures in a democracy are designed to "produce the best answers to the essentially moral question of what the democratic conditions actually are," Justice Tension acts democratically when she is sure that she can produce a democratic outcome better than a majority of citizens.[6]

[5] Dworkin, *Freedom's Law*, 32. For Dworkin, this entails that democratic outcomes have three characteristics. In his words: "A political community cannot count anyone as a moral member unless it gives that person a part in any collective decision, a stake in it, and independence from it" (ibid., 24). For Dworkin a "part" means that there is room for democratic participation in community and that participants have a chance to affect the outcome of decision making. In this category Dworkin includes speech rights as well as the right to vote in elections. A "stake" means that decisions that are made through democratic processes must ultimately recognize each citizen's status as an equal member. Wealth, for instance, must be distributed consistently with the recognition of this status. Finally, Dworkin suggests that it is essential that each member of the community have some independence from it. To use his metaphor: while members of an orchestra must adopt a single musical interpretation while working together under the direction of a conductor, they must also have the space to develop their own musical tastes; see ibid., 25. Waldron considers Dworkin's position when majoritarian legislation is struck down by courts: "Is there a loss to democracy? The answer, Dworkin says, depends entirely on whether the court makes the right decision" (Waldron, *Law and Disagreement*, 291). I agree with Waldron's analysis of Dworkin but resist the alternative he draws.

[6] Dworkin, *Freedom's Law*, 34.

The merit of the pure outcomes view lies in its recognition that any evaluation of the degree to which a policy outcome is democratic must make reference to democratic values. For Dworkin, the primary democratic value is the equal status of citizens. I agree with Dworkin that democratic procedures at times can undermine this value, as well as others such as political autonomy, that are essential to the meaning of self-rule. In such cases, there is a loss to democracy. An exclusive focus on outcomes, however, neglects the intrinsic democratic value of majoritarian procedures. The core value of political autonomy requires that actual persons have a role in deciding which laws will govern them. This value should be protected on democratic grounds, in part by striking down legislation that threatens the very rights that allow citizens to make autonomous personal decisions. But the value of autonomy also is realized through political rights that allow individuals to participate in policymaking. At minimum, majority affirmation of a good democratic outcome enhances its value, but Justice Results's view and other pure outcomes-based views neglect the intrinsic worth of individual participation in favor of what I regard as an excessive focus on democratic outcomes. These views are too strong in that they fail to recognize that there is a loss to democracy every time a nonmajoritarian institution is needed to protect substantive democratic rights.

The importance of democratic procedure, like the importance of democratic outcomes, is based on the core values of democracy. Democratic procedures that allow the citizenry as a whole to participate in democratic decision making give legitimacy to the procedural aspect of autonomy I identified in chapter 1. Specifically, such procedures include structures that enhance deliberation and participation.

The importance of actual participation by persons in a majoritarian procedure is demonstrated best by comparing the ideal circumstances of democracy, in which majorities affirm democratic outcomes, to those present in Justice Tension's dilemma. In her particular case, Justice Tension must decide whether to overturn a bad democratic outcome. From the standpoint of democracy, it is better when a majority does not make a mistake. Democracy is at its most ideal, according to the value theory, when a democratic procedure produces the democratic outcomes required by the core values.

Ronald Dworkin's analysis of a 1989 flag-burning case demonstrates how pure outcomes theories fail to acknowledge that democratic procedure can add even the slightest amount of legitimacy to a political decision. In *Texas v. Johnson* the Court considered whether the First Amendment required a judicial override of a Texas law prohibiting citizens from burning the American flag.[7]

---

[7] 491 U.S. 397 (1989).

The Court reasoned that because the Texas law restricted politically symbolic speech, the First Amendment required them to strike it down. In Dworkin's view, such a decision was only a gain for democracy. In his words:

> No one's power to participate in a self-governing community has been worsened, because everyone's power in that respect has been improved. No one's equality has been compromised, because equality, in the only pertinent sense, has been strengthened. No one has been cheated of the ethical advantages of a role in principled deliberation if he or she had a chance to participate in the public discussion about whether the decision was right.[8]

For the purpose of argument, let us stipulate that an outcome like the one Dworkin defends—one that protects free speech—manifests the core democratic value of political autonomy. Given that a variety of procedures could have produced this outcome, surely it would have had added legitimacy if a plebiscite rather than a court had secured it or, indeed, if the Texas legislature never had passed the law restricting free speech in the first place.

Specifically, the added legitimacy that comes when majorities affirm good democratic outcomes, for instance through a plebiscite, is that persons actually endorse, or some would say ratify, the core values of democracy. This reflects the core value of political autonomy in two senses. First, autonomy is reflected through the participation of persons in policymaking. If persons in a democracy have the status of rulers, there should be some merit to considering what they actually think when it comes to ruling. The core value of autonomy demands respect for citizen's capacity to rule, and actual persons' decisions embody this capacity. Second, the core value of autonomy is reflected in an outcome that affirms autonomy itself—the very value that justifies persons' participation in the first place. In the previous quotation, Dworkin claims that no individuals were "cheated" out of a chance to participate because, regardless of the Court's decision, they were able to participate in "public discussion." Dworkin, however, fails to recognize that autonomy would have been enhanced if political participation had involved ratifying a decision that was right from the standpoint of democracy. In his rush to support the right to free speech as a central democratic outcome, Dworkin actually undercuts the democratic value that is upheld when democratic procedures affirm this right.

The added significance that comes with a majority's or supramajority's affirmation of the core values indicates that procedure has some intrinsic worth. Specifically, the intrinsic value of procedure is located in its relationship to a core democratic right. Following Jeremy Waldron, I call this the "right

[8] Dworkin, *Freedom's Law*, 32.

143

to participate."[9] Like democratic rights that are substantive and therefore limit outcomes, it is a direct manifestation of the core values of political autonomy and equality. When citizens participate in political decision making, they exercise their autonomy by the very act of making a decision. Their equality is recognized when their vote is regarded as equal to all of their fellow citizens' votes.[10]

The intrinsic importance of democratic outcomes and procedures explains why these two aspects of democracy rightly are balanced. When majorities undermine the very values of democracy that give rise to their right to participate and decide, they rightly are regarded as having, on balance, acted undemocratically. Occasionally, the threat to the core values is so extreme that it calls for a correction. Any democratic correction results in some loss to democracy. This is why Justice Results's approach to judicial review cannot be sustained. It is too cavalier in evaluating only outcomes and ignoring the processes by which they are reached. The very fact that a majority makes a decision gives it weight from the standpoint of the core democratic values.

Alon Harel defends the pure outcomes theory and the "no loss" thesis on the grounds that the Court actually is making citizens live up to their deepest convictions when it enforces a democratic outcome.[11] Since citizens embrace the core values of democracy, Harel suggests that in some sense they actually participate in judicial overrides because these overrides ensure that their deepest convictions are enacted at the policy level. I believe that Harel makes a mistake similar to that made by Rousseau, however, in failing to distinguish between the values and policies essential to democracy that citizens *should* accept and those values and policies that they *do* accept. Some actual persons reject the core values, and a good democratic theory should not mistakenly claim that such persons really will or participate in the right democratic outcomes. Rather, recognizing that democracy is about core values sometimes requires overriding individuals' beliefs when they deeply threaten these values. In such circumstances, there is a loss to the democratic ideal. When a polity produces good democratic outcomes through democratic procedure, it ratifies the core values of democracy at the same time that persons exercise the right to participate. Such instances should be celebrated as gains for democracy.

In this section, I have explained why the notion that democracy requires the protection of individual rights is consistent with recognizing an intrinsic value

[9] Waldron, *Law and Disagreement*, 232.

[10] See "Participation: The Right of Rights" in ibid., 232–54, for the capacity argument: "The attribution of any right, I said, is typically an act of faith in the agency and capacity for moral thinking of each of the individuals concerned" (250).

[11] Alon Harel, "Rights-Based Judicial Review: A Democratic Justification," *Law and Philosophy* 22, nos. 3–4 (July 2003): 247–76.

to participation in majoritarian procedures. In the next section I consider pure proceduralism, which holds that these two claims are incompatible. This position, I argue, has a flaw similar to that of pure outcomes-based theories.

III. The Failure of Pure Procedural Theories

I have stipulated that majoritarian procedures plausibly are a part of a legitimate democratic state because they reflect the core values. Both pure proceduralism and my theory suggest that collective self-government calls for citizens to be granted equal status in their right to make decisions. Both theories also argue that the value of political autonomy is enhanced when majoritarian procedures actually result in an enacted policy that is not overturned. Justice Process's view, however, endorses majoritarianism as a sufficient condition for democratic legitimacy, not merely a necessary one. Thus, it is a pure procedural theory. Justice Process contends that majoritarianism must serve not only as democracy's core principle but also as its only principle in political decision making. Such pure proceduralists believe that courts should defer to majorities even when they make incorrect or unjust decisions. In our example, Justice Process thus concludes that judicial review is not merely a loss to democracy but incompatible with it. He holds that nonmajoritarian decisions violate the right to participate and therefore are incompatible with recognizing the intrinsic value of majoritarianism.

To some degree, these arguments are consistent with my case against pure outcomes-based theories. The conclusion, however, that any instance of judicial review is a loss to democracy is flawed in the same way that pure outcomes-based theories are. A pure procedural theory, which claims that whatever outcomes result from a majority vote are democratic, fails to recognize that some of these outcomes could undermine core values of democracy. The core values reflect the status of a people as self-rulers. They thus justify the very right to participate upon which majoritarian procedures are based. For instance, when these procedures produce outcomes that disenfranchise part of the citizenry, not only are the core values undermined, but the right to participate itself also is undermined. Such an outcome clearly would be a loss to democracy.

The core values also can be undermined when democratic rights other than the right to participate are attacked. Some of these rights might be regarded as preconditions of democracy. For instance, many democratic theorists have argued that restrictions on free speech would detract from citizens' ability to formulate well-developed democratic opinions and would cut off access to the information—factual and moral—needed for a good democratic decision. Thus, outcomes of majoritarian procedures that undermine speech rightly are regarded as losses to democracy. Equally harmful are attacks on substantive rights derived from the core values that justifiably limit state coercion. For instance, I argue in chapter 4 that laws violating democratically justifiable privacy, such as restrictions on whom one can marry or with whom one can engage in sexual relations, are examples of substantive rather than procedural attacks on the core values of democracy.

Ultimately, my concern is to show that attacks on such rights so undermine the core values of democracy that majoritarian procedures sometimes should be overturned to protect them. Before I make this argument, however, one which clearly is in tension with the pure procedural view, I want to make a less ambitious point. As I stated, the pure proceduralist not only rejects judicial review but also fails to recognize that violations of rights required by the core values can ever be losses to democracy. In the same way that Dworkin fails to recognize how a majoritarian procedure that affirms good democratic outcomes enhances democratic legitimacy, the pure proceduralist cannot acknowledge that unreasonable violations of the core values by majorities are worse, from a democratic standpoint, than affirmation of these values by majorities.[12] The problem with pure procedural views, including majoritarianism, is not that they identify the value of participation as central to democracy, but that they exaggerate the importance of participation by failing to give any weight to democratic outcomes.

So far in this chapter, I have shown the problems with purely procedure-based and purely outcomes-based theories of democracy. In particular, I have suggested that both procedure and outcomes deserve weight in accord with their case-by-case impact on the core values. Both procedural and outcomes theorists can respond to this account by amending their theories. Procedural theorists can recognize that outcomes have weight, but never more weight than the procedures themselves. Similarly, outcomes theorists can recognize that procedures have weight, but never more than outcomes. I reject these amended positions in the next section.

IV. Impure Procedural and Outcomes-based Theories

Even if one rejects purely outcomes-based or purely procedure-based theories of democracy, the question remains of how best to make a democratic decision

---

[12] There is some ambiguity about whether Jeremy Waldron holds a pure procedural view or the impure view I sketch in the next section. Although he defends democratic procedures as the exclusive implication of the capacity to decide, he does not deny that there is a loss to democracy when procedures undermine the capacity to decide; see Waldron, *Law and Disagreement*.

when majoritarian procedures produce bad democratic outcomes. One can recognize that there inevitably is a loss to democracy in such a circumstance. But the democratic theorist's task is to offer an explanation of how to minimize this loss. To illustrate, consider an instance of Justice Tension's dilemma. I suggested in chapter 2 that free speech is a paradigmatic democratic right, and I examined earlier in this chapter Dworkin's argument that the decision to restrict flag burning inevitably violates that right, regardless of how it is made. If Justice Tension is confronted with legislation that restricts democratic free speech, she cannot avoid a loss to democracy. A decision to uphold the restriction would harm democracy because the legislation would produce a bad democratic outcome. On the other hand, Justice Tension would undermine the right to participate were she to strike down the legislation. Accordingly, the question for Justice Tension is not how to avoid a loss to democracy but how to minimize this loss.

Both Justice Process's and Justice Results's views can be reconstructed to recognize that there will be a loss regardless of how Justice Tension decides. They could agree that although both outcomes and procedures matter, the democratic theorist always must prioritize one of these two aspects of democracy when they conflict. Justice Process could claim that majoritarian procedures always are more fundamentally important from the standpoint of democracy than any loss to the core values that results from bad democratic outcomes. Therefore, he could argue that the right to participate in majoritarian procedures always should be upheld. At the same time, Justice Results could argue that although there is a loss to democracy when majoritarian positions are overturned, the need to protect against bad democratic outcomes is more fundamental than the right to participate. On these grounds, she could retain her position that majoritarian procedures always should be overturned when they result in outcomes that at all negatively impact democratic values. Since this version of Justice Results's view gives weight to an intrinsic value of procedure but never dispositive weight, it follows that any bad democratic outcome would be reason to overturn a majoritarian procedure.[13]

Justice Process's reconstructed view is impure in that it admits that outcomes can have moral weight according to the core values, yet retains his commitment to proceduralism by refusing to allow for instances in which bad outcomes require overturning majoritarian procedures.[14] Similarly, Justice Results's reconstructed view is tainted because it admits that majoritarian procedures have

---

[13] Arguably, thinkers such as David Estlund and Ronald Dworkin also deny that democratic procedures have any dispositive intrinsic weight; see Estlund, *Democratic Authority,* and Dworkin, *Freedom's Law.*

[14] By "moral weight," I mean significance, but this does not mean that anything that has moral weight will be cause for a particular decision. In this sense, moral weight is *pro tanto.*

moral weight according to the core values, yet retains its commitment to democratic outcomes by refusing to admit that they ever can be trumped by a concern for majoritarian procedure. The problem here is that Justice Results's view cannot explain why participation could trump undemocratic outcomes, even when the outcomes represent a trivial loss to democracy. Certain zoning restrictions might fit this description. One could argue that a law prohibiting holiday lights of a certain brightness inhibits one's autonomy and freedom of expression and thus constitutes an undemocratic outcome. If one thinks majoritarian zoning decisions negatively impact the core value of autonomy, then they always will require an override according to the impure outcomes-based theory. This example suggests why the impure outcomes-based theory insufficiently values the intrinsic merit of majoritarian procedures.

Less trivial examples also highlight why impure outcomes-based views do not give enough weight to the intrinsic merit of majoritarian procedures. In chapter 6, I argued that certain welfare rights were necessary to an ideal democracy. However, there is still the question of whether majoritarian procedures that fail to guarantee these rights should be overturned. Given reasonable disagreement about how best to secure welfare rights, the intrinsic value of majoritarian procedures might be reason enough not to overturn legislation that fails to guarantee these rights. Moreover, much literature suggests that if courts were to attempt to instantiate these rights, they would undermine further legislative enactment of them.[15] Although welfare rights might be necessary to democratic legitimacy, the judiciary, given the economic complexity of this process, might do better to leave their implementation to legislators. The impure outcomes-based theory cannot, however, concede that majoritarian policy should be allowed to stand although it violates democratic rights.

These impure accounts of procedural and outcomes-based theories have similar flaws to their pure versions. The problem is that these theories already admit that the core values of democracy can be manifested within both procedures and outcomes. This clearly recognizes that both outcomes and procedures have some weight. Unless these theorists fall back upon a pure procedural or outcomes-based view, this recognition undermines the claim that the decision should be made solely on the basis of whether it is majoritarian or results in a democratic outcome. At a minimum, these two impure theories should leave open the possibility that in a particular instance, either outcomes or procedures might be more decisive in light of the core values; however, they do not.

In contrast to these impure theories, my account not only accords moral

---

[15] For a good discussion of non-court-enforced welfare rights, see Mark Tushnet, "Social Welfare Rights and the Forms of Judicial Review," *Texas Law Review* 82, no. 7 (June 2004): 1895–920.

weight to both procedure and outcomes, but also allows for the possibility that in any given case, a balance might need to be struck either in favor of a particular majoritarian procedure or in defense of a democratic outcome. The pure procedural theory, while perhaps wrong, nonetheless is internally consistent in denying any moral weight to outcomes and in repudiating the notion that the protection of basic democratic rights could necessitate overriding a procedure. A similar point holds for the pure outcomes view. If, however, an outcome can have weight because it affects the core values, the most theoretically plausible view (barring additional argument) would leave open the possibility that this weight might be enough to require an override of democratic procedure. It also would allow for the opposite possibility: in a case where the outcome insufficiently threatens the core values, the most democratic decision would be the one resulting from democratic procedure.

At this point critics might object that I have abandoned the chief virtue of both the pure procedural and pure outcomes-based views. Those accounts offer a simple way of determining whether a decision is democratic. One claims that we should look to procedures, the other to outcomes. In contrast, my view leaves us only with the assertion that we need to balance the two. But ease of decision making is not the chief virtue in normative political theory. The evaluation of what is the most democratic decision inevitably involves balancing democratic values. Moreover, transparency about value conflicts should count as a virtue. These conflicts between values should not be ignored for simplicity's sake.

A strategy for balancing democratic outcomes and procedure can be found in the Supreme Court's current approach to judicial review. Although the Court does not couch it in democratic terms, the approach offers a model for balancing majoritarian procedures with individual rights and can help answer the challenge that balancing democratic outcomes and majoritarian procedures is impractical. The Court's practice is to regard legislation passed through legitimate procedures as presumptively valid. If there is a "rational purpose" to a law, which primarily means that it is not based in animus, the Court assumes it is valid when all procedures that are necessary to legal enactment have been followed. However, when legislation implicates basic rights—for example, a law that potentially threatens privacy—the Court presumes it is invalid. Here the burden is on the defenders of the law to show a "compelling interest" in overcoming this presumption and allowing the law to stand. Similarly, justices in Tension's position can recognize the right to participate by presuming that majority-affirmed legislation is valid on democratic grounds. But when majoritarian procedure violates a democratic right, the right can be given weight by presuming the legislation invalid.

V. The Flaws with Formal Democratic Arguments and the Need for Examples in a Theory of Democracy

In the previous sections, I demonstrated the limitations of a purely procedural or purely outcomes-based theory. The following table helps to elucidate my claims. Each of the four quadrants represents a possible scenario if a legislative enactment is left to stand or overridden by the courts. I sort such enactments according to whether they have been passed by a majoritarian procedure and enacted into law (quadrants 1 and 2) or overridden by courts and thus struck down (quadrants 3 and 4). This latter process not only is nonmajoritarian but countermajoritarian, in that it happens after a majoritarian institution has authorized a particular law. While decisions are grouped by their procedure, they also are grouped by whether their content would constitute a democratic outcome. As I have done throughout this book, I classify democratic outcomes as those that manifest the core values of democracy and nondemocratic outcomes as those that undermine these values.

Both the pure procedural and pure outcomes-based accounts of democracy suggest that a political decision's democratic legitimacy depends entirely on which quadrant it falls into. I suggest in the remainder of this section that this characteristic makes both theories too formal. For instance, the question of whether a decision is democratic in the pure procedural theory depends entirely on whether it falls in quadrants 1 or 2, in which case it is democratic, or in quadrants 3 or 4, in which case it is not. The problem with this theory is that it

Table 1

Procedure vs. Outcomes in Political Decision Making

	Democratic Outcome	*Non-Democratic Outcome*
Majoritarian Plebiscite	1. Majorities ratify democratic outcome. Core values reflected in both procedure and outcome.	2. Majorities produce outcome that violates core democratic values. Core values reflected in procedure but not outcome.
Countermajoritarian Plebiscite Overruled	3. Plebiscite overruled to prevent outcome that undermines core values. Core values undermined in procedure, but reflected in final outcome.	4. Plebiscite overruled for bad democratic reasons. Both procedure and outcome undermine the core values.

cannot account for the differences in democratic legitimacy between examples that fit quadrant 1 and those that fit quadrant 2, and similarly between examples fitting quadrants 3 and 4. Specifically, I argued against the pure procedural theory that instances in which majoritarian plebiscites affirm core democratic values are more democratic than instances in which a majority undermines the core values. Quadrant 1 thus represents a more democratic scenario than quadrant 2. Furthermore, the pure proceduralist cannot account for the difference between instances in which a plebiscite is overruled for good democratic reasons and instances in which it is overruled for bad democratic reasons. The pure procedural theory thus cannot account for distinctions between democratic legitimacy in quadrants 3 and 4.

Pure outcomes-based theories face a similar problem because they cannot account for the loss to democracy that occurs when a court is needed to ensure a democratic outcome. On this account, the question of whether a decision is democratic depends entirely on whether it is in quadrants 1 or 3, in which case it is democratic, or quadrants 2 or 4, in which case it is not. The pure outcomes-based theory therefore cannot distinguish between examples that fit quadrants 1 and 3.

The table also reveals limitations on the more sophisticated impure variants of both procedural and outcomes-based theories. The impure procedure-based theory cannot acknowledge that in some instances, the impact of a bad democratic outcome could be so great that it would require overriding a plebiscite. In terms of the table, even this impure theory fails to recognize that a decision in quadrant 3 may be more democratic than a decision in quadrant 2. For example, the impure theory denies that a judicial override of so-called miscegenation laws is democratic. Similarly, the impure outcomes-based theory cannot recognize that decisions that negatively impact the core values sometimes should not be overturned because majorities deserve some deference. The impure theory cannot recognize that quadrant 2 decisions sometimes are more democratic than quadrant 3 decisions. As I reasoned earlier, the impure outcomes-based theory always would require an override of majoritarian zoning ordinances that restrict holiday lighting if they were judged to impact negatively the core value of autonomy.

Thus far I have discussed a hypothetical example in which a jurist and democratic theorist, Justice Tension, must decide whether striking down a majoritarian plebiscite would, on balance, be the most democratic decision. The simplicity of this hypothetical example helps explain why both majoritarian procedures and the protection of certain rights have democratic weight. But the conflicts within actual institutions in the United States do not directly match Justice Tension's dilemma of whether to strike down a plebiscite. Congress, for instance, is not equivalent to a plebiscite, although the right to participate is used to select representatives. Rather, Congress is a representative institution that only sometimes reflects the actual views of persons within the polity. At the same time, while the Court sometimes acts counter to the majority of persons' actual views, it, too, can be defended as a representative institution.[16] This observation can be linked in part to the fact that justices must be confirmed by the Senate, a representative body.

In the last part of this section, I draw on actual Supreme Court cases to demonstrate the complications that arise in applying Justice Tension's hypothetical dilemma and the democratic solution I have crafted to actual institutions. While the Court sometimes acts in a countermajoritarian way to preserve the core values, at times it also protects rights of participation necessary for majoritarian procedures. As I have argued, the Court rightfully protects majoritarian decision making when such decisions do not threaten basic democratic rights. Therefore, the Court can act democratically in two ways. At times it strikes the balance between procedural and substantive values in favor of individual rights, and at times it protects majoritarian decision making in the name of democracy.

To illustrate how the Supreme Court can act democratically by overriding majoritarian decision making, one need only look to the case of *Loving v. Virginia*.[17] Here, the Supreme Court overturned legislation endorsed by a majority of Virginians that prohibited interracial marriage. The Court argued that this prohibition undermined the substantive due process right to make autonomous individual decisions in intimate matters. It also argued that the law violated the right of citizens to equal protection. I argued in chapter 4 that privacy is an important democratic right required by the core values. Indeed, given that the right to privacy is fundamental to one's status as a citizen, the loss to democracy is minimized by overturning laws that violate this right. In this case, judicial review preserves a basic democratic right. The Court's appeal to substantive due process in striking down the Virginia law can be understood as a reference to the core value of autonomy, while the appeal to equal protection can be understood in terms of the core value of equality of interests.

The Virginia law's threat to these core values was more significant to the status of democratic citizens than any particular right to participate. The law undermined the value of autonomy by unreasonably limiting one of the most important decisions in a person's life, thus demeaning any other decisions a person might make. It directly violated the value of equality by giving legal sanction to

---

[16] Christopher L. Eisgruber, *Constitutional Self-Government* (Cambridge, Mass.: Harvard University Press, 2001), 48.

[17] 388 U.S. 1 (1967).

racial bigotry. Finally, it undermined the value of reciprocity by limiting citizens' ability legally to recognize each other's marriages and thus denying public recognition of their autonomous decision making.

The general point suggested by *Loving* is that legislative bodies can act undemocratically even when they enact the will of the majority of their constituents if their policies threaten the core democratic values. Thus, countermajoritarian institutions, such as courts, act in a democratically legitimate manner when they strike down such laws. Courts also can be understood to act democratically when they limit certain types of cruel and unusual punishment—punishments that, I have argued, are incompatible with the democratic ideal for treating criminals as citizens. I have used the American case as one example, but it extends to other cases of countermajoritarian judicial review; my point, however, concerns the ideal of democracy and is not limited to a claim about democracy in one constitutional culture. Constitutional courts act not only legally, but also democratically, when they strike down legislation that threatens democratic values. For instance, my arguments in chapter 4 suggest a possible democratic defense of the Constitutional Court of South Africa's decision to extend the right to marry to gay couples despite widespread public opposition.[18] Moreover, the Constitutional Court of South Africa's decision in *State v. Makwanyane* that capital punishment is unconstitutional is defensible not only because the practice is widely condemned by the population, but also because it is incompatible with the core values of democracy.[19]

Judicial review also can be used for nondemocratic purposes, however. The Supreme Court acts undemocratically when it strikes down popular legislation that does not threaten the core values of democracy. In *Lochner v. New York*, the Court overturned popular legislation that limited the hours of bakers.[20] It did so in the face of a movement among a majority of persons to increase the autonomy of workers by ensuring some room to have a life outside of work. The Court acted undemocratically in two senses. First, there was a loss to democracy insofar as the Court invalidated a majoritarian decision. In this sense, its action was similar to that in *Loving*. But the Court's decision here also was undemocratic in a way that *Loving* was not; namely, it undermined, rather than promoted, the core values of democracy. In chapter 6, I argued that democracies that protect property also should require basic rights to welfare. The pieces of legislation at issue in *Lochner* and its progeny were part of a general attempt to guarantee rights to basic welfare and to secure a decent economic minimum for all workers. The decisions of the *Lochner* era, therefore, can be understood as

[18] "South Africa's Top Court Blesses Gay Marriage," *Washington Post*, December 2, 2005.
[19] 1995 (6) BCLR 665 (CC).
[20] 198 U.S. 45 (1905).

153

judicial attempts to undermine majoritarian institutions' ambitions to secure the basic welfare rights that I argued are essential to ideal democracies.

The *Lochner* era often is used as an example of the danger of judicial review and its potential to undermine welfare rights. But on my account, the *Lochner* Court can be criticized because it undermined democratic outcomes, not because there is something inherently wrong with judicial review. The general point is that countermajoritarian institutions are illegitimate when they use their power to act against the core democratic values. The Court acts most illegitimately when it strikes down democratic procedures that aim toward advancing these rights. The danger seems acute in the American case because of the Court's history of illegitimate action in the early twentieth century. The South African Constitution's explicit appeal to welfare rights would seem to preempt Lochner-type decisions.[21] But of course in any constitutional regime, including South Africa, the danger still exists that courts will exercise judicial review in a way that undermines basic democratic rights.

One implication of the welfare rights I argued for in the previous chapter is that *Lochner* and its progeny are illegitimate instances of judicial review. A distinct question, however, is raised by certain postapartheid litigation in South Africa that suggests that constitutional courts should play an active role in guaranteeing citizens' basic welfare rights.[22] This litigation echoes theoretical arguments popular in the United States of the 1970s.[23] In the case of South Africa, the fact that welfare rights are enshrined in its constitution suggests that its courts have a role to play in these matters. There is reason, however, to think that courts generally do not offer the best means to secure basic welfare rights despite my argument that these rights are essential to ideal democracies. As I argued in the previous section, judicial review should not override democratic procedures on the grounds that they fail to provide basic welfare given the significant empirical controversy about how best to secure welfare rights. In other words, despite *Lochner*'s illegitimacy as a quadrant 4 decision, legislative failures to secure welfare rights might be understood best as quadrant 2 decisions that are not rightly overturned by the courts.

[21] For a discussion of welfare rights and South African constitutionalism, see Patrick Lenta, "Democracy, Rights Disagreements and Judicial Review" *South African Journal on Human Rights* 20, no. 1 (2004): 1–31.

[22] For example, the Constitutional Court of South Africa has ruled that welfare rights, such as a right to housing, are justiciable. See *Minister of Public Works and Others v. Kyalami Ridge Environmental Association and Others* 2001 (7) BCLR 652 (CC).

[23] Frank Michelman, "The Supreme Court, 1968 Term—Foreword: On Protecting the Poor through the Fourteenth Amendment," *Harvard Law Review* 83 (1969): 7–59. See also idem, "Welfare Rights in a Constitutional Democracy," *Washington University Law Quarterly* (1979): 659–93.

In *Loving* the Court struck down legislation on grounds that could have been expressed in democratic terms because legislation prohibiting interracial marriage is a fundamentally antidemocratic outcome. Sometimes, however, the Court acts democratically by protecting democratic procedures instead of substantive democratic rights. In these cases the Court should oppose state legislatures and Congress to affirm citizens' procedural right to participate. This is what takes place when the Court strikes down legislation that undermines the principle of "one person, one vote."[24] In contrast to instances in which the Court acts democratically by striking down majoritarian procedures, here the role of the Court is democratic because it defends democratic procedural guarantees.

A more complicated question concerns the relationship between representative institutions, the Supreme Court, and the right to participate. For example, consider the dilemma that the Court has faced in deciding whether federal law preempts or invalidates state law.[25] In some of these cases, the Court considers whether Congress has the authority to overrule majoritarian decisions of states or other localities. When the Court upholds the decisions of smaller governmental units against congressional decisions, it can be said to protect the decisions of local majorities against Congress. The Court's decisions in these cases could be defended on the grounds that they accord majoritarian decisions greater weight than any potential gain from the substantive outcomes of congressional decisions, assuming the congressional outcomes to be more substantively democratic than the local decisions.

So far I have suggested that the Court strikes down legislation on democratic grounds for two reasons. First, as in *Loving*, it can override representative and majoritarian decisions that threaten a fundamental democratic right. Second, it can defend the right to participate when this right is more fundamental than the negative impact of a policy on the core values of democracy. Another institutional question about the balance between procedural and substantive values regards amendments to the United States Constitution. The legal scholar Walter F. Murphy famously asked whether some constitutional amendments, which require supramajorities for passage, could so undermine the core values of the Constitution that they themselves should be declared unconstitutional.[26] The same question can be recast in democratic terms. Could a particular

[24] *Reynolds v. Sims,* 377 W.S. 533 (1964).

[25] The Court decides preemption cases by reference to the Supremacy Clause of the United States Constitution: "This Constitution, and the Laws of the United States which shall be made in Pursuance thereof; and all Treaties made, or which shall be made, under the Authority of the United States, shall be the supreme Law of the Land" (U.S. Const., Art. VI).

[26] Walter F. Murphy, "An Ordering of Constitutional Values," *Southern California Law Review* 53, no. 2 (1980): 703–60, esp. 754–57.

constitutional amendment so undermine the core values of *democracy* that it should be struck down by the Supreme Court on *democratic* grounds?

This question is more complicated than the issue of how to balance majoritarianism and individual rights. The very passage of such an amendment suggests that it enjoys far greater than majority support among the electorate.[27] Thus, if majoritarian decisions have democratic weight, supramajoritarian ones should have even greater moral force.[28]

Despite this added weight, however, some constitutional amendments nevertheless should be struck down on democratic grounds because they so greatly undermine democratic values.[29] An amendment to repeal the Eighth Amendment guarantee against cruel and unusual punishment, for instance, could be struck down on democratic grounds because it would undermine the rights I argued in chapter 5 were central to democratic legitimacy. Despite the deference that the Court should show to constitutional amendments, we cannot rule out, a priori, the possibility that some amendments might so undermine the values of democracy that they should be struck down on democratic grounds. The question of whether a constitutional amendment is democratic, like the question of when majoritarian decisions should be struck down, ultimately depends on the success of arguments about specific democratic rights.

A good theory of democracy should recognize that a democratic evaluation requires balancing the protection of democratic rights and majoritarian procedures. In practice, the Supreme Court has the potential to uphold substantive democratic rights when majorities threaten them. In addition, it can affirm the right to participate when representative institutions such as Congress challenge it. But an appropriate evaluation of whether the Court has acted democratically depends on the substantive issue at stake and its relationship to the core values of democracy.

[27] This is evidenced in part by the difficulty Congress has in passing many constitutional amendments that clearly have the support of the majority of Americans. For instance, at the time of writing, the proposed amendment against flag burning has not been passed despite apparently enjoying majoritarian support among Americans; see Carl Hulse, "Flag Amendment Narrowly Fails in Senate Vote," *New York Times,* June 28, 2006.

[28] For instance, *Stanley v. Georgia,* 394 U.S. 557 (1969), in my view, rightly extended the right of privacy to ensure an ability to possess pornography in one's home. But if a supermajority were to pass a constitutional amendment in an attempt to overturn such a decision, it would be harder to argue that this outcome is undemocratic and that the amendment should be declared unconstitutional.

[29] Walter F. Murphy argues that a constitutional amendment that undermined values associated with inherent human dignity could itself be unconstitutional. In his words: "A change so fundamental as to destroy a central value of the 'constitution' would be radical in the true sense of the word, going to the root of the nation's reason for being. Such a change would make the United

VI. The Objection from Benevolent Dictatorship

Critics might object that nothing in my theory requires an institution accountable to the public to enforce democratic rights. According to the value theory, what, if anything, would prevent an unaccountable set of unelected guardians from enforcing these rights?

To explore this question, consider a judiciary that intends to protect basic rights but is structurally unaccountable—if, for instance, the judges choose their own successors.[30] Similarly, we could imagine a situation in which an enlightened hereditary monarch has been entrusted to protect fundamental rights. Some might argue that my view commits me to defending such institutions as democratic.

However, my claim that outcomes can be more or less democratic concerns the content of particular decisions instead of the authority that institutions have. The implication is that institutions (both private and public) and officials (both unelected and elected) can work to bring about democratic outcomes. The democratic legitimacy of decisions, therefore, is not solely about *who* is acting, but also is about what is decided. Private institutions and powerful unelected individuals can act more or less democratically according to the quality of the outcomes that they help to secure, both through direct political participation and through more indirect means.

It is important, however, that judicial review differs from "democratic dictatorship" in its structure. The aim of judicial review is to ensure democratic outcomes while preserving popular participation in democratic processes. Neither

---

States a different nation, its people a different people" (Murphy, "The Right to Privacy and Legitimate Constitutional Change," in *The Constitutional Bases of Political and Social Change in the United States*, ed. Shlomo Slonim [New York: Praeger, 1990], 213–35, quotation on 227). See also idem, "An Ordering of Constitutional Values," 754–57. For an attempt to reconcile the notion of unconstitutional constitutional amendments with popular sovereignty, see Akhil Reed Amar, "Philadelphia Revisited: Amending the Constitution Outside Article V," *University of Chicago Law Review* 55, no. 4 (Autumn 1988): 1043–104, esp. n. 1. Judicial review of constitutional amendments is an important part of Indian constitutionalism, articulated by the Supreme Court of India in 1973 in *Kesavananda Bharati v. State of Kerala*. This decision held that the Parliament could not pass constitutional amendments that violated the "basic structure" of the Constitution and asserted a right of judicial review over amendments to guarantee this substantive limitation; see Gerald E. Beller, "Benevolent Illusions in a Developing Society: The Assertion of Supreme Court Authority in Democratic India," *Western Political Quarterly* 36, no. 4 (December 1983): 513–32.

[30] I take this criticism and these examples from Chris Eisgruber's response to my paper on the panel "Substance of Democracy" held at a meeting of the American Political Science Association, Philadelphia, Pennsylvania, September 2003.

the U.S. Supreme Court nor the constitutional courts of South Africa and Germany dictate policy. More precisely, judicial review involves striking down legislation that majoritarian institutions then can debate once again and reformulate. This process can be understood as a dialogue between courts with the power of judicial review and legislative majorities, insofar as legislatures can acknowledge their mistakes and rewrite legislation to respect basic rights while still achieving their legislative goals. It is these courts' role as participants in a wider procedural process that led me earlier in this chapter to question the wisdom of court-directed economic policy to secure welfare rights.

I concede that a dictator could bring about outcomes that are more or less democratic. But nothing in this claim implies that democratic outcomes are sufficient for democratic legitimacy. By definition, dictatorship entirely ignores the intrinsic value of actual persons making decisions. Such a regime would undermine democratic procedure, thus failing to uphold an essential aspect of the core values. The objection that my account of democracy is compatible with dictatorship is valid only insofar as it allows for the distinction between dictators, or unaccountable elected officials, who make democratic decisions and those who do not. My account, however, also explains why a benevolent dictatorship would lack an essential aspect of democratic legitimacy.

VII. Conclusion

The view I have defended in this chapter identifies and embraces the tension between commitments to democratic procedures and to substantive democratic outcomes. I do not seek to resolve this fundamental tension in favor of a narrowly procedural or narrowly outcomes-based conception of democracy. Rather, I have shown why the idea of self-government requires a balance of both the procedural right to participate and substantive individual rights. It explains why the democratic tradition rightly engages persons in majoritarian processes in which they are free to make decisions about policy. It therefore recognizes the intrinsic value of the majoritarian procedure commonly associated with democracy. At the same time, however, it demonstrates why some majoritarian decisions can be not only unjust but undemocratic. For instance, a majoritarian decision that violates the privacy rights of individuals, like the Texas legislation at issue in *Lawrence*, rightly is overridden through the process of judicial review. Some countermajoritarian decisions by the Court can be justified directly by reference to the core values of democracy and do not present pragmatic problems of implementation. In contrast, the Court's role in implementing welfare rights, such as those I argued for in the previous chapter, is more ambiguous. Because of the economic and policy complexity involved in implementing these rights, the Court is not the most effective institution to do so. This reason, coupled with the intrinsic value of democratic procedure, suggests that judicial review is not always the best way to minimize the loss to democracy that occurs when majorities fail to secure some democratic rights.

Although both democratic procedures and substantive democratic rights are necessary to ideal democracies, these aspects of democracy will conflict in non-ideal circumstances. This chapter has endeavored to demonstrate how, when these conflicts do happen, the majoritarian procedures that manifest the core values should be balanced against the protection of substantive democratic rights through judicial review.

Conclusion

Democratic Rights and Contemporary Politics

I have argued in this book that the ideal of democracy should not be limited to guaranteeing the right of individuals to participate in fair procedures. Polities that are truly democratic also must offer basic respect for, and an institutional defense of, other fundamental rights. In chapter 1, I proposed the value theory of democracy: the idea that three core values underlie democratic procedures and should underlie the outcomes of those procedures. These values—equality of interests, political autonomy, and reciprocity—serve as a procedure-independent standard for articulating the fundamental democratic rights of citizens. In chapter 2, I demonstrated why paradigmatic democratic rights associated with the rule of law and free speech should be understood in both a procedural sense (guarantees to citizens as authors of law) and in a substantive sense (limits on coercion of citizens as addressees of law). In chapter 3, I presented democratic contractualism as a framework for evaluating the legitimacy of state coercion. This framework, comprising democracy's public reason and the inclusion principle, is a means of ensuring that coercive institutions and policies respect democratic rights. In chapters 4 and 5, I discussed two substantive democratic rights: the right to privacy and the rights of the punished, respectively. I argued in chapter 4 that the Court's decisions in *Lawrence v. Texas* and several related cases could be defended by reference to the core values of democracy. In chapter 5, I argued that even those who have flouted their most basic duties as citizens must be treated in accordance with the democratic ideal. Those convicted of crimes should not be viewed as enemies "at war" with democratic polities but rather as members of those polities who retain some basic rights.

In addition to respecting the points of view of gay citizens and convicted criminals, a democracy also should recognize the legitimate claims that can be made by the economically least well-off. Democratic regimes often have coexisted with the capitalist institutions of private property and the free market, but the legitimacy of this coexistence by no means is self-evident and must be justified in the same manner as all other coercive institutions. I argued in chapter 6 that private property should be legitimated by appeal to its advantages for the least well-off. Democratic justification, therefore, requires a right to basic welfare for all citizens.

The core values outlined in the value theory of democracy—equality of interests, political autonomy, and reciprocity—constitute an independent standard against which actual democracies should be judged. The closer actual democracies are to this ideal, both in their procedures and in the substance of their outcomes, the more legitimate they are. In chapter 7, I argued that substantive democratic rights ideally would be affirmed and protected though democratic procedures. In nonideal circumstances, however, polities should limit losses to democracy by balancing the intrinsic values of democratic procedures and substantive rights. I suggested that judicial review sometimes is justified when it protects substantive democratic rights, even though it overturns the outcomes of majoritarian procedure.

Given the plethora of polities across the world that claim to be democratic, there is a central need in political theory to elaborate upon what the democratic ideal entails. This discussion of democracy should not remain abstract, however. The core values, and the substantive democratic rights they support, serve as a means of measuring the legitimacy of actual democracies. How, then, do contemporary democracies measure up to the democratic ideal articulated by the value theory of democracy? There are at least two trends in contemporary American politics potentially at odds with one another. On the one hand, the Supreme Court has protected the basic rights of citizens, as in *Lawrence*. On the other hand, certain federal policies associated with the "war on terror" suggest that the protection of the basic rights I have defended can be exchanged for other social goods, such as security. One might argue that privileging security over liberty is democratically legitimate because of its basis in democratic procedure. I have undertaken to show, however, that the basic rights of criminals and the privacy rights of all citizens cannot be discarded without a great loss to the democratic ideal. Moreover, despite the popular notion that free markets are required for the establishment of new democracies, I have sought to illustrate that private ownership alone is illegitimate if it is not accompanied by a commitment to welfare rights. The fundamental democratic rights I have argued for—privacy, limits on punishment, and guaranteed welfare—are entailed by the democratic ideal itself. When any one of these rights is sacrificed, so, too, is the level of democratic legitimacy that a polity can claim. It would be both ironic and tragic if at the very time that democracies committed themselves to war in the interest of defending or expanding democracy, they dismantled their own basic democratic institutions at home.

✦ Bibliography ✦

BOOKS, ARTICLES, AND SPEECHES

"Gettysburg Address (1863)," *Basic Readings in U.S. Democracy*, United States Department of State. Available at http://usinfo.state.gov/usa/infousa/facts/democrac/25.htm. Reprinted from Roy P. Basler, ed., *The Collected Works of Abraham Lincoln*, volume 7 (New Brunswick, N.J.: Rutgers University Press, 1953), 22.

"The Official Colonial Protest: The Declaration of the Stamp Act Congress (October 19, 1765)." In *Colonies to Nation 1763–1789: A Documentary History of the American Revolution*, ed. Jack P. Greene. New York: Norton, 1975.

"South Africa's Top Court Blesses Gay Marriage," Washington Post, December 2, 2005.

Ackerman, Bruce, and Anne Alstott. *The Stakeholder Society*. New Haven: Yale University Press, 1999.

Ackerman, Bruce, and James S. Fishkin. *Deliberation Day*. New Haven: Yale University Press, 2004.

Amar, Akhil Reed. "Philadelphia Revisited: Amending the Constitution Outside Article V." *University of Chicago Law Review* 55, no. 4 (Autumn 1988): 1043–104.

American Civil Liberties Union. "National Death Penalty Fact Sheet." 2005. Available at <http://www.aclu.org/capital/facts/10593res20050216.html> (accessed June 23, 2006)

Barton, Len. "The Struggle for Citizenship: The Case of Disabled People." *Disability, Handicap and Society* 8, no. 3 (January 1993): 235–48.

Bedau, Hugo Adam. "Abolishing the Death Penalty Even for the Worst Murderers." In *The Killing State: Capital Punishment in Law, Politics, and Culture*, ed. Austin Sarat. New York: Oxford University Press, 1999.

Berlin, Isaiah. "Two Concepts of Liberty." In *Liberty*, ed. Henry Hardy. Oxford: Oxford University Press, 1997.

Blanchard, Olivier, and Lawrence F. Katz. "What We Know and Do Not Know About the Natural Rate of Unemployment." *Journal of Economic Perspectives* 11, no. 1 (Winter 1997): 51–72.

Brettschneider, Corey. "Balancing Procedures and Outcomes Within Democratic Theory: Core Values and Judicial Review." *Political Studies* 53, no. 2 (June 2005): 423–41.

———. "Dignity, Citizenship, and Capital Punishment: The Right of Life Reformulated." *Studies in Law, Politics, and Society* 25 (2002): 119–32.

Brown, Wendy. *States of Injury: Power and Freedom in Late Modernity*. Princeton: Princeton University Press, 1995.

Callan, Eamonn. *Creating Citizens: Political Education and Liberal Democracy*. Oxford: Clarendon, 1997.

Carole Pateman, "The Equivalent of the Right to Life, Land, and Liberty?: Democracy and the Idea of Basic Income." Lecture available online at http://www.sscnet.ucla.edu/polisci/faculty/pateman.

Christiano, Thomas. *The Rule of the Many: Fundamental Issues in Democratic Theory.* Boulder, Colo.: Westview, 1996.

Cohen, Jean. *Regulating Intimacy: A New Legal Paradigm.* Princeton: Princeton University Press, 2002.

Cohen, Joshua. "Democracy and Privacy." In progress.

———. "For a Democratic Society." In *The Cambridge Companion to Rawls,* ed. Samuel Freeman. Cambridge: Cambridge University Press, 2003.

———. "Procedure and Substance in Deliberative Democracy." In *Democracy and Difference: Contesting the Boundaries of the Political,* ed. Seyla Benhabib. Princeton: Princeton University Press, 1996.

Cole, David. *Enemy Aliens: Double Standards and Constitutional Freedoms in the War on Terrorism.* New York: New Press, 2003.

Constant, Benjamin. "The Liberty of the Ancients Compared with That of the Moderns: Speech Given at the Athénée Royal in Paris." In *Political Writings,* trans. and ed. Biancamaria Fontana. Cambridge: Cambridge University Press, 1988.

Dworkin, Ronald. *Freedom's Law: The Moral Reading of the American Constitution.* Cambridge, Mass.: Harvard University Press, 1996.

———. "Liberalism." In *A Matter of Principle.* Cambridge, Mass.: Harvard University Press, 1985.

Einhorn, Lois J. "[Abraham Lincoln's] Gettysburg Address (1863)." In *Abraham Lincoln the Orator: Penetrating the Lincoln Legend.* Westport, Conn.: Greenwood, 1992.

Eisgruber, Christopher L. *Constitutional Self-Government.* Cambridge, Mass.: Harvard University Press, 2001.

Ely, John Hart. *Democracy and Distrust: A Theory of Judicial Review.* Cambridge, Mass.: Harvard University Press, 1980.

Estlund, David. "The Democracy/Contractualism Analogy." *Philosophy and Public Affairs* 31, no. 4 (October 2003): 387–412.

———. "The Insularity of the Reasonable: Why Political Liberalism Must Admit the Truth." *Ethics* 108, no. 2 (January 1998): 252–75.

Exdell, John. "Feminism, Fundamentalism, and Liberal Legitimacy." *Canadian Journal of Philosophy* 24, no. 3 (September 1994): 441–64.

Feinberg, Joel. "The Classic Debate." In *Philosophy of Law,* 5th ed., ed. Joel Feinberg and Hyman Gross. Belmont, Calif.: Thomson Wadsworth, 1995.

Finnis, John. "Law, Morality, and 'Sexual Orientation.'" In *Same Sex: Debating the Ethics, Science, and Culture of Homosexuality,* ed. John Corvino. Lanham, Md.: Rowman and Littlefield, 1997.

Freeman, Samuel. "Illiberal Libertarians: Why Libertarianism Is Not a Liberal View." *Philosophy and Public Affairs* 30, no. 2 (April 2001): 105–51.

———. "Deliberative Democracy: A Sympathetic Comment." *Philosophy and Public Affairs* 29, no. 4 (Autumn 2000): 371–418.

Fuller, Lon. *The Morality of Law.* New Haven: Yale University Press, 1965.

George, Robert P. *In Defense of Natural Law.* Oxford: Clarendon, 1999.

164

Goodin, Robert E., and David Schmidtz. *Social Welfare and Individual Responsibility.* Cambridge: Cambridge University Press, 1998.

Grey, Thomas C. "The Disintegration of Property." In *NOMOS XXII: Property,* ed. J. Roland Pennock and John W. Chapman. New York: New York University Press, 1980.

Gutmann, Amy, and Dennis Thompson. *Why Deliberative Democracy?* Princeton: Princeton University Press, 2004.

———. *Democracy and Disagreement.* Cambridge, Mass.: Harvard University Press, 1996.

Habermas, Jürgen. *The Inclusion of the Other: Studies in Political Theory,* ed. Ciaran Cronin and Pablo De Greif. Cambridge, Mass.: M.I.T. Press, 1998.

———. *Between Facts and Norms: Contributions to a Discourse Theory of Law and Democracy,* trans William Rehg. Cambridge, Mass.: MIT Press, 1996.

Hanisch, Carol. "The Personal is Political." In *The Radical Therapist,* ed. Jerome Agel. New York: Ballantine, 1971.

Harel, Alon. "Rights-Based Judicial Review: A Democratic Justification." *Law and Philosophy* 22, nos. 3–4 (July 2003): 247–76.

Hobbes, Thomas. *Leviathan.* New York: Macmillan, 1962.

Holmes, Stephen, and Cass R. Sunstein. *The Cost of Rights: Why Liberty Depends on Taxes.* New York: Norton, 1999.

Kant, Immanuel. *Metaphysical Elements of Justice: Part I of the Metaphysics of Morals.* 2d ed. Trans. John Ladd. Indianapolis, Ind.: Hackett, 1999.

Kateb, George. "What do Citizens Owe Their Constitutional Democracy?" Lecture Delivered at the Center for Human Values Twentieth Anniversary Celebration. (Unpublished, 2000).

———. *The Inner Ocean: Individualism and Democratic Culture.* Ithaca: Cornell University Press, 1992.

Katz, Michael B. *The Price of Citizenship: Redefining the American Welfare State.* New York: Metropolitan, 2001.

Koppelman, Andrew. "Homosexual Conduct: A Reply to the New Natural Lawyers." In *Same Sex: Debating the Ethics, Science, and Culture of Homosexuality,* ed. John Corvino. Lanham, Md.: Rowman and Littlefield, 1997.

Larmore, Charles. "Political Liberalism." *Political Theory* 18, no. 3 (August 1990): 339–60.

Lenta, Patrick. "Democracy, Rights Disagreements and Judicial Review." *South African Journal on Human Rights* 20, no. 1 (2004): 1–31.

Locke, John. "An Essay on the Poor Law." In *Political Essays,* ed. Mark Goldie. Cambridge: Cambridge University Press, 1997.

———. *Two Treatises of Government,* ed. Peter Laslett. Cambridge: Cambridge University Press, 1988.

Macedo, Stephen. *Diversity and Distrust: Civic Education in a Multicultural Democracy.* Cambridge, Mass.: Harvard University Press, 2000.

———. "Homosexuality and the Conservative Mind." *Georgetown Law Journal* 84 (December 1995): 261–300.

MacKinnon, Catharine A. *Only Words.* Cambridge, Mass.: Harvard University Press, 1993.

———. "Privacy v. Equality: Beyond *Roe v. Wade* (1983)." In *Feminism Unmodified: Discourses on Life and Law.* Cambridge, Mass.: Harvard University Press, 1987.

Madison, James. Federalist 44. In "The Bounds of Legislative Specification: A Suggested Approach to the Bill of Attainder Clause (in Notes and Comments)." *Yale Law Journal* 72, no. 2 (December 1962): 330–67.

Mainardi, Pat. "The Politics of Housework." In *Sisterhood is Powerful: An Anthology of Writings from the Women's Liberation Movement,* ed. Robin Morgan. New York: Vintage, 1970.

Mansfield, Harvey. *America's Constitutional Soul.* Baltimore: Johns Hopkins University Press, 1993.

Meiklejohn, Alexander. *Political Freedom: The Constitutional Powers of the People.* New York: Harper and Brothers, 1960.

———. *Free Speech and Its Relation to Self-Government.* New York: Harper and Brothers, 1948.

Michelman, Frank. "Democracy and Positive Liberty." *Boston Review* 21, no. 5 (November 1996).

———. "Law's Republic." *Yale Law Journal* 97, no. 8 (July 1988): 1493–537.

Mill, John Stuart. "Considerations on Representative Government." "On Liberty." In *On Liberty and Considerations on Representative Government,* ed. R. B. McCallum. Oxford: Basil Blackwell, 1948.

Morris, Herbert. "Persons and Punishment." *The Monist* 52, no. 4 (October, 1968): 475–501.

Murphy, Liam, and Thomas Nagel. *The Myth of Ownership: Taxes and Justice.* Oxford: Oxford University Press, 2002.

Murphy, Walter F. "An Ordering of Constitutional Values." *Southern California Law Review* 53, no. 2 (1980): 703–60.

Nagel, Thomas. "Concealment and Exposure" and "Personal Rights and Public Space." In *Concealment and Exposure and Other Essays.* Oxford: Oxford University Press, 2002.

Ober, Josiah. "The Democratic Animal: Nature, History, and Politics." Stanford University, Wesson Lectures, 2004.

Okin, Susan Moller. "Political Liberalism, Justice, and Gender." *Ethics* 105, no. 1 (October 1994): 23–43.

———. *Justice, Gender, and the Family.* New York: Basic, 1989.

Pateman, Carole. "Freedom and Democratization: Why Basic Income is to be Preferred to Basic Capital." In *The Ethics of Stakeholding,* ed. Keith Dowding, Jürgen De Wispelaere, and Stuart White. London: Palgrave Macmillan, 2004.

Pettit, Philip. *Republicanism: A Theory of Freedom and Government.* Oxford: Clarendon, 1997.

Plato. "Crito." In *Five Dialogues,* 2d ed., trans. G.M.A. Grube, rev. by John M. Cooper. Indianapolis, Ind.: Hackett, 2002.

Posner, Richard. *Law, Pragmatism, and Democracy.* Cambridge, Mass.: Harvard University Press, 2003.

———. "Security versus Civil Liberties." *Atlantic Monthly* 288, no. 5 (December 2001): 46–48.

Rawls, John. *Political Liberalism.* New York: Columbia University Press, 2005.

———. *Justice as Fairness: A Restatement,* ed. Erin Kelly. Cambridge, Mass.: Harvard University Press, 2001.

———. "The Idea of Public Reason Revisited." In *The Law of Peoples with "The Idea of Public Reason Revisited."* Cambridge, Mass.: Harvard University Press, 1999.

———. A Theory of Justice, rev. ed. Cambridge, Mass.: Harvard University Press, 1999.

Reiman, Jeffrey H. "Justice, Civilization, and the Death Penalty: Answering van den Haag." *Philosophy and Public Affairs* 14, no. 2 (Spring 1985): 115–48.

Rorty, Richard. *Contingency, Irony, and Solidarity.* Cambridge: Cambridge University Press, 1989.

———. "Democratic Sex: *Reynolds v. U.S.,* Sexual Relations, and Community." In *Sex, Preference, and Family: Essays on Law and Nature,* ed. David M. Estlund and Martha C. Nussbaum. New York: Oxford University Press, 1997.

Rosenblum, Nancy L. *Membership and Morals: The Personal Uses of Pluralism in America.* Princeton: Princeton University Press, 1998.

Sarat, Austin. *When the State Kills: Capital Punishment and the American Condition.* Princeton: Princeton University Press, 2001.

Scanlon, T. M. *What We Owe to Each Other.* Cambridge, Mass.: Harvard University Press, 1998.

Schrecker, Ellen. *The Age of McCarthyism: A Brief History with Documents.* Boston: St. Martin's Press, 1994.

Sedgwick, Eve Kosofsky. *Epistemology of the Closet.* Berkeley: University of California Press, 1990.

Shklar, Judith. *American Citizenship: The Quest for Inclusion.* Cambridge, Mass.: Harvard University Press, 1991.

Smith, Rogers M. *Stories of Peoplehood: The Politics and Morals of Political Membership.* Cambridge: Cambridge University Press, 2003.

Sreenivasan, Gopal. "Interpretation and Reason." *Philosophy and Public Affairs* 27, no. 2 (Spring 1998): 142–71.

Tushnet, Mark. "Social Welfare Rights and the Forms of Judicial Review." *Texas Law Review* 82, no. 7 (June 2004): 1895–920.

Van Parijs, Philippe. "Competing Justifications of Basic Income." In *Arguing for Basic Income: Ethical Foundations for a Radical Reform,* ed. Philippe Van Parijs. London: Verso, 1992.

———. "Why Surfers Should be Fed: The Liberal Case for an Unconditional Basic Income." *Philosophy and Public Affairs* 20, no. 2 (Spring 1991): 101–31.

Waldron, Jeremy. *Law and Disagreement.* New York: Oxford University Press, 1999.

Walzer, Michael. *Spheres of Justice: A Defense of Pluralism and Equality.* New York: Basic, 1983.

Warren, Samuel D., and Louis D. Brandeis. "The Right to Privacy." *Harvard Law Review* 4, no. 5 (December 1890): 193–220.

Wenar, Leif. "Original Acquisition of Private Property." *Mind* 107, no. 428 (October 1998): 799–819.

———. "Political Liberalism: An Internal Critique." *Ethics* 106, no. 1 (October 1995): 32–62.

Wiebe, Robert H. *The Opening of American Society.* New York: Knopf, 1984.

Young, Iris Marion. "Inclusive Political Communication." In *Inclusion and Democracy.* Oxford: Oxford University Press, 2000.

LEGAL CASES

Baker v. Carr, 369 U.S. 186 (1962).

Bowers v. Hardwick, 478 U.S. 186 (1986).

Eisenstadt v. Baird, 405 U.S. 438 (1972).

Furman v. Georgia, 408 U.S. 238 (1972).

Gitlow v. People of the State of New York, 268 U.S. 652 (1925).

Griswold v. Connecticut, 381 U.S. 479 (1965).

Herrera v. Collins, 506 U.S. 390 (1993).

Lawrence v. Texas, 539 U.S. 558 (2003).

Lochner v. New York, 198 U.S. 45 (1905).

Loving v. Virginia, 388 U.S. 1 (1967).

Meyer v. Nebraska, 262 U.S. 390 (1923).

Miller v. California, 413 U.S. 15 (1973).

Minister of Public Works and Others vs. Kyalami Ridge Environmental Association and Others 2001 (7) BCLR 652 (CC).

New York Times Co. v. United States, 403 U.S. 713 (1971).

Planned Parenthood of Southeastern Pennsylvania v. Casey, 505 U.S. 833 (1992).

Reynolds v. Sims, 377 U.S. 533 (1964).

Reynolds v. United States, 98 U.S. 145 (1878).

Romer v. Evans, 517 U.S. 620 (1996).

Stanley v. Georgia, 394 U.S. 557 (1969).

State v. Makwanyane, 1995 (6) BCLR 665 (CC).

Texas v. Johnson, 491 U.S. 397 (1989).

Trop v. Dulles, 356 U.S. 86 (1958).

United States v. Quinones, 205 F. Supp. 2d 256 (S.D.N.Y. 2002).

Index